PHL

KU-724-391

THE ARCHAEOLOGY OF
BUILDINGS

Richard K. Morriss

TEMPUS

First published 2000

PUBLISHED IN THE UNITED KINGDOM BY:

Tempus Publishing Ltd
The Mill, Brimscombe Port
Stroud, Gloucestershire GL5 2QG

PUBLISHED IN THE UNITED STATES OF AMERICA BY:

Arcadia Publishing Inc.
A division of Tempus Publishing Inc.
2 Cumberland Street
Charleston, SC 29401

Tempus books are available in France, Germany and Belgium
from the following addresses:

Tempus Publishing Group	Tempus Publishing Group	Tempus Publishing Group
21 Avenue de la République	Gustav-Adolf-Straße 3	Place de L'Alma 4/5
37300 Joué-lès-Tours	99084 Erfurt	1200 Brussels
FRANCE	GERMANY	BELGIUM

© Richard K. Morriss, 2000

The right of Richard K. Morriss to be identified as the Author
of this work has been asserted by him in accordance with the
Copyrights, Designs and Patents Act 1988.

All rights reserved. No part of this book may be reprinted or reproduced or utilised in any form
or by any electronic, mechanical or other means, now known or hereafter invented, including
photocopying and recording, or in any information storage or retrieval system, without the
permission in writing from the Publishers.

British Library Cataloguing in Publication Data.
A catalogue record for this book is available from the British Library.

ISBN 0 7524 1429 1

Typesetting and origination by Tempus Publishing.
PRINTED AND BOUND IN GREAT BRITAIN.

Contents

To Mary

The pyramids themselves, doting with age,
have forgotten the names of their founders.
(Thomas Fuller, 1608-1661)

Preface

The book is not intended as a definitive textbook but merely as an introduction to the subject within a relatively small compass. It attempts to cover the key evidence for buildings archaeology — materials and construction techniques — and the basics of the recording and interpretation of that evidence.

It is written for anyone with an interest in studying buildings archaeologically, whether amateur or professional; the difference between the two is seen as immaterial. It is also written for the vast majority of buildings archaeologists who do not have access to the latest 'high-tech' EDMs or CAD systems and hopes to demonstrate that, however useful these can be, they are by no means essential. To paraphrase, and to make printable, what an old master builder told me too many years ago when I worked for him in Staffordshire, 'The tools don't matter, it's how you use them.'

Buildings archaeology — the study of the archaeology of buildings — is not a subject that most people have heard of. Even in academic circles it is virtually unknown. No university runs an undergraduate course in it, and there are only a handful of postgraduate courses that teach it. In the broad field of study that is archaeology it is usually seen as a new fringe subject, on the edge of archaeological respectability and needing to be brought into line. Ironically, only the name is new; the subject itself can claim a documented history of six centuries and origins in the Italian Renaissance. It is, in fact, by far the oldest form of archaeology.

In a sense, part of the problem facing buildings archaeology as a respectable subject is the difficulty in pinning it down and putting it into the right academic pigeon hole. Is it a Science, an Art, or a Social Science? Such academic niceties sometimes matter more to

ANTIQUITIES of England and Wales.
The FRONTISPIECE.

EXPLANATION

The figure Seated in the foreground represents HISTORY Recording an Account of the Original & present state of the ANTIQUITIES of England & Wales. She is also engaged in resisting the Ravages of TIME, who advances to destroy these beautiful Monuments of Antient Magnificence. The figures viewing the Monument of an illustrious Warrior, the Monastic Edifice behind them, together with a distant Glimpse of Stonehenge, and the other parts of the plate very properly point out the general nature of this Useful & Entertaining Work

Published according to Act of Parliament by Alex Hogg

1   This engraving, well over two hundred years old, still perfectly sums up the role of modern
    building archaeology. In this case the archaeologist is called 'History' and wears rather less clothes
    than her modern successors, but she is engaged in 'recording an account of the Original and
    present state of the Antiquities' she is studying. The 'ravages of time' that she resists is ever
    present, along with the ravages of some planners and some developers — though the built heritage
    is safer now than it has ever been

academics than they should do. In this case the unhelpful answer is quite simple; it is all three. It is a Science, because it involves the accurate recording and objective analysis of part of the physical world; it is an Art because it deals directly or indirectly with that most public of the Arts, architecture; and it is a Social Science because it deals with people and their environment.

As a subject it cannot be seen as fully-fledged and independent. It cannot be separated from the other aspects that make up the wider study of architectural history: documentary research, the history of design, and the development of structural technology to name just three. It is, instead, and like them, an autonomous subject with its own specific purpose and methodologies. The multidisciplinary nature of architectural history is both inevitable and apt. Nearly two thousand years ago, Vitruvius began his *Ten Books of Architecture* by stating that 'The architect should be equipped with knowledge of many branches of study and varied kinds of learning, for it is by his judgement that all work done by the other arts is put to the test'. The same applies to the architectural historian, and to the buildings archaeologist.

It is impossible to understand any building adequately without at least a basic knowledge of architectural styles, building types, and regional characteristics. Yet, whilst there must be an awareness of these other sometimes parallel and sometimes intertwined strands of architectural history, the buildings archaeologist should nevertheless be aware of the parameters of his or her specific subject, blurred and undefined as those may be.

As an 'archaeology', buildings archaeology is the study of the physical remains of the past, its material culture; in this case, buildings or structures. The archaeological study of buildings can be the basis of many different types of research, but it is important to know where the evidence being used ceases to be purely archaeological. This does not mean that a buildings archaeologist cannot undertake work that develops the results of the fieldwork. Indeed, the study of buildings requires an holistic approach and a freedom of thought not restricted by the straight jacket of scientific methodologies. Nevertheless, the distinction between the raw archaeological evidence and other source material needs to be well defined.

To a certain extent this book takes a simple, fundamentalist, line. The role of the buildings archaeologist is, after all, really a very straightforward one — the study of the archaeology of buildings. Its subject is the fabric, form and function of buildings, nothing more and nothing less. Its purpose is to understand the way buildings were built, and how they have subsequently been changed. The buildings archaeologist needs to be observant, objective and open-minded and the information produced becomes just part of the overall evidence available.

As a consequence this book is broadly divided into two basic sections; the first is about the archaeological evidence of the buildings, what they were built of and how they have changed. The second is about trying to record and to understand them. It is not intended to be a study of anything else. It is not concerned, for example, with the philosophy of the subject, or research strategies, or comparative analysis. All of these are dealt with in the Institute of Field Archaeologist's Buildings Special Interest Group's *Buildings Archaeology: Applications in Practice,* published in 1994.

PART I: INTRODUCTION

VIEW of the ARCH or GRAND ENTRANCE to the TEMPLE of the SUN as now Standing among the RUINS at PALMYRA

2   *The ruins of Palmyra, as published in the* Gentleman's Magazine *in 1754. This town on the edge of the Roman empire is in modern-day Syria. The drawing is a typical mixture of measured archaeological survey and art work, and the influence of such engravings on the higher echelons of British architecture was quite profound*

1   What is buildings archaeology?

Until recently buildings archaeology, whatever the term used to describe it, had always been considered to be a branch of something else. For centuries it remained largely within the span of what might be called 'pure' architectural history. Then, almost by accident, by the middle of the twentieth century, it gradually came under the expanding and increasingly professional world of archaeology. Not everyone engaged in more traditional (i.e. excavating) archaeology accepted that buildings archaeology was archaeology at all, and a few still don't. Most, however, do and it has been embraced as a new field of archaeology. Unfortunately that is where many of its problems begin.

At one time in the 1980s, it seemed as if it would be totally assimilated by the archaeological world. The price of acceptance into the fold was an implicit acceptance of the methodologies and philosophies of 'traditional' archaeology, including 'value-free' recording, context-based stratigraphic interpretation, and an essentially scientific approach to the subject. Archaeology has advanced tremendously in the past twenty or thirty years, but whilst the study of buildings has benefited from some of these advances, by no means all of them are appropriate and some are actually counterproductive. Now, most of those involved with this type of study of historic buildings have realised that, whilst they have much in common with the excavating archaeologist, they have there own separate needs too.

It was only as recently as 1993, at a special conference of the Buildings Special Interest Group of the Institute of Field Archaeologists, archaeology's professional body, that there was broad agreement on its name. Prior to that, building archaeologists had been called several different things: building recorders, architectural archaeologists, or archaeological surveyors amongst others.

In one sense the 'new' name has been rather unfortunate, because of the assumption that techniques used in excavations can and should be applied to buildings. This is simply not the case. Nor is it true that building archaeology is a new subject. It is not only a distinct subject in its own right with its own distinct methodology, it is one with a very long heritage. The name may have changed, but the archaeological study of buildings has been going on for at least six centuries.

Architectural history is slightly different from other histories in that it not only consists of the study of documents, it also includes the study of art, style, structure, and the development of ideas. To a degree this relies on the study of the buildings as well as documentary sources. In general, this has been undertaken in a different way than that used by the archaeologists, and one in which the buildings are almost used as physical documents in their own right, providing examples of the development of decorative carving, or mouldings, or plan forms for example.

It was in this area that the foundations of buildings archaeology as a separate subject

3 *A typical example of the excellent pioneering archaeological work of Robert Willis, in this case in illustrating the development of the nave of Winchester Cathedral, Hampshire. This was published in 1846; Willis is not to be confused with another pioneer, Browne Willis, of a century earlier*

ELEVATION OF TWO BAYS OF THE NAVE, SHOWING ITS
TRANSFORMATION.
[From Willis's " Architectural History of Winchester Cathedral," 1846.

lie. It is well known that in ancient times, one civilisation copied the buildings of another, sometimes building replicas or sometimes adding their own particular innovations. The most obvious example is the manner in which the Romans copied the Greeks. Despite their exaggerated reverence for past cultures they did not really study buildings in any depth but simply copied favoured motifs and basic ideas. The best example of their approach is in the Coliseum in Rome. This magnificent structure utilised new structural techniques and materials that the Greeks did not have — the arch, the dome and mass concrete — and yet still had applied pilasters and entablatures that have no more structural purpose than the off-the-shelf 'period' features tacked onto a modern suburban semi.

Perhaps appropriately it was in Rome that we have the first documented evidence of buildings being studied in a more archaeological manner, and thus it is there that the origins of buildings archaeology as a subject lie. The Florentine architect and goldsmith Fillippo Brunelleschi was born in 1377; he is known to have visited Rome on several occasions in the early fifteenth century to study and draw some of the ruins of the Imperial city. It was his understanding of the structural techniques used in these ruins, formed

*4   Until fairly recently most of the archaeological study of buildings was concentrated on those
considered to be the most important — castles, stately homes and, especially, churches — such as
Tintern Abbey, Monmouthshire. Ironically these can often be far simpler structures than more
humble fare*

from an archaeological interpretation of them, that allowed him to solve the problem of
building the dome of Sta Maria del Fiore in his home city, one that had foiled the best
architects and engineers of the day. This was a pioneering use of archaeological study to
solve a contemporary structural problem, which is an underrated and often overlooked
benefit of modern buildings archaeology.

The first great architectural theorist of the Renaissance was another Florentine, Leon
Battista Alberti, a little younger than Brunelleschi. He also used the ruins of Rome as
evidence for his theories of the principles of ancient architecture but his book, *De re
aedificatoria* pre-dated the printing press. A century later, it was the work of a Paduan,
Andrea Palladio, that marked the first major published treatise on architecture and also
included large numbers of illustrations and reconstructions based on reasonably accurate
scale drawings of Roman ruins. His *Four Books on Architecture* had an enormous influence
on western architecture, particularly after his death and in England where the classical
style based on his work in the seventeenth and eighteenth century became known as the
Palladian style. His recording was archaeological to a degree, and his methodology
involved not only accurate surveying but also interpretation and occasional extrapolation
of the information he was finding. To that extent he could be called a buildings
archaeologist. Curiously, despite the fame and influence of his *Four Books,* the most recent
translation into English, in 1997, was the first for over 250 years.

By the eighteenth century, close and accurate study of the ancient ruins of antiquity

5 *There is a growing realisation that our built heritage is broad based; it includes all types of structures from pigsties to palaces. Archaeological study of even humble sites, such as these rare surviving examples of back-to-backs in Birmingham, continue to add to our knowledge of the past. In this case the survey and analysis showed that the development was far more complicated than had been thought beforehand, altering the understanding of early nineteenth century housing in the city*

was well established, and there was a move also to start to record some of the more historic buildings in Britain as well. Much of the work was purely illustrative, such as the illustrations of the Buck brothers, with varying degrees of accuracy. Amongst the best, particularly in relation to cathedrals, were the plans and drawings of Browne Willis in the 1720s and '30s.

By the start of the nineteenth century the accuracy of such drawings had improved dramatically and so had the interpretation of the manner in which buildings had developed. Men like John Britton were to the fore with his monumental six volume *Cathedral Antiquities of Great Britain* published between 1814 and 1835. Up until the twentieth century the buildings studied continued to be mainly high status, defensive or religious but this began to change gradually as there was a greater interest in the vernacular buildings of both town and country. Amongst the pioneers of this new branch of study was J H Parker, who finished the work started by T H Hudson and produced *Some Account of Domestic Architecture in England* in 1859.

It is doubtful if Britton, Parker, or their contemporaries considered themselves to be archaeologists as such. They were architectural historians that simply used what we would regard as archaeological techniques as an aid in helping them to understand the architectural development of a particular building. Archaeology was, even until the mid-twentieth century, considered to be the study of the ancient past, not of the more recent.

So what, exactly, is buildings archaeology, and how does it differ from the rest of architectural history? In very simple terms archaeology, of whatever kind, is one of the two main strands of what we can broadly term 'history', the other being documentary research. Both provide evidence and information, the difference being that archaeology is the study of the physical remains of the past and, theoretically at least, more reliable. Documents can lie, either intentionally or unintentionally. Scribes can make mistakes or the story is told by only one side of a particular historical divide. The skill of the documentary historian is based in no small part on the ability to decide on the trustworthiness of the written word. The archaeological resource, above or below ground, cannot lie; it can confuse, it can certainly frustrate, and it can unintentionally mislead, but if studied properly the information that it produces will be the unadulterated truth. The only limits to understanding the archaeology of buildings or of excavations are the skills of the archaeologist.

Buildings archaeology, then, is the study of buildings as archaeological objects in their own right; the building is the archaeological resource and the evidence for its archaeological interpretation is contained within it. Buildings archaeology is the study of structure, and the development of structure. All structures have three main interlinked elements, the keys to their interpretation. These can be called, for the sake of convenience, the three 'Fs': fabric, form, and function.

The fabric is the material (or, more commonly, materials) of which a building is constructed; understanding the manner in which these materials were used and their structural capabilities and limitations is the first step in any analysis. The form is the physical shape of the building in all dimensions and its internal layout; form is dictated both by the fabric, and by the third self-explanatory 'f', the function, of the building. The form has to meet the requirements of the function in a way that can be achieved by the available fabric. The relationship between form and function is most obvious in an industrial buildings such as a blast furnace or a windmill, but Le Corbusier's dictum that 'a house is a machine for living in' is as relevant for the buildings archaeologist as it is for the modern architect. A house, be it a hovel or a Palladian mansion, has a function too, as do all structures, even follies.

To study the three 'Fs' the building archaeologist needs, in this age of the pithy soundbite, to be observant, objective, and open-minded — the three 'Os'. Observant, to accurately record and note all the relevant structural information; objective in assessing that available evidence; and open-minded enough not to let the perceived wisdom of experience overrule the physical evidence, no matter how odd the conclusions may appear.

Like any form of archaeology, buildings archaeology is the study of material culture. But the study of any building cannot be simply based on the study of its nuts and bolts. Buildings are more than that, and any study of them has to be far more inclusive and holistic, though care has to be taken in appreciating the difference between the objective and subjective evidence. Excavation archaeology has become more and more scientific in its methodology as advances in technique have developed and it is now firmly in the Science camp of academia. Building archaeology is less easy to categorise and

6   Sometimes the loss of parts of our built heritage is sudden — when a building is demolished, or
    destroyed by fire, or radically altered. Sometimes erosion of this heritage is both slower and more
    avoidable. A car park is hardly the best modern use for this medieval undercroft in York!

7   Another historic building is destroyed. This was Newdale foundry, Shropshire, a unique mid-
    eighteenth century complex built by the Coalbrookdale Company but hidden within a farmstead
    for two centuries. On the edge of a World Heritage Site it was rediscovered in 1987 and
    immediately listed. The government overturned the listing and it was demolished — though an
    archaeological record was made

8 *Buildings archaeology is not always a passive exercise. This complex of timber-framed buildings in Ludlow, Shropshire, was recorded archaeologically and assessed. The developers then used the information to reinstate many of the missing timbers as an economic and structurally practical alternative to a full steel support frame*

straightjacket.

There are two fundamental differences between excavating archaeology and buildings archaeology which need to be appreciated. The first, which will be dealt with in more detail later on, is that whilst the excavator is largely dealing with the two-dimensional shadows of the past, the buildings archaeologist mainly deals with the three-dimensions of the present. Not only does this affect the suitable methodologies for the work, it also means that understanding space and the use of space is as important as the fabric enclosing that space; the interpretation has to be in three dimensions as well.

The second difference is in the differing roles of the archaeologists in the present day. For the most part, excavations inevitably destroy the archaeological evidence that they encounter. This is the price of progress — both in redevelopment work and in the much rarer research excavations. Usually, excavations are a last resort, designed to at least 'preserve by record' a particular part of the past and, at the same time, add to our growing body of knowledge. The results of excavations can also help to highlight any particularly important archaeological 'hot-spots' and to a certain extent inform planners and developers of the potential risks and thus minimise the effects of subsequent developments. Nevertheless, their main role is to record what is to be lost.

Conversely, building archaeologists do not (or should not) destroy what they record, despite the inevitable temptation to rip out Regency plasterwork to expose a possible medieval timber-frame beneath. Certainly, part of their role can be to preserve by record buildings that are to be pulled down. More often it is to provide a better understanding of ones that are to be conserved. Sometimes this work may simply be for research purposes but that is a rare luxury for the professional building archaeologist. He or she will usually be dealing with planning or heritage related issues where the continuing survival of a building will depend on a degree of change, whether that be simple patch repairs or a major conversion and adaptive reuse.

By providing a better understanding of the building, the archaeologist can help to inform the decision-making processes; historic divisions identified within the building can be used as a basic for subdividing a large house being converted into apartments, for example. In the best schemes, the buildings archaeologist becomes part of the project team, and a necessary one. Few architects these days are taught a comprehensive knowledge of historic building techniques or architectural history, and the input of the archaeologist can be vital. Surprisingly, that advice can even help the other specialists, such as the structural engineers. For example, in the 1980s the usual answer to stiffening timber-framed buildings was to introduce new steel frames and supports. An archaeological understanding of the evolution of the original timber-frame and the original stresses and strains acting on it usually gives the engineers the better option of simply reinstating the original timbers in their original locations. An understanding of the building's archaeology can help its long-term future, and the building archaeologist is often, therefore, not just a recorder of a building's past, but part of its long-term future.

So far, and in the rest of the book, the terms 'archaeologist' and 'buildings archaeologist' have been used frequently and without any indication of what their specific skills and qualities should be. There is no ready answer, because the skills and qualities of building archaeologists vary so much. One thing should be made clear; these do not depend on whether they are professional or amateur.

There are surprisingly few full-time professionals and we have a distinct disadvantage over the amateurs. To earn our corn we mostly work in a competitive market place. We do not have the luxury to spend more time and effort than our clients are willing to pay for in studying the buildings in question. Apart from heritage bodies such as the National Trust, the Landmark Trust and English Heritage, and a few genuinely interested owners, most of our work will be for private clients understandably reluctant to fund someone else's academic research. Providing the archaeologist produces enough information to satisfy the 'brief' set out by the relevant planning authority, the client will be happy. Nor does the professional have the luxury of picking and choosing the buildings he or she works on, and will seldom be able to undertake interesting research projects.

The amateur building archaeologist, on the other hand, can select any desired building or group of buildings, providing their owners are in agreement, and study and dissect them for as long as they want. They can, often in groups of like-minded people, carry out surveys of whole villages or groups of buildings of a specific type. Unlike the professional, they can also follow to the logical conclusion any 'lead' they find during their analysis.

9 *Building materials give towns, and individual buildings, much of their character. Some towns, like those of the Cotswolds, owe their homogenous appearance to homogenous materials whilst others enjoy much more diversity. This corner of Sandwich, an historic Cinque Port in Kent, shows the use of flint, stone, brick and timber-framing*

What has to be emphasised at this point is that there should be no difference in the quality of the work of the professional or the amateur building archaeologist. The term 'amateur' is all too often taken in vain, but there are many in this particular field of study that can put some of us professionals to shame with their expertise and depth of knowledge.

As with most subjects, there is a risk that enthusiastic but unskilled people get put off attempting to get involved because there is an assumption that only the skilled and experienced will do. One of the admirable things about the best amateur groups is the pooling of a tremendous amount of diverse expertise, and of the training of complete beginners. The more people that can be involved in buildings archaeology, the better — at whatever level. Providing the basic rules are followed and people work within their hopefully expanding limitations, any building survey and analysis is better than none. There are simply too many buildings in the country that deserve some form of record before they disappear for ever or are changed beyond recognition, and too few buildings archaeologists to do the work.

There has been a growing awareness of our rich architectural heritage since the nineteenth century and in the twentieth century a realisation that this heritage included not just the great houses, castles and cathedrals. Pioneering bodies such as the Society for

10 Buildings, too, can be made of many different materials, such as the unusually named church of St. Wendreda, March, Cambridgeshire. This small portion is a real mix of dates and materials, which include rubble, ashlar, flint, flushwork and even brick — in the voussoirs of the clerestory windows. The church also has one of the finest timber roofs — a double hammer beam — in the country

the Protection of Ancient Buildings and the National Trust have been followed by other bodies dealing with specific periods or specific types of buildings. The all-too real threat of wholesale destruction of towns and cities through bombing during the Second World War led indirectly to the listing of buildings of importance, and these 'lists' are now one of the key records for planning purposes.

More recently, the importance of actually understanding listed buildings was set out in the government's 'PPG15' *Planning Policy Guideline: Planning & The Historic Environment*, published in 1994. Perhaps typically, the importance of the buried archaeological resource had until then attracted more official attention and the guidelines relating to it, in PPG16, had been issued *before* PPG15. PPG16 was also clearer and potentially gave local authorities more support than the relatively toothless PPG15. Both are only guidelines and, frustratingly, their implementation varies considerably from planning authority to planning authority.

PART II:
THE MATERIAL EVIDENCE

Most buildings contain a variety of different building materials, used for different purposes in their construction. It is these materials that give buildings, and regions, their character and also the core evidence for the building archaeologist.

Until the development of good and cheap internal transport links in the middle of the nineteenth century, most builders utilised local materials simply because the cost of importing better or cheaper ones would have been exorbitant. Materials could and often were transported long distances, if the client had sufficient wealth to fund such extravagance. The fine quality Caen stone from Normandy used in some of the greater twelfth-century churches in England is a typical example of this. Nevertheless, until the development firstly of the national canal system and then of the steam railway, local materials gave a distinct flavour to the fabric of a building, even if the form was influenced to a greater or lesser extent by ideas — far cheaper to transport — from elsewhere.

This section has been loosely divided up into main chapters relating to walls, roofs and floors, with a shorter section on glass and glazing. Some of the materials discussed inevitably overlap so that the divisions between sections are inevitably blurred.

2 Walls

The walls are the main structural elements of most buildings. The manner of their construction can be divided into two broad categories; solid or framed. It could be argued that the only true solid walls are of earth or concrete but for most purposes walls of stone and brick can be included as well. Apart from the obvious basic difference between the two categories there is another. Stone and, especially, brick-walled buildings were generally (though not always) held together by their floor and roof structures without which they would have no lateral stability. In contrast framed construction, whether it be of timber, iron or reinforced concrete, unites walls, floors and often roofs within the basic structural skeleton of the building and it is impossible to divorce one from the others.

Materials used for walling also fall into two broad types, natural and man-made. Despite these distinctions it is not at all unusual to find single-phase walling incorporating elements of both categories of construction and both types of materials. As fashions changed and available supplies dictated, it was not unusual to find buildings with rear walls of brick and a front wall of stone and, conversely, to find buildings of stone faced with contemporary brick facades. Whilst the brick facings of most timber-framed buildings are usually the result of later changes, some examples have been found where such a front was built at the same time as the frame. Sometimes this primary mix can be even richer; for example, the walls of the main buildings of Chirk Castle Home Farm in Clywd, built in 1736, have solid rubblestone ground-floor sections and a timber-framed first-floor, the panels of which were infilled from the start with brick nogging.

Even more widespread was the use of contrasting materials for decorative or structural purposes. Brick buildings from the Tudor period onwards would often have architectural details such as quoins, string courses and window surrounds made of stone, stone being seen as the more important material. In buildings with rubblestone walls, bricks were often used for the same purposes, though these also had a structural purpose in providing strong straight corners and jambs in an otherwise fairly rough material. Similarly, brick would also be used in flint and sometimes cob buildings and, very commonly, for chimneys.

SOLID WALL CONSTRUCTION

Stone

The natural materials for solid walling are surprisingly varied, ranging from — literally — mud to the highest quality ashlared masonry. By far the most important of these is stone, used by man for millennia. Apart from the obvious use as a walling material it could be

11 *The front of a building is not always, and indeed seldom, indicative of what the rest is built of. This Shrewsbury example is a fairly typical example of the refronting in eighteenth-century brick of a much older timber-frame*

12 *Brick, when it was fashionable, was often used on the front of an otherwise stone-built building. The archaeologist's role is to distinguish whether or not the brick and stone were contemporary or whether the brick is a later alteration. Not all are as simple to unravel as Royal Hotel in Ashby-de-la-Zouch, Leicestershire of 1826*

13 *In most periods, stone was preferable to brick — so the grand frontage of the late-sixteenth-century range of Moreton Corbet, Shropshire, is really only stone* appliqué *to a brick carcass. The house was never properly finished*

utilised in many different ways, including the footings for other types of walls, especially brick, clay and timber-framed. It could also be used to decorate brick buildings in the form of quoins, string courses, entablatures and the surrounds of windows and doorways. Certain types of stones, and not just slates, could be cut into sufficiently thin sections to be used as tilestones on roofs and even for the louvers in the windows of bell chambers in some of the greater churches.

In Britain, the earliest and most impressive surviving stone buildings, as opposed to ceremonial stone structures such as Stonehenge, Avebury or barrows, are in the Highlands and islands of Scotland. The most dramatic site of all is Skara Brae on mainland Orkney, a Neolithic settlement of stone huts complete with stone 'furniture', preserved remarkably intact by being buried for two thousand years under the ever-shifting sand. At the opposite end of Britain, in Cornwall, are the remains of the eight Iron Age houses at Chysauster near Penzance, built a little later but still before the arrival of the Roman legions.

Prehistoric man had an intimate knowledge of stone in a slightly different way, but his cave habitations were scarcely man-made. Later on caves, natural or partly or wholly man-made, were used for both domestic and commercial purposes. As late as the eighteenth and nineteenth centuries, people were still living in caves in several parts of England,

14 Quality tells. Most of the lower section of this part of the town wall of Chester is of Roman date, and most of the ashlared facework and parts of the cornice survive. Above, and to the right, the work is medieval with nineteenth- and twentieth-century repairs (Ken Hoverd/Archive)

particularly where the rock could easily be cut away to form roughly regular living spaces. Examples existed in the rock outcrops of the Severn valley in Shropshire and Worcestershire even up until the mid-twentieth century. At Kinver, Staffordshire, the National Trust has recently recreated the eighteenth-century brick front of the largest of several such dwellings, after the caves had been surveyed, not without difficulty, by building archaeologists.

The Romans built in stone, and built big. Their most famous legacy is Hadrian's Wall; over 72 miles long and crossing some of the most forbidding terrain at the edge of their Empire, it stands as a feat of both civil engineering and endurance. Most of their other surviving examples of stonework are also defensive, including the walls around such towns as Colchester, Portchester, Chester and Richborough. Noticeably, after the legions left these shores in the fifth century, stone ceased to be used to any extent, despite the availability of the material in the usually deserted Roman towns. Even within the towns that were still inhabited, new and clearly very grand timber buildings replaced the old stone Roman ones, this being the case at Wroxeter, Shropshire, for example.

From the surviving archaeological evidence it appears that the Saxons built mainly in wood and that only their grander churches were built in stone. Houses and even town defences were mainly built of timber. The arrival of the Normans in the later eleventh century reintroduced the concept of high-quality and ambitious masonry, and this was no longer confined simply to their new churches.

15 *Surviving Saxon
stonework, such as the
walls of this
particularly fine church
at Sompting in West
Sussex, is quite rare,
largely because Saxon
architecture appears to
have mainly been
timber based. Stone
was used only for the
highest status
structures, almost
invariably the greater
churches*

Nevertheless stone was, until the end of the medieval period, generally seen as a prestigious building material and usually confined to the great churches, castles, town walls, and the houses of the very wealthy. Even in the areas where stone was common and could be easily picked up from the surface, poorer houses continued to be of less substantial materials until well into the seventeenth century. This was no doubt in part at least because of feudal property laws that did little to encourage peasants to build permanent structures that their children could inherit. In part, too, it was because all stones belonged to the landowner.

The decay of the feudal system gradually led to greater security of tenure and freehold and the Dissolution of the monasteries brought about an unexpected cheap source of good quality building stone. Abbeys were sold for their building materials and often quickly dismantled, particularly when they were within or near the larger towns. In Shrewsbury, stones from demolished abbey buildings were used to build a large new house on the edge of the town; originally thought to be whitewashed to hide the provenance of its walls it is still called the Whitehall. At least parts of Shrewsbury Abbey survive; Winchcombe Abbey in Gloucestershire has disappeared and virtually no traces of reused stonework had been found. In a rear range of the nearby George Inn, recently converted to housing, an

16 *Some buildings appear to grown out of the natural rock. Stirling Castle perches on a volcanic outcrop. Behind the grim walls are some of the finest fifteenth-century buildings in Britain, part of the palace developed by the Scottish kings until the union of the thrones in 1603*

17 *Natural rock outcrops in a typical drystone-walled landscape surround the surviving tower of Crook old church, Cumbria. In the distance, and closer to the present village straggling along the main road, is its Victorian replacement*

archaeological survey found that parts of its stone walls incorporated moulded stone from the abbey, laid so that their delicate carved ends were hidden in the core of the masonry.

From the seventeenth century onwards stone ceased to be such an exclusive material, especially in areas where it was common and readily available. As with other building materials it was then subject to fluctuating fashions and regional tastes. In the western Midlands and the Welsh Marches, timber framing continued to be more popular until the Restoration, despite the availability of stone and brick. In England in particular, many towns have examples of stone facades to what are essentially brick buildings. In some areas the opposite is true. Ludlow, superficially a town of brick, is really a town of timber framing and rubblestone behind applied or sometimes contemporary brick facades. In general, good quality ashlared stonework continued to be considered the best material of all, and became more and more available to all parts of the country with the transport improvements of the nineteenth century. This had the inevitable effect of eroding much of the regional character developed in the earlier centuries.

TYPES OF STONE

For its size, Britain has an exceptional variety of building stones but although there are all manner of hues and textures, there are only a few basic types. Stone is classified as being either Sedimentary, Igneous, or Metamorphic. All classes of stone are also sometimes referred to by their geological date — the period in which they were formed. These are, in order of antiquity: Ordovician, Silurian, Devonian, Carboniferous, Permian, Triassic, Jurassic, Cretaceous and Tertiary.

The Sedimentary Rocks

Sedimentary rocks were formed over millions of years. As the name suggests, they were formed from the sediments derived from weathered and eroded rocks transported and deposited by water or, occasionally, wind. These particles accumulated in layers and were cemented together in a new matrix. The make-up of that sediment can vary enormously but because of the way it was slowly built up layer by layer, the stones formed share one common trait; they are stratified. Because of this, they are generally easier to work and more convenient to build with. Sedimentary rocks are divided, in turn, into two broad categories, the *limestones* and the *sandstones*.

Limestones

Limestones are essentially composed of calcium carbonate ($CaCO_3$), but vary enormously in character depending on their constituent parts. Some are organic limestones made up mainly of the crushed remnants of tiny sea creatures, shells, and other organic matter. Others are inorganic and formed from the chemical precipitation from solution of calcium carbonate and can be devoid of all organic matter. Both types contain, to a lesser or greater degree, impurities trapped and crushed at the time they were formed; by far the most common of these is sand. They vary in toughness from the younger and softer chalks to the rugged mountain limestones.

18 *Cotswold stone is a distinctive oolitic limestone that occurs in a broad swathe across middle England from Somerset to Lincolnshire. Easily quarried and easily worked, it was used for high status and low status buildings alike. Chipping Campden's fine church overlooks the former outbuildings of Campden House, destroyed by fire in the Civil War*

The main band of limestone crosses England in an unevenly broad sweep from Dorset in the south-west to Yorkshire in the north-east; it is made up mainly of two parallel formations, both of the Jurassic period, the *oolitic* and *liassic*. It is generally considered that the best building limestone is the oolitic, made up of minute spherical carbonate particles called *ooliths* cemented together. They were formed by chemical precipitation and accumulation on ancient sea floors and the surface texture of oolites is rather like that of fish roe. They have produced some of the finest building stones, including Barnack, Chilmark, Clipsham and Portland as well as the many varieties of the far-famed Bath and Cotswold stones.

The nearly contemporary *liassitic* limestones are less predictable in quality, colour and texture, but the best quarries, Ham Hill and Hornton, produced stone as good as many of the oolitic quarries. Much harder than either of these Jurassic limestones are the older Carboniferous ones, sometimes referred to as *mountain limestone* because they are found mainly in upland areas such as the Peak District, the Yorkshire Dales and the Mendips. Being much harder, these are difficult to work and are usually used as rubble, often with sandstone decoration.

The English *chalks* are mainly in the south east of the country, exposed most famously in the fine cliffscapes of Kent and Sussex. They are almost pure calcium carbonate, but are given their individual colour and character by the relatively small amount of impurities in them. Because of chalk's softness it is easy to quarry and to work but at the same time it is not usually very durable if exposed to the weather. It was often used purely for internal work, in vaults and decoration. The best building chalks were the least pure, the most famous being quarried at Totternhoe in the Chilterns and at Beer in Devon. In parts of Cambridgeshire and Bedfordshire a more compact and thus harder type of chalk, *clunch* was quarried. Because the local stone was difficult to work, this clunch was often used for decoration in band courses and window surrounds.

One of the more unusual types of limestone used by medieval builders is *tufa*, also sometimes known as *travertine*. There are technical and visually subtle differences between the two types, travertine being slightly more dense than tufa. Both were usually formed by carbonate saturated spring water bubbling through existing limestone rock and hardening when it came into contact with the air. As more and more of the deposit formed this gradually compacted and turned into a light, soft and porous rock with a very characteristic speckled and pitted texture. Its main attribute for the builder was its lightness, after it had been quarried and been allowed to dry thoroughly. It was thus ideal for the vault infills of medieval churches, and was used, for example, in Canterbury, Gloucester and Worcester cathedrals. Being easy to work, it was also often used for quoins and jambs in rubblestone buildings, including several churches in Kent and in the Teme valley in Worcestershire; one of these, the Norman church at Eastham, was built entirely of ashlared tufa. The only other large building constructed of it is Berkeley Castle in Gloucestershire.

Sandstone

Technically, sandstones are *arenaceous* (literally 'sandy') rocks whose commonest ingredient is quartz. Unlike limestone, they have little or no organic element. The particles of quartz are held in a matrix or natural cement, the nature of which dictates the character of the stone. Thus *silicaceous sandstone* has a matrix mainly composed of silica, and is generally the best for building purposes, and *calcareous sandstone* has a matrix of calcium carbonate. Sandstone, like limestone, varies considerably in texture, colour and durability, and, as a result, in its suitability for building purposes.

The Old and New Red sandstones provide the best known of building sandstones in Britain, the former particularly in the western midlands of England, eastern Wales, and the midland belt of Scotland, and the latter from the midland England up to Cumbria in the north-west and County Durham in the north-east. Older Jurassic sandstones were extensively quarried in the North Yorkshire Moors and the North East. Older still is the *gritstone* of parts of the Peak District of northern Staffordshire and Derbyshire, and on both flanks of the southern Pennines; it is very durable but difficult to work. As its name suggests, this is a stone containing angular and often quite coarse grains. Finer-grained gritstone occurs further north, particularly in Wensleydale.

Other Sedimentary Rock

Other sedimentary rocks include the finely-grained *argillaceous* or 'clayey' types. These consist of crushed clay layers and include the types of *siltstone, mudstone* and *shale* that are

19 *Scotland, traditionally, is a country of stone or clay buildings, where timber framing was rare and brick a mainly a product of the railways. Granites and sandstones were the main building stones. This nineteenth-century tenement block in Dundee, of local sandstone, is like many others in the towns of eastern Scotland in particular. Externally grim, many of those that have survived have been restored to become quite fine apartments*

found in much of Wales and the Welsh Marches. Siltstone contains a higher proportion of quartz and so has a rougher texture; depending on its bedding it can look similar to both mudstone and shale. Shales are composed of silt and clay, is finely grained, and splits easily along their bedding planes. Mudstone splits far more erratically. These stones were generally easy to work but could weather quite badly if exposed.

Breccia is a coarsely grained sedimentary rock, formed from jagged fragments in detritus washed down from other areas, compacted and held in a fine-grained calcareous sandy matrix. Technically the fragments are called *clasts* and breccia is thus a *clastic* rock. Its quality is variable and it is only occasionally used for building — in west Shropshire, for example. Other types of clastic sedimentary rocks have rounded fragments and are called *conglomerates*. Examples include *septaria* and *pudding-stone* in the south-east of England but both are poor building stones.

Flint

Flint is one of England's more idiosyncratic and unusual building stones, seldom seen to such an extent elsewhere. Even in England it was found only in the chalk districts of the south-eastern half of the country where better building stone was rare. It is seldom if ever seen in the Midlands or the North. Although obviously associated with the chalks in which they are found, flints stand somewhat apart from the other main walling materials.

The flints are small stones or nodules of siliceous rock a few inches long; they were sometimes called *popples*. The flint nodules are extremely hard but very brittle and so can be easily chopped. Inland flint varied enormously in shape but in some coastal areas flints derived from the chalk cliffs were smoothed and rounded by the action of the sea and infinitely easier to work with. Because of their small size, flints could only be used in walls with a large amount of mortar. Usually, flint walls also incorporated other building materials for strength.

Allied to flint in some respects, another unusual type of rubble walling occurs in some villages near the Humber estuary and in coastal areas of northern Lancashire and Cumbria. Large numbers of glacier-worn stones or cobbles formed by many different varieties of rocks could be picked up from the fields and used for house building. The rounded cobbles are generally laid in a herringbone pattern and needed large amounts of mortar as well as brick surrounds to openings and brick quoins to corners.

Metamorphic Rocks

As their generic name suggests, metamorphic rocks are those rocks, either sedimentary or igneous, that have been metamorphosed into something else. Their original character has been changed by forces way beyond our comprehension; huge upheavals in the earth's crust and extraordinary heat, the one often following the other. By far the most important metamorphic rock in the United Kingdom is *slate*. The only others of significance are *quartzite* and *marble*, but true geological marble is only found on Iona; the rest of English 'marbles' are really forms of limestone. Marble is metamorphosed limestone and most so-called marbles are fine-grained fossiliferous limestones that take an attractive polish.

Slate is found in the upland areas of Britain: in England in much of Devon, Cornwall and Cumbria, and, to a lesser extent, in the Charnwood Forest of Leicestershire; in the north-west of Wales; and in the southern part of Scotland. It originated as a fine-grained sedimentary rock, usually shale, but due to heat and pressure when still buried below later rock strata, it was transformed.

Its hardness and the fact that it can be split easily to leave smooth surfaces made it ideal as a roofing material. It is also virtually impervious, so resists weathering. Fragments of slate roofing tiles have been found in North Wales at the Roman fort of Segontium, near Caernarfon.

Quartzite consists of a quartz sandstone that, through heat and pressure, has been altered. Quartzite was a useful road stone material but generally only used for building where no other stone was readily available as it is quite hard to work with in anything but rubblestone. It was used, for example, in the uplands of south-western Shropshire, particularly around the Stiperstones.

Igneous Rock

Igneous rocks are formed when molten lava or magma cools and solidifies and mainly consist of silica. *Plutonic* or *intrusive* rocks cool and crystallise below the earth's surface. Rocks formed from material actually spewed out into the air during volcanic action are

20 *Typical slate-walled and slate-roofed cottages near Boscastle, Cornwall. Note the very thin courses of the fissile metamorphic rubblestone. The limewash finish is a local tradition, the brick top to the chimney is not*

called *extrusive* or *volcanic*. The intrusive rocks usually have larger crystals because they have cooled more slowly.

Granite

The only important igneous rock used for building in Britain is an intrusive rock, granite, which is coarse-grained and made up of quartz, feldspar and mica. Its colour varies from shades of greys to pinks depending on the amount of feldspar. It is an extraordinarily durable building stone but also one that, because of that, is very difficult to carve decoratively. Conversely, most varieties can be polished to a shine. In the British Isles, granite is mainly found in the south-west of England, particularly in the moors of Devon and Cornwall, the Charnwood Forest area of Leicestershire, parts of Cumbria, and the Highlands of Scotland.

Building in stone

Stone in building varies from the crudest rubblestone to the finest wrought ashlar, with innumerable gradations in between. By the medieval period there were well-established quarries in most of the good stone areas of Britain, producing material for the larger local buildings, notably churches and castles. Although this produced distinct local

21 John Wood the Younger's Royal Crescent overlooking Bath, Somerset, is one of the most famous eighteenth-century set pieces in Europe. However, its effect is achieved only by a grand unified facade to many disparate and separately built terraced houses, and the rear of the crescent is both less grand and uniform (Ken Hoverd, Archive)

characteristics, it did not mean that even at this time stone could not be moved surprisingly long distances if sufficient money was available to do so. Indeed, stone was imported from France soon after the Norman Conquest for many of the country's most prestigious buildings, notably the beautiful white limestone from Caen. Most long-distance transport of stone would be by sea or river, with only the last few miles being overland.

Unless particularly large blocks of easily cut stone were available, it was unusual to have solid stone walls. Even in a simple drystone boundary wall, there are usually two separately-built sides knitted together at the centre. In a typical medieval stone building, each wall consisted of a sandwich of rough rubble and mortar fill, or 'hearting', between two faces of masonry. In the same way the huge round piers of Norman cathedrals are actually hollow cylinders of ashlar filled with rubble.

The general method of construction was to build up the two outer faces to an agreed level and then pack the gap between with a layer of rubble and mortar. The next phase of the outer 'leaves' of the wall would then be built up, and then the gap between them would be filled in as before, and so on until the wall reached its full height. In normal walls there would be larger blocks laid between the two faces at intervals, either in courses or randomly, to add rigidity to the structure, prevent differential settlement in the two outer faces, and to even the loadings upon it. However the detailed study of such buildings often shows that the rubble core was one area in which cost cuts were made.

Sometimes it is possible to see the horizontal joins between each 'lift' of masonry,

22 *This redundant Greek Revival Methodist church in Dumfries, Dumfries & Galloway, was photographed in the early 1990s prior to the redevelopment of the site. Note the contrast between the smooth façade and the rougher rubble work of the main carcass of the building*

particularly in worked stone or ashlar. The opportunity was sometimes taken to level up the work if it was beginning to get out of true, and one or more courses may taper in height one way or the other as the horizontal is re-established. Commonly the evidence of the fixing of the timber scaffolding may survive in a series of small infilled 'putlog' sockets. Usually the scaffold support would be built into the masonry and then be removed when no longer needed; the resultant gap would then be filled in either by a small surface block of stone or rubble, and as many medieval buildings would be limewashed inside and out, this would not show. Over time, however, these blockings will have fallen out, leaving a telltale socket in the stonework.

Few buildings were built with 'drystone' walls that had no bedding material between the stones. In even the simplest the individual stones of the outer leaves of masonry would usually be bedded onto earth or clay; lime mortar was preferable but more costly and tended to be used by the more prestigious buildings until the seventeenth century, apart from 'pointing' the gaps between the stones on the outer faces of the wall.

Even the best lime mortars were not always seen as being adequate for keeping a masonry wall together and in the larger and more ambitious buildings a variety of cramps — of iron, lead and even slate — were often introduced. These were needed in particular on sloping features such as pediments. An empty shallow slot, often single or double dovetailed, in the surface of a worked piece of stone is usually an indication that it had been cramped in the past.

Stone construction is generally divided into just two basic types, rubble and ashlar, though the degree of regularity covered under the broad heading of the former is very

23 *The ruins of the late fifteenth-century gateway to Ramsey Abbey, Cambridgeshire, show the typical formation of high-status masonry work. The crisp ashlar facing and decoration hides the rubble core work; Ramsey, like several other local abbeys, obtained much of their stone from the famed quarries at nearby Barnack*

24 *Not a spectacular ant hill or stalagmite, but the rubble core of one of the once soaring columns of the abbey of Bury St. Edmund's, Suffolk. All of the ashlar facing stone around the core has been 'quarried' for use elsewhere, leaving only these amorphous — but still impressive — masonry spears*

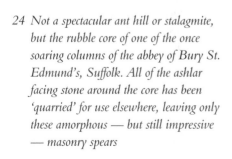

25 *The ventilation slit in this eighteenth-century stone barn near Raglan, Monmouthshire, is framed in reused ashlar, part of which includes an 'oillette', part of an arrow or gun loop. The logical 'quarry' for this stone is Raglan Castle, slighted after being taken in the Civil War*

varied. The best varieties of 'worked stone' rubble on a fine stone like Bath stone can be almost as good a finish as true ashlar work on others. The choice of rubble or ashlar depended on many factors, from the nature of the local stone to the status of the building.

Rubble or rubblestone is usually formed of relatively small stones, generally irregular in shape and only roughly cut to any shape, if worked at all. Rubblestone walls rely either on the careful laying of the stones (as is the case in a well-built dry stone wall), or on their weight and the mortar in which the stones are laid. In most forms of rubble construction, special attention has to be paid to the corners of the building and to the surrounds of windows and doorways. Depending on the size of the available stone, larger corner stones, or quoins, may have to be selected or possibly even brought in from elsewhere. There are several variants of rubble walling of differing quality.

Random Rubble is the most primitive of all stonework and in it the individual stones are laid only roughly horizontal. They may be cut to fit the wall but little attention is made to coursing and any large gaps between stones can be infilled with smaller stones. Ironically, this type of masonry requires a great deal of skill if the wall is to last. Boundary walls of random rubble 'set dry', i.e. without mortar, are the work of skilled craftsmen and form a distinct feature of the upland landscapes of much of Britain.

In *Coursed Random Rubble* the stones are still only very roughly dressed but care is taken to try and bring them to proper courses every foot (0.3m) or so. This helps to prevent too many continuous vertical breaks in the bonding.

Snecked, or Squared, Rubble consists of stones roughly cut to shape so that they can be laid with straight horizontal and vertical joints. It was, and is, particularly common in areas

26 Basic types of stone wall: a random rubble; b snecked rubble; c coursed rubble; d ashlar; e tufa; f rusticated ashlar

where the quarried stone was highly stratified and straight cuts along the bed line could be easily obtained but where uniform vertical heights were not. The *snecks* are smaller stones added to the bond to fill in between stones of different heights and help create a degree of regularity in the coursing A better quality variant of this is the *Coursed Snecked,* or *Squared Rubble*, essentially snecked rubble brought to even more regular courses.

Coursed Rubble is one of the superior forms of rubble in which the individual blocks of stone are worked sufficiently to ensure that each separate course of stones is of a consistent height and that there are tight straight joints between each stone of each course and between the courses. The height of courses can and does vary, as does the quality of the worked stones. The best type of such work is sometimes called *Hammer dressed ashlar* and was often used in industrial buildings and in railway engineering in the nineteenth century.

Two of the more unusual forms of rubble are *Kentish Rag* and *Flint*. Kentish rag, also, in the nineteenth century at least, called *Rustic* or *Polygonal Ragwork*, is a type of rubble that is not even roughly horizontally bedded. It usually consists of a heavy unstratified type of limestone, a type of stone relatively common in Kent, a county not rich in good building stone.

A rare form of stone construction, used in the Saxon and early Norman period, was *herringbone masonry*. The term itself describes the manner in which individual worked stones were laid in alternate diagonally-set courses in the walls, producing a quite distinct pattern.

Flint is difficult to categorise but is essentially another type of rubble, albeit one in which the size of the individual 'stones' was very small. It was used by the Romans who laced the walls with horizontal binding courses of their large flat bricks. Saxons and Normans used it for their churches and flint was common from the thirteenth century in even the most prestigious of buildings, including the Tower of London. Nevertheless it was always a fairly difficult material to work with and was largely replaced by brick in the eighteenth century. It did enjoy a revival in the Regency and early Victorian period and is still used in some buildings today. However, its use is now limited to applied decoration; flint panels were used, for example, to good effect in the otherwise severe design of the new Winchester Crown Court, opened in 1974.

Flints could be used just as they were dug out of the chalk, usually referred to simply as *roughwork*, or they could be split. Splitting flint is called *knapping*. With knapped flint the roughly straight cut side was laid flush with the face of the wall. The exposed cross-section of the flint has a glazed texture and is of various shades of grey surrounded by a chalky crust. The curious effect was commented on in the diary of Celia Fiennes at the end of the seventeenth century when she noticed that Sittingbourne church, Kent, 'is all built with flints headed so Curiously that it looks like glass and shines with ye suns Reflexion'.

Normally the facing flints were laid first, up to a height of a few inches or so; the less ordered core of the wall, or the *hearting*, was then added — often consisting of a mix of poorer flint and chalk rubble in a stiff mortar or grout. Because so much relied on the strength of the mortar, each lift had to dry out properly before the next one could begin. The procedure continued until the wall was finished, but it was slow and was stopped by damp weather.

27 *Despite being a difficult material to work with, very large buildings could be built of flint, as were the medieval defences of several towns and cities in south-eastern England, including the walls and bastions around Canterbury, Kent*

The corners of flint-walled buildings were almost invariably of stone or brick, for strength, as were the jambs or doors and windows. In the better work lacing courses of stone, brick or tile were added to link the two faces of the wall and to stiffen its structure. These could be made deliberately decorative, for example forming a pattern of contrasting horizontal stripes of the dark flint and light coloured stone on the face of the building. A not uncommon variant of this was the use of a chequer pattern of squares of flint and stone. Perhaps the most attractive combination of two materials is *flushwork* in which blank patterns of dressed stone were incorporated into the flint.

In the best quality work the flints are cut to form small squares and can then be laid in regular courses. This was particularly popular in the late eighteenth and early nineteenth centuries. Flintwork is often *galleted*, with thin slithers or wedges of flint being rammed into the mortar between the whole flints. In less regular flintwork, the galleting was not simply decorative but partially structural, infilling what would otherwise have been large areas of mortar.

Ashlar consists of carefully selected, smoothly worked and laid stone and is thus generally the most expensive form of masonry. For this reason, and if possible, it was only used on the principal elevations of a building. It is thus very common to see that the side and rear walls of a splendidly fronted ashlared building are of rubble. Some of the most dramatic examples of this are in the great sweeping terraces of Georgian Bath, including the Royal Crescent itself.

28 *The four main types of flintwork, clockwise from top-left: rough; knapped; chequer work; brick coursed (Ken Hoverd, Archive)*

29 Mixing flint with stone can produce rather attractive results, especially in the informal chequer work, seen here in Harnham Mill near Salisbury, Wiltshire. It also made the construction of the walls stronger than if they had been entirely of flint (Ken Hoverd, Archive)

As previously mentioned most walls were not solid ashlar and in many ashlared walls only the outer skin of the wall was proper ashlar, and only the outer face of the outer stones at that. The inner skin, usually covered with plaster or limewash, could be any type of stone (or indeed brick), and the inner side of the ashlar blocks themselves would adhere better to the rubble and mortar core of the wall if they were left completely irregular.

Ashlar could only be created from suitable stone; some stones, such as the famed oolitic limestones, were very easy to cut and carve and ideal for ashlar. Others were virtually impossible to work until the advent of mechanised cutting and smoothing machinery in the nineteenth century.

In construction, the coursing of ashlar varied. In the best quality work regularity of stone and course height were seen as being paramount, but mostly the sizes of either or both varied. Providing the courses were even and the stones worked smooth most clients were probably quite happy. In some buildings a degree of irregularity, particularly in the form of snecking, was deliberate.

Not all ashlar work consisted of a simple smooth flat surface. The influence of the Renaissance in higher-status architecture led to the shaping of the edges or surfaces, or both, of ashlared stones. The result, is usually referred to under the general, if inappropriate name of *rustication*. In its simplest form the edges of the ashlared stones were chamfered or plainly rebated, creating light and shade in an otherwise flat surface. This became particularly fashionable for the lower storeys of Palladian buildings from the eighteenth century onwards, and these lower stories were called the *rustics*.

Ashlar was not used just for complete walls. Ashlar stones were also used for decoration and for structural strength. Thus it was common to use ashlar in the quoins, door and window surrounds in rubblestone, flint and brick buildings. Because of the quality of the workmanship required, the cost of ashlar work was always higher than that of the rougher rubblestone. The masons had to be better paid and the setting out of the work more carefully planned. A direct result of these issues has left a legacy to the modern archaeologist in the form of the various *masons' marks* often associated with ashlar.

Masons' marks are not generally as useful to the buildings archaeologist as carpenters' marks are. This is partly because they are usually cut into the top of individual stones, and thus hidden once these have been laid, and partly because, generally, they do not say a great deal about how a building was built, and only a little about those craftsmen who built it. The usual masons' marks probably originated to identify the stones worked by individual banker masons. Only a fully time-served mason was entitled to his own mark. Such a mark would allow the master mason or overseer to calculate the necessary payments and, at the same time, ensure that, if a stone was not up to standard, the mason responsible could be quickly found and told to rectify the matter.

Most masons would have, like the rest of the population of medieval Britain, been illiterate, so simple initials were seldom used. Instead, quite elaborate individual patterns evolved. These were mostly based on straight lines simply because they were easier to cut, though segments of circles could sometimes be included as well. Some of the more elaborate marks were no doubt embellished versions of simpler designs, perhaps in some cases passed down from father to son and 'differenced' in the same way as the heraldic coats of arms of the aristocracy. Few marks have ever been definitely identified with individual masons. Occasionally other marks will be found on stones, including quarry marks and check marks but again these are not usually seen in a complete building.

Visible masons' marks should usually be recorded during a building survey if they are thought to be significant, but it is not necessary to do more than take full size 'rubbings' with tissue paper and soft pencil, or take a photograph, or draw a simple sketch. Obviously, if the money and time are both in abundance, more detailed treatment is possible but the additional information gleaned will be small. The size of identical marks can vary on the same building, so precise sizes are not generally relevant.

Sometimes study of the mason marks can be of greater benefit to the understanding of a building or site. For example, exposed masons' marks could indicate reused stones laid on their sides, and if they are also found in the ruins of an older building in the vicinity, could suggest their source. Similar masons' marks on historic buildings in the same area this could suggest the same team of masons working at the same time; masons' marks on Apley Castle, a fourteenth-century fortified mansion in east Shropshire, were similar to those found at Lilleshall Abbey nearby, for example.

In more rare examples when masons' marks were deliberately cut into the face of the stones, they can be used to identify primary masonry and later replacement. One remarkable example of this is Hardwick Hall in Derbyshire, built at the end of the sixteenth century. In that building, normal rules of subtly hidden masons' marks were completely dispensed with. Apart from the internal stone carvings, every inch of ashlar, including all the individual facing blocks, the doorways inside and out, and the windows, was marked. Each block of facing stone actually had two marks; one was the banker masons, inscribed at many different sizes, and the other, a segmental check mark. It was clear that the check mark came after the banker mark and was probably cut after each stone was put in place. It was as if every piece of work had not only to be checked but had to be seen to be checked.

Quite how much this had to do with the redoubtable owner of the Hall, Bess of Hardwick, is open to speculation. In archaeological terms, it allowed for a swift and positive identification of surviving primary stonework and gave some idea of how much work on each face was done by individual masons, though these anonymous craftsmen could be identified only by their marks.

A second type of mark sometimes found on stones, but almost invariable on their top or bottom beds, are the setting out marks. These are simple scratches in the surface of the stone designed to show the masons how the stone should be laid. Unfortunately they are seldom of great value in the interpretation of a standing building.

Mud and clay

Apart from timber and stone, one of early man's most widely available walling materials was the earth, or, more specifically, earth mixed with water — mud. As a material it transcends the boundary between the natural and man-made, for in its more sophisticated use it was transformed by man into building blocks. Whilst the traditional view of the primitive mud hut is one with some basis in fact, mud, particularly in the form of unbaked brick, was also used to produce some of the finest buildings of antiquity, including the great palaces of Egypt and Babylon.

In Britain today it is often surprising to realise that several thousand houses are built of little more than mud, and that this was a technique once fairly widespread even in a relatively damp climate. The variety of quality and status of such buildings has changed hugely over the centuries. The fact that most of the surviving examples have now achieved a state of picturesque respectability should be treated with a great deal of caution.

Conversely, it is always important to remember that what we now regard as cottages, whether of mud or more substantial materials, have mainly survived because they were built as the homes of the relatively well-off. Over time they have descended the social order simply because of the increasing aspirations of society, or by obvious subdivision. True peasant dwellings were, until surprisingly recently, quite ephemeral structures and have seldom left much trace of their passing; these were often the true 'mud-huts' of history.

At the same time mud is still used in parts of the world and in Britain in the early part of this century architects were seriously recommending a more sophisticated use of the material as being both economical and practical. This was particularly so after the First World War when there was a shortage of other building materials, and due in no small measure to the efforts of the self-styled 'architect-errant', the eccentric Sir Clough William-Ellis, founder of the fantasy village of Portmeirion, Gwynedd, and more established architects such as Edwin Lutyens.

The way in which the natural mud and clays have been used in building over the centuries has varied tremendously from the primitive to the sophisticated. Basically three separate methods evolved — turf, using the earth with its grass cover still in place; solid clay or mud walls — often all now labelled *cob*; and finally, lumps of mud and clay used like stone or brick and in essence continuing the long tradition of the unfired bricks of the ancient world.

Turf

According to Nathaniel Kent, writing in 1775, over half of the poor in the United Kingdom lived in '*shattered hovels*'. A large percentage of these would have been ephemeral structures with solid turf walls, or others of flimsy timberwork covered with turves. Whilst they were evidently very common in the medieval period, their occupants were of no importance to the record keepers of the day and our knowledge of them is limited mainly to what little archaeological evidence they have left behind. Even in the post-medieval period the true extent of such buildings is still not properly understood.

Near Cheadle, north Staffordshire, in 1686 Robert Plot, noticed a hovel 'built only of turf in a Conical manner, much like the houses of the Indians near the Straights of Magellan'. It was sufficiently unusual in that area to have warranted his notice, but in other parts of Britain such structures seem even then to have been common at the end of the seventeenth century and well into the eighteenth, particularly further north. In the southern outliers of the Cheviot Hills, on the northern edge of England, there are the ruins of many *shielings*, temporary huts used by herdsmen looking after summer grazing cattle. Most of the surviving examples were built of stone but a few have been found with solid turf walls; these were probably still being built in the seventeenth century.

In Scotland, and particularly in the central Highlands, small turf huts were still common in the eighteenth century. Gradually, more permanent stone buildings replaced them but even these sometimes had wall tops and gables of turf. On many large Scottish estates, especially where agriculture was marginal at best, tenants suffered from the neglect of their usually absentee landlords. In the 1820s the Duke of Sutherland was one of the wealthiest men in the kingdom, benefiting in particular from his industrial activities in Shropshire. His peasant tenants in Scotland, however, were still living in little more than turf-walled and turf-roofed huts that they shared with their pigs and poultry. Cottages at Glencalvie, Sutherland, were described in 1845 as being 'apparently low heaps of turf', with a central hearth, though 'everything within them is clean and orderly'.

Of all the natural walling techniques, turf was the most primitive. It was used in two different ways, the more long-lasting being in the form of solid walls up to three feet thick with the turves literally used as organic building blocks and laid on top of each other in rough courses. There could be vertical timbers at the corners for additional support, and primitive crucks structurally separate from the walls to support the roof, which itself was commonly covered in more turves.

Walls built in the other method were of composite construction, the thinner turves laid grass-side inwards and fixed onto a simple framework of thin timbers or branches. The branches could be earth-fast or simply held in place by a ring of stones. Sometimes there would be wattles between the uprights, as was the case at the small inn where Boswell and Dr Johnson stayed on the way to Glenelg on their Scottish trip in 1773.

Such buildings were obviously not long-lived, have often left few traces, and will be of more interest to the excavating archaeologist rather than the building archaeologist. Even less traces remains of the hovels built by those made landless in parts of southern England by the Enclosure Acts of the eighteenth century. A Board of Agriculture survey towards the end of that century showed that many lived in turf-walled huts in counties such as Surrey and Hampshire. In the mid-nineteenth century there are records of the navvies building the new railways living in turf-walled hovels, though these were designed to be temporary. Nevertheless, the existence of such insubstantial dwellings needs to be recognised in order for the better built and surviving ones to be placed in their true historical and social context.

Solid Mud Walls

Mud and clay are effectively the same thing. Mud-walled buildings are known to have existed in Britain in the Roman period, Viking York, and medieval London. Despite the length and extent of the mud wall tradition, the nature of their construction inevitably means that, once demolished, their archaeological traces are ephemeral.

Presumably Sir Thomas More was thinking about English examples in 1516 when he wrote in his *Utopia* of 'homely cottages or poor shepherd houses, made . . . of every rude piece of timber that came first to hand, with mud walls and ridged roofs thatched over with straw'. Nevertheless, as late as the mid-sixteenth century some mud-walled houses were still of reasonably high status, such as Hayes Barton, Devon, an E-shaped cob-walled manor house of some pretensions and the birthplace, in 1554, of Sir Walter Raleigh. Curiously, nearly two centuries later, in 1728, another great seafarer, Captain James Cook, was born in a mud-walled labourer's cottage in Marton, Yorkshire.

By that time mud-walled buildings in most areas were generally, but not exclusively, homes for the lower agricultural classes. Other materials, particularly brick and stone, had become more widely available and it was only in the south-west of England that clay, locally called *cob*, was still being used for some relatively high-class buildings. In Exmouth, for instance, quite grand cob houses were being built at the very end of the eighteenth century. These were the exception rather than the rule and a few years later one of William Cobbett *Rural Rides* took him through Leicestershire. 'Look at these hovels', he fumed, 'made of mud and straw, bits of glass or of old cast-off windows'.

The old West Country word now generally used to describe most walls built of solid mud is *cob*. Earlier terms include *clob*, *clom*, and *witchert*, though in other areas, such as the English Midlands and the Carse of Gowrie in eastern Scotland, they seem to have been known more prosaically as *clay* or *mud* walls. Depending on the local geology the mud usually has chopped straw and lime added to it. These help to stop it shrinking too much and to set harder. Sometimes other aggregates were added, such as gravel or sand and, if at all possible, chalk.

Chalk was a particularly useful ingredient for mud or cob walls, and was often added

30 This house in Haddenham, Buckinghamshire, looks to be a typical seventeenth-century building of whitewashed stone or brick. Only where the external render has fallen away — underneath the brick left-hand gable — is the true construction revealed. It is mostly built of wichert, a type of mud walling specific to this area. Note the stone plinth to prevent rising damp

in a crushed form to the ordinary mud and straw mix. The greater the percentage of chalk the stronger the resultant wall. Some of the sturdiest can be found in parts of Wiltshire and Dorset, northern Hampshire and adjoining Berkshire. A small area of around Aylesbury, Buckinghamshire, which also just crosses the Oxfordshire boundary, has a particularly hard subsoil containing both chalk and clay and is known locally as *witchit* or *wychert*. Walls of this material were made in the same way as the standard cob wall but because the material was stronger they could be a little thinner.

As exposure to water will inevitably return the dried mud back to its semi-liquid state, the walls of cob buildings must be kept dry. A much repeated if varied traditional saying was that all cob walls needed for a long life was a 'good pair of shoes and a good hat'. For this reason they have solid plinths, usually of the local stone rubble or flint, and overhanging roofs. The solid plinths had the added benefit of deterring vermin.

Once the plinth was ready, the cob section of the wall could be started. The subsoil had previously been dug up and was often allowed to weather over winter to break it up and make it easier to work. It was then laid out and watered, well trodden by man and beast, and, in the process, blended with the cut straw, dung, and anything else that seemed appropriate including, if possible, the lime or gravel. This process was called *tempering*. The clay for the first layer was then forked onto the plinth and trod down by the builders.

31 A cob boundary wall in the Leicestershire village of Billesden, with the necessary 'good pair of shoes and a hat' in the form of a stone plinth and a tiled coping — possibly replacing an original one of thatch. In this part of the English Midlands the material is simply called 'mud'

Once finished and reasonably level, the sides would be straightened and straw would be put on the top. It would be left to dry before the next layer could be added.

It was a necessarily slow process. The walls were usually very thick, generally around two to three feet or more, though slightly narrower and much broader walls can also be found. The height of each layer of cob seems to have varied from region to region and from century to century. Surviving houses of the sixteenth and seventeenth centuries in Devon, for example, have recognisable layers up to a foot high, whilst in nineteenth-century Yorkshire they can be around 6in (15cm).

The amount of time it took for each layer to dry would vary according to the locality and depth. Recent research suggests that there were two distinct methods. In most of England this was the 'slow method', in which each layer could take several weeks to properly dry out. In these buildings the clay walls were structural, in that they supported a standard design of roof, albeit one usually carrying a thatch cover rather than one of stone or tile. Such buildings could take months to complete and two storey examples might take well over a year to finish.

Once each succeeding layer had dried out the next one could be added until the wall reached its desired height. Then the outside of the wall would be either coated with a lime plaster or painted with several layers of limewash to help protect it from the weather. It was common practice to build the walls solid, without openings, but to place within the clay the lintels for the doors and windows. When the wall had fully dried out, the openings could then be carefully cut through the clay wall, leaving the lintels with sufficient bearing on either side. Sometimes the door and window frames would be built of more substantial materials, such as stone, and the cob would then be built up against them. Cob buildings could be built two-storeys high with no obvious difficulty; the walls just took much longer to build. If there was an upper floor, horizontal timbers were usually added in the inner face of the cob as the walls were being built ready to support the ends of the joists.

The lack of any form of shuttering during construction meant that cob buildings lacked any angularity at all but instead had almost organic, sinuous lines, usually complemented by their equally organic roof coverings. Most cob-walled buildings seem to have had thatched roofs, which had the benefit of being lighter than tiled or slated ones and so added less weight onto the walls. The thatch was designed to overhang the walls to help protect them from the weather.

Not all clay buildings took so long to build. In northern Cumbria and elsewhere some were, structurally, composite and a 'fast method' could be used. The roofs were supported on crucks standing on the stone plinths and were thus independent of the clay walls. The plinths were built first and then the crucks raised on top of them before work on the mud walls started. The courses of clay were quite thin and interleaved with more straw than is usual elsewhere. There is some evidence to suggest that this allowed for a much faster way of walling and even apocryphal tales that, by working together, neighbours could finish a house in a day.

This faster walling technique may once have been more widely used. There are some examples of jointed cruck roofs in cob-walled buildings in the south-west of England and isolated examples have been identified in Lancashire, Warwickshire and Leicestershire. Whilst in these buildings the mud walls and the cruck-framed roof structure were clearly structurally separate, in others, the distinction between mud wall, timber-framing, and masonry becomes a little blurred.

Several examples are known of mud walls which are built up around an armature of wattles tied to ephemeral timbers hardly worthy of the term 'timber-framed'. In Lancashire, these *clam-staff and daub* houses generally have thin cruck-framed roof structures and in the early nineteenth century William Hutchinson wrote that in Northumberland the cottages of the poor were 'deplorable, composed of upright timbers fixed in the ground, the interces wattled and plastered with mud'. Similar *mud-and-stud* walls have been found in Lincolnshire.

A technique in the Speymouth area of Scotland, known as *Auchinhalrig Work*, was similar to the standard method of mud wall construction, but large lumps of stone were incorporated as well; a couple of years after completion, the surface mud of the outside would fall away and the external face of the wall would be harled — a northern term for rendering.

Another, and usually later, variant on the solid clay wall was the technique of *puddled clay* or *shuttered earth*. The undulating sides and rounded corners of cob buildings that now make them so attractive to the modern eye was out of step with the straight-lined symmetry of the late Georgian period. To improve matters, timber shuttering was placed on top of the plinth and the first layer of clay was forked into it and rammed down tight in the usual manner. Once that layer was dry, the shuttering was raised up for the next, and so on until the all was finished. Although there is evidence to indicate that the Romans used timber shuttering in a similar manner for mud-walled buildings in Verulamium (St. Alban's), most surviving English examples are from the nineteenth and twentieth centuries.

The shuttered earth method was particularly effective with a chalky soil. In some areas the clay and chalk would be watered and the resultant mixture was virtually poured between the planks of the shuttering. Once dry, the resultant walls were extremely hard and there are obviously affinities with the later technique of cast concrete.

A more sophisticated variant of shuttered earth construction is *pisé*, or, properly, *pisé de terre*. It had been used by the Romans but despite its use in much of north Africa and parts of Europe, including France, it never became widespread in Britain. The architect Henry Holland used this method in the 1790s for some estate cottages at Woburn, Bedfordshire, but it acquired only a brief popularity. It seems mainly to have been used only in those parts of southern England where chalk was readily available.

No straw and little or no water was added to the mud being used. The technique of pisé requires much higher pressure tamping down than the normal shuttered earth method and this in turn required stronger shuttering. A portable shuttering box was used and moved along as each section of wall was complete. As the walls rose this was fixed in place through the upper levels by small putlogs through the wall. Modern improvements to the technique, including adding concrete to the mix, were tried in the early twentieth century but it still failed to attract the attention of many builders.

At the end of the eighteenth century there was a revival of one of the ancient forms of mud building, the unfired brick as used thousands of years ago in Sumeria and Babylon. In post-medieval England, this occurred mainly in East Anglia, where it was called *clay lump* or *bat*, although isolated examples have been recorded elsewhere. Because of the regularity achieved in the process, and its comparative cheapness in comparison to fired brick, it became quite common in the nineteenth century in Norfolk and Suffolk, with other examples being found in Cambridgeshire and parts of Essex, Northamptonshire and Hertfordshire.

The process effectively died out towards the end of the nineteenth century, but enjoyed a brief revival in the 1920s; some small council estates were built of clay lump in the 1920s in mid-Norfolk, but now the tradition seems to have virtually ended again.

The technique was very simple and much quicker than the other types of mud wall construction. The clay was dug up, laid on the ground, watered, and then trodden. The larger stones were taken out and straw mixed in with it to stabilise it and to prevent excessive cracking. The clay was then formed into wooden moulds and left to dry, or *cure*, in much the same way as handmade fired bricks were. Clay lump blocks were substantially larger than fired brick though, generally being about the same size as a modern breeze block, but wide — big enough without being unmanageable during construction.

Once dry, the clay lump could be used in virtually the same way as the standard fired brick, using puddled clay as a mortar. It needed to be built on a stone or fired-brick plinth, but only needed to be one 'leaf' deep. Door and window openings were dealt with in the same way as in brick buildings and topped by normal wooden lintels. Once the wall was completed it was protected from the wet by being plastered or rendered and colour washed. Occasionally, and especially in farm buildings, the walls would be tarred and sanded instead. A finished clay lump building is difficult to distinguish from one of rendered brick, though the fact that it could be built quite regularly meant that it can easily be distinguished from one built of cob.

BRICK

The humble brick is one of the most basic, but most versatile, of all building materials. It is the earliest example of a building material that was *manufactured* from natural ingredients rather than *wrought* from them. An early eighteenth-century guide to building rightly describes the brick as 'a fictitious or artificial kind of Stone'. By that time brick was established as the most important of all building materials in Britain, but there is still a general and mistaken assumption that it was a relatively late arrival on the architectural scene.

Bricks developed about 5000-6000 years ago from the baked mud or clay blocks of the ancient world, when the use of fire was used instead of the heat of the sun. This resulted in a more regular, much harder and more resilient product. The Romans made and used both mud-bricks and fired bricks in their Italian cities and it was through them that the brick first arrived to Britain in the first century AD.

Generally these Roman bricks were used not for whole structures but usually for arches and vaults, or to strengthen walls of rubblestone or flint, mainly as narrow bands or 'lacing courses'. This can still be seen in many of the surviving walls of Roman sites, such as Richborough, Colchester and Wroxeter. The bricks were commonly about a foot square in plan but very thin (seldom more than 1in [2.5cm] high) and not dissimilar to nineteenth-century quarry tiles. Partly as a result of this they were usually well fired and, consequently, extremely durable.

After the withdrawal of the legions in the fifth century AD, brick-making seems to have died out in Britain despite continuing in parts of continental Europe. Whilst the making of bricks may have stopped, the use of bricks did not. The abandoned Roman towns became convenient quarries of all types of building materials, particularly in the later Saxon period. Much of Verulamium, for example, was pulled down in around AD900 on the orders of the Abbot of St.Alban's and the materials were set aside for new building. After the Conquest, the great new church of St Albans was built almost entirely of reused Roman brick, originally plastered over to resemble stone. Similar examples of architectural salvage were repeated around most of the major Roman settlements on buildings great and small, though mainly religious: such as the Saxon churches of Brixworth, Northamptonshire, Bradwell, Essex, and the late tenth-century church of St Mary-in-Castro, Dover, which also reused the adjacent Roman *pharos* as its detached belltower.

It was the strength of these Roman bricks that attracted the late Saxon and early Norman builders, and they were reused in quoins, arches, jambs, and, in St Botolph's

32 The Romans brought brick to Britain and it was used extensively by them in the defences of their towns as well as in the more important buildings. The wall built in the early second century AD around Colchester is one of the finest surviving examples and this section shows the typical use of brick lacing courses within rubble stonework

Priory, Colchester, stairs. St Botolph's also has a particularly ambitious west front decorated with brick-built blind arcading, originally plastered.

Perhaps the wide availability of salvaged Roman brick delayed the re-establishment of a native brick-making industry, but the reduction in the relative cost of good quality stone may also have had some effect. Whatever the reason, the earliest known examples so far of new, post-Roman, brick in Britain are thought to be in the church at Polstead, Suffolk, built around 1160. It is a mainly flint building, but the voussoirs of the chancel arch and nave arcades are thin red bricks. A better-known and better-documented site is the former Cistercian abbey at Little Coggeshall where the flint rubble abbot's lodging and gatehouse were built about 1190 and have brick dressings. The bricks used in both buildings were remarkably similar, roughly 13in (32.5cm) long, 6in (15cm) wide and 2in (5cm) deep.

The shape and size of these so-called 'great bricks' set them apart from the smaller and narrower 'Flemish' bricks that were imported in fairly large numbers during the thirteenth and fourteenth centuries. The brick industry in Flanders and northern Germany had developed because of the lack of good local stone and timber for building. These same criteria existed in much of the east of England and there were also strong trading links between the ports on either side of the North Sea, particularly through the Hanseatic League. Not surprisingly, Flanders had a huge influence on the English brick industry, though the amount of bricks imported into England is easy to exaggerate. One famous shipment is the 202,500 bricks sent from Nieuport in 1278 for use in the Tower of London; the cost of transport was considerably more than the cost of the bricks.

A more significant import from Flanders than the bricks were some of the brickmakers. The differences between imported bricks and native bricks made by immigrant craftsmen or their apprentices are almost impossible to distinguish, apart from in their relationship to the local clay. By the late 1270s, when the first substantial surviving brick house, Little Wenham Hall, Suffolk, was built, the bricks used were mainly of Flemish type, but made locally. On average they were 9in (23cm) long, 4in (11.5cm) wide and 2in (5cm) deep — almost identical to the standard brick of today.

The name 'brick' only appears in the surviving documents from 1340, when a stair made of *brikis* is mentioned at Windsor Castle. It does not become common until the fifteenth century. Up until that time the bricks are generally called 'wall tiles', 'Flemish tiles', and sometimes, more confusingly, 'tegulae', which could mean either bricks or roof tiles. Leland noted in the early sixteenth century that 'the buildings of Hulle for the most part be . . . buildid with brike' and that the bricks had been made in an area called the *Tylery*.

Although since the late fourteenth century the texture and colour of brick has become more varied, the basic size has remained the same with only minor differences. The reason for this is quite simple; there was no reason to change from a size of brick that was not too heavy and could be lifted easily in one hand and laid from a narrow scaffold. Over the years there have also been attempts to officially regulate the size of bricks, and as early as 1425 there was an official brick mould kept in the Moot Hall at Chelmsford, Essex to ensure that all 'tylers' made bricks of the same size. Despite this, bricks continued to vary in size but the differences were seldom great. Overall, the height of bricks gradually increased from the fourteenth century onwards, whilst their length has generally remained more or less the same.

As a fashionable building material, brick really blossomed at the start of the sixteenth century especially after being used in the great palaces of Cardinal Wolsey and, more importantly, Henry VIII. By the end of that century, even most of the middling yeoman houses had at least a brick (and fireproof) chimney. In 1587 Harrison noted, that in the south east of England at least, that many new houses 'as be lately built are commonly either of brick or hard stone, or both'. In other areas of the country timber-framing and stone continued to flourish nonetheless well into the second half of the seventeenth century.

The great age of brick was undoubtedly the eighteenth century, for whilst the greater houses may be built of stone, most middling houses were of brick, and, by the end of the century, even working-class houses were being constructed of this material in some areas of England. As usual, the government tried to capitalise on success and, after earlier attempts had failed, introduced a Brick Tax in 1784. The tax was levied on green unfired brick whatever their size, so some enterprising brickmakers simply manufactured larger bricks — a loophole not closed until 1803. These *tax bricks* can sometimes be seen in late-eighteenth century buildings but most bricks continued to be of the standard size.

In a sense brick became a victim of its own success and at the end of the eighteenth century it began to become a little unfashionable. Because it was relatively cheap, it was then being used for much of the new working class housing of the towns and for the huge new factories, often designed to ape the houses of the great and the good. Ashlared stone had never ceased to be at the pinnacle of architectural taste but was expensive. Architects began to imitate it, covering ordinary brick walls with *stucco,* a lime-based cement lined to resemble ashlar, and this fashion continued until around the 1840s until there was a Victorian moral backlash against such 'deceit'. Subsequently 'honest' brickwork became the most important material for buildings ranging from outhouses to Gothic Revival churches and town halls.

Until the end of the nineteenth century, the colour and texture of bricks usually reflected the local clays and gave buildings a distinct regional character. Through most of

33 *Detail of the early sixteenth-century brickwork of Hampton Court, Middlesex, the palace begun by Cardinal Wolseley and finished by his master, Henry VIII. The diaper pattern was made by using the burnt ends, or headers, of standard red handmade red bricks*

the country, bricks were varying shades of red, from the subtle reddy-brown hues of the Midlands to the strident cherry reds of the Lancashire shales. In the south-east, there were two main colour palettes, the reds, and the greys. The 'greys' varied from russet red to pale yellow and true grey bricks were rare; by the later eighteenth century the standard colour of brick in London and the home counties was a dull beigey yellow.

Builders were quick to realise the decorative potential of mixing up the different coloured bricks. In the early clamps and kilns, it was common for many of the bricks to be more burnt than others, which usually resulted in partially vitrified ends; though accidental at first the effect was later deliberately created in the firing. These burnt-ended bricks, or *flared headers,* were often blue or grey on a typical red brick, and the use of diaper work in these blue headers was well established on the grander buildings by the end of the sixteenth century. Later, simple colour combinations were used on much humbler houses. In Sussex, for example, the wood-fired kilns gave a gentle blue-grey hue to locally produced bricks, which could be enhanced by using red bricks for quoins and window surrounds. Red bricks were similarly used with yellow stocks in the south or vice versa in the north.

Better transport facilities meant that from the middle of the nineteenth century bricks from different areas could be transported all over the country, and architects began experimenting with elaborate colour patterns in brick. This *polychrome brickwork* was seen as a cheap way to enliven cheap buildings and, in conjunction with stone and other materials, was also used on some of the grandest. Mass-produced bricks made in large specialist brickworks began to dominate the market. This was particularly true of the common-or-garden *flettons* from Bedfordshire, and the durable 'pressed' engineering bricks — the 'Staffordshire Blues' and 'Accrington Bloods'. Brick is still a popular material for 'traditional' style buildings but since the middle of the twentieth century it is literally

34 Sissinghurst, Kent, is world-famous for the gardens laid out in the early twentieth century, but it also possesses this fine brick-built prospect tower or gatehouse, the main remnant of the Elizabethan mansion that stood on the site. Unusually, when the turret roofs were repaired in the twentieth century they were covered with wooden shingles instead of tiles

only skin deep on most new buildings.

Brickmaking was a fairly simple but labour intensive and seasonally dependant process, and remained so up until the middle of the nineteenth century. In the autumn the clay or brick earth first had to be dug, initially from close to the surface or even in river or estuary beds. The clods were then piled into heaps in the open to be *weathered* over the winter, during which frosts, in particular, and rain helped to break down the clay. In the early spring the clods were turned and beaten to extract any stones or other impurities. After that the clay was laboriously *tempered* or *puddled* (i.e. sluiced with water and trodden on by men and animals), and any remaining contaminants removed. It was usually then left under cover for a few more weeks to properly *cure* before being ready for the *moulder*.

Up until about the middle of the fourteenth century some medieval bricks were made without moulds. Instead, the clay would be rolled evenly onto a bed of straw, which prevented it from sticking to the ground, and then cut up into the individual bricks, which was a process used by the Romans and one that in some ways anticipated the wire cut bricks of this century. The resultant bricks varied considerably in size and meant that the courses in which they were laid varied too.

35 By the eighteenth century brick was a fashionable material in most of England and extensively used. The Crown Hotel in Devizes, Wiltshire, is a typical building of the time, built of brick with stone decoration in the window sills, keystones and porch. The tall room over the gateway to the left is of a slightly later build than the rest

Moulded bricks, although more time consuming to make, were much preferable. The clay was simply pushed into a wooden mould, or *form,* of the required dimensions and the excess was removed. The unfired, or *green,* bricks were then taken from the mould and stacked in *hacks* to finish curing before being burnt in a *clamp* or a proper *kiln* or *tilehouse.* Permanent kilns were expensive to build and maintain and needed to be used all the time to be viable. They tended to be built only in the major towns where there was a ready market. Clamps, on the other hand, were only temporary, involved little or no capital, and were built of the bricks that were to be fired anyway; they were thus ideal for single projects.

One of the earliest mechanical innovations in brickmaking was the development of the *pugmill* at the end of the seventeenth century. This was a machine for blending clays and consisted of paddles or blades attached to a vertical shaft within a barrel into which the clays were loaded. The shaft was turned by a revolving beam pulled round and round by a horse and improved version of these horse-powered pugmills continued in use until the start of the twentieth century. By that time far more sophisticated steam powered pugmills had evolved. Some mechanisation of the brickmaking process, such as the rolling of clay, occurred in the eighteenth century, but until the mid-nineteenth century it was still labour intensive and quite primitive.

The most important changes to brick manufacture did not take place until the mid-nineteenth century. In 1858 the Hoffman Kiln was invented, which allowed for a continually fired brick kiln that avoided the waste of time and fuel in having to constantly fire-up and cool down the kiln as each batch of bricks were made. New improvements in

36 By the nineteenth century brick had become an almost universal building material, helped by the canals and railways. It was one of the commonest materials for farm buildings by this time. This brick barn, at Glan Hafren near Welshpool, Powys, is of particularly good quality and was also innovative in its technology, the machinery within originally being powered by a water turbine

steam-powered machinery evolved at around the same time and included new types of pugging mills and brick presses.

Brick-making also became more concentrated in larger and larger works in specific areas, particularly after huge reserves of Lower Oxford clays around the Cambridgeshire village of Fletton were found to contain up to 10% carbon, and were thus almost self-firing. They also had relatively little water content and could be taken directly to the kilns without having to dry out first. The Hoffman kilns were modified to cope with the new type of brick, resulting in taller chimneys that are now an integral part of the landscape of Cambridgeshire and Bedfordshire.

Flettons has become a generic word for cheaply made brick, and their discovery has been likened to that of North Sea Oil in that it provided a bonanza of very cost-effective domestic brick that meant despite the huge increases in demand, British bricklayers did not have to resort to the cheap hollow clay bricks used on much of the Continent.

Hollow bricks were advocated by some architectural reformers on the basis of cost — including Henry Roberts who, with Prince Albert's encouragement, patented several types and used them for the prince's model dwellings at the Great Exhibition of 1851 and in some workers houses in Windsor and elsewhere. Despite Royal patronage they were never widely used for domestic buildings. One rare example of their adoption was in the walls of munitions factories. For example, in the main iron-framed and brick buttressed 'sheds' of government munitions depots built in the First World War, the rest of the side

37 *A small brick house in Kimbolton, Cambridgeshire, probably of early nineteenth century date. The reason that the bricks seem rather tall is that they are laid on their sides rather than flat — in a 'rat-trap' bond. This saved on the number of bricks used but was not as strong as more traditional bonds. The building also has a pantiled roof*

38 *From the mid-nineteenth century glazed bricks became fashionable, particularly for commercial and industrial buildings. White-glazed tiles were useful in dark spaces, but the plum reds used at the start of the twentieth century by Leslie Green for his London Underground stations were chosen as part of a distinct, and still recognisable, house style. This is Chalk Farm station near Camden, London*

39 *The brickwork on the front wall of a building is often of a better quality than on the rest of the walls, and sometimes even the bricks on the front face of a wall are better than the rest of the wall — as in this mid-eighteenth-century building in Walsall, West Midlands, where the outer face is only crudely bonded into the rest*

walls were made of hollow bricks to prevent too much collateral damage if there was an explosion.

Allied to the brick industry was the production of *terracotta*. This had been used in the late medieval period but its use expanded greatly in the second half of the nineteenth century. The finest brick clay was used in moulds and fired at high temperatures. The moulds could be elaborate or fairly plain, allowing for the mass production of decorative features such as consoles or band courses, or for individual works including cartouches with a firm's name included, or a date. Terracotta panels were usually unglazed but a second firing allowed a glaze to be added; usually the panels (or tiles) were hollow and quite lightweight, but extremely durable. A generic glazed form of terracotta is faience, also popular at the turn of the twentieth century.

Brickwork

Bricks are a conveniently hand-sized building block and obviously had to be properly laid if the building was going to be strong and long-lasting. The individual bricks were laid in mortar, usually consisting of lime and sand until the start of the twentieth century when cement replaced lime. The mortar not only bound the individual bricks together, but also helped to distribute the loading of the wall evenly through the masonry. As in stonework, mortar could be laid thick enough to act as the bedding for the bricks and have enough extruding out from the surface to be properly 'pointed' back flush with the wall face; this was sometimes referred to as *common mortar*. In better quality work this bedding mortar was separate from the later pointing and not always of the same mix. In Georgian buildings in particular a finer lime mortar or even a lime putty was used for the pointing instead.

40 *The main bonds:*
   a English bond
   b English Garden Wall Bond
   c Flemish Bond
   d Flemish Bond with burnt
   headers and stone quoins

41 *Part of the terracotta decoration of Sir George Gilbert Scott's Midland Hotel, the grand Gothic Revival pile attached to St. Pancras' station, London and opened in 1876. Built of brick it is richly decorated in stone and terracotta.*

The pattern in which the bricks are laid is called the *bond*, and these vary according to the thickness of the wall and taste. In the earliest examples of solid brick walls, the irregular shaped bricks were laid in fairly thick mortar and in a quite haphazard bond. Gradually, experience showed that by using a more regular bond, greater strength could be achieved along with an economy of brick use and walls began to be thinner.

In practise there have been two main families of bonds, now known as English and Flemish, and differentiated by the way in which the bricks are arranged in the main elevation. English bonds are expressed as alternating courses of *stretchers* (bricks showing their full length in the wall), and *headers* (brick ends in the wall). Flemish bonds, on the other hand, consist of alternating stretchers and headers in the same course. English bonds are simpler and thought to be stronger, but Flemish bonds became more fashionable, especially from the end of the seventeenth century. It is quite common to see Flemish bond used on the principal elevations of a building and English bond on the rest. Despite their name, this is a bond seldom seen on historic brick buildings in Flemish towns like Ghent or Bruges.

Apart from slight differences in the placing of the bricks in an elevation, the main variants on these are the 'Garden Wall' bonds. In English bond walls these usually have two or more courses of stretchers between each course of headers. In Flemish bonds there are two variants, one in which there are two or more stretchers between each header in the same course, and a second in which there may be one or more stretcher courses between each 'bond' course of stretchers and headers. These are known respectively as Flemish Garden Wall and Flemish Stretcher bond.

Even in the best-planned buildings it was virtually impossible to ensure that every corner and every opening was designed so that each adjacent course ended in a full brick. This meant that other lengths of brick had to be introduced into the bonding, known usually as *closers*. A *queen closer* is a brick cut straight across, whilst a *king closer* is usually longer and has an angled cut. Closers could also accommodate the changes in the bond at corners between the inner and outer faces of thicker walls.

Not all brickwork is quite what it seems. It became common practise to build the main outer 'leaf' or face of brick in the better quality *stock* brick and the inner leafs (one, two or more depending on its thickness), in cheaper *place* bricks. These often contained as much common ash, swept from countless fireplaces, as proper clay and were extensively used where they would not be seen.

Unscrupulous builders would not even use the headers of the outer leaf of stock bricks to bond the front of the wall into these inferior bricks. Instead, to save money, they would use *snap headers* in the facade, which were just proper bricks cut in half and used as if they were full ones. Only an occasional full brick header would tie in the two parts of the wall. Even some walls nominally solid and $1^1/_2$ bricks thick have been found in which the outer and inner faces are only linked by occasional through bricks across what is essentially a brick-rubble filled void, a technique echoing medieval masonry walling. Worse still, some builders did not even *have* an inner leaf of place bricks, but faced lath and plaster covered studwork with a single outer leaf of brickwork. Many of the elegant stuccoed Georgian terraces, in particular, were appallingly built.

By the end of the nineteenth century some architects had realised the potential benefits of introducing a cavity into brick walls, improving insulation, sound-proofing and preventing damp. This was initially produced to save paying too much brick tax; standard-sized bricks were laid on their sides rather than on their bottoms but the bond pattern produced inevitably created gaps in the masonry. Despite some serious attempts at using cavity walling, until the 1930s brickwork was, if properly built, generally solid. Since the Second World War cavity walls — with two single leafs of brick with a gap between them — have become the norm, with the two 'skins' joined by metal ties at intervals. More recently, the inner 'skins' have been replaced by cheaper and stronger blockwork, of concrete or 'breeze', and the outer skin of brick has become a mere facing. In larger buildings of steel or reinforced concrete framing, the brickwork forms a non-load-bearing screen wall.

FRAMED CONSTRUCTION

Timber-framing

In 1587 William Harrison wrote that 'The greatest part of our building in the cities and good towns of England consisteth only of timber'. The quality and design varied enormously, from buildings in areas where quality wood was plentiful that were 'commonly strong and well timbered' to those 'slightly set up with a few posts . . . in the

42 *The famous Wheat Barn at Cressing Temple, Essex, has been dated by tree-ring analysis to the second half of the thirteenth century. This aisled building is built of square sectioned oak timbers and uses mainly half-lapped joints. It is a magnificent survival of early medieval carpentry techniques*

43 *Unlike the Cressing Temple barn, most medieval buildings had larger sized panels until the fifteenth century. These are seen clearly in the mid-fifteenth-century Chesil Rectory, Winchester, Hampshire. It is an early example of vernacular building conservation, having been restored in 1892-3 (Ken Hoverd/Archive)*

fenny countries and northern parts . . . where for lack of wood they are enforced to continue this ancient manner of building'.

Harrison's distinction between the quality of timber-framed buildings is important, and not only for the inherent regional differences. There was also a huge variety in the quality of timber-framed buildings, from the hovel to the great mansion, and it is important to realise that the buildings that we study today exist not simply because they have escaped fire, war, or replacement, but also because they were amongst the better built buildings of their day. The vast majority of the timber-framed buildings — certainly up until the later seventeenth century — were simply not as long-lasting.

Although wood was an obvious and readily available material with which ancient man could build his huts, the manner in which carpentry developed in Britain is unknown. Unfortunately we have very few timber structures of any kind that can definitely be dated to before the twelfth century. Even the famous tree-trunk walls of the small Essex church of Greensted-juxta-Ongar, once thought to be of the ninth century AD, have been scientifically dated to the late eleventh century. However, the sophistication of design in our earliest surviving structures clearly shows that they were born of an already long and well-established craft tradition. Although 'solid' timber walls, of horizontal or vertical logs, have been identified through excavation they appear to have been very rare in Britain, and instead the use of timber for walling has generally been in the form of timber-framing.

Today we generally think of this timber-frame tradition dying out in the face of the competition of brick in the seventeenth century, but it is important to realise that this was not the case. High-status timber-framed buildings were still being built after the English Civil War and the technique was still commonly being used for homes and other buildings in rural areas throughout the eighteenth century. Often these were of quite poor quality, partly for reasons of cost and partly because of the difficulty of obtaining decent sizes of timber. At the same time a gradual awareness of better design evolved by the end of the century, and in the eighteenth century the architect Samuel Wyatt even designed prefabricated timber-framed hospitals that could be shipped to anywhere they might be needed.

In July 1913 the editor of the *Spectator*, John St Loe Strachey, exhibited a three-bedroom cottage costing just £150 and made of a simple timber frame, weatherboarded externally and plastered within. In a sense the techniques used were still as simple as they had been two or three centuries earlier but greater sophistication of design continued through the twentieth century and by the end of it large numbers of timber-framed buildings were still being built all over Britain, from the south-east of England to the north-east of Scotland.

The raw material for timber-framed buildings came originally from the forests that swathed most of Britain, and England in particular, up until the medieval period. As these were being cleared and the demand for timber grew there is some evidence to suggest that timber was beginning to be properly 'harvested' in managed woodlands.

By far the most common timber found in timber-framed buildings, and presumably the most desirable, is the native *oak*. Widespread, plentiful, slow growing, close-grained, easy to work and long-lasting, it was used for construction of both buildings and ships. The best

44 *A fine close-studded framed first-floor guildhall, now part of Lord Leycester's Hospital in Warwick. Close-studded was structurally unnecessary and purely for display. Lavish use of timber indicated wealth. Built in the mid-fifteenth century, for centuries it was subdivided into four apartments, being restored to its present state in 1950. (Ken Hoverd, Archive)*

timber came from trees around 200 years of age that had reached their maturity and an oak, if allowed to grow unrestricted in our climate, could reach a height of well over 120 feet. Baulks of large scantling oak well over 50ft long were not uncommon in medieval buildings; for example, at the end of the fourteenth century the timber posts of the new octagon of Ely cathedral were each 63ft in length and came from huge oak trees felled in woodlands belonging to Chicksands Priory in Bedfordshire many miles away.

The accelerating depletion of the oak forests in the later sixteenth century sometimes led to the need to use other hardwood trees for framing. *Ash*, another close-grained timber, was used in some cases but its flexibility meant that it was used only when oak was not available. *Elm* is known to have been used for this purpose, though its main attribute, resistance to damp, meant that it was also a particularly suitable timber for use in water mills, lock gates, pile footings for bridges and wharves, and even early water pipes. Its twisted grain resists splintering and yet it cuts easily into boards, used both for floors and, in the south-east of England, for weatherboarding. Framed buildings of *beech, larch, poplar* and *chestnut* have also been identified and several other native species found diverse use in the building industry, especially in areas where the choice was limited.

Usually the timber was used soon after it was felled, rather than being left to season. When the felled wood is still 'green' it is wetter, softer, and easier to work. Using the limited tools available to them principally the axe, the saw and the adze in manifold ways, the carpenters were able to 'convert' the raw timber into the beams, posts and joists for the building. The way in which the cut tree trunk, bough or branch was converted depended on its size and on the size, or 'scantling', of the elements needed in the framing or elsewhere in the new building.

Typically the main methods involved *boxing* (or *hearting*), *halving, quartering,* or *slabbing*. As far as possible every bit of the tree was used, so that even a fairly thin branch could be 'boxed' to create a rafter or a joist. Where timbers were halved or quartered it was common sense for the builders to use the timbers cut from the same tree in similar positions, such as in matching end posts or tie-beams. This can sometimes be checked visually by matching the visible rings of the timbers. Carpenters were also careful to use the natural contours of a tree bough or branch where it suited them, particularly, for example, in curving braces for example and, above all, in crucks.

Cruck construction is one of the simplest forms of any type of framing, and its use was not confined just to buildings that were wholly timber-framed. It is a technique once considered to be fairly primitive and ancient but one that more recent research has demonstrated could conversely be extremely sophisticated and survive for far longer than might have been anticipated. Many medieval cruck buildings were of high status, particularly in the western Midlands and the Welsh Marches, and the sheer size and decoration of some crucks can be surprising. It was a type of building contemporary with the more common forms of framing, rather than a predecessor, and one that shared many of the developments in jointing techniques and changes in architectural decoration. In a much debased form it continued in some poorer parts of Britain until the nineteenth century.

In a cruck building the main structure is based on pairs of crucks, or *blades,* usually cut from the same piece of timber and thus virtually identical in size, shape, and alignment. Joined at the top and usually tied by one or more horizontal *collars,* each pair forms an 'A'-frame structure that supports the ridge-piece and purlins of the roof structure. The feet of the crucks were usually stood onto stone padstones set into the ground. The side walls, usually linked by horizontal timbers (*spurs*) to the main cruck blades, are virtually freestanding and carry little load. They could be of almost any material, including timber-framing; in lesser vernacular buildings where only poor walling materials were available — poor quality rubble, mud or turf for example — crude cruck pairs were used to support the roof structure, and the walls simply kept out the weather.

Other variants of crucks include *jointed crucks,* with blades made up of more than one piece of timber; *raised crucks,* in which the blades rise from well above ground level (generally 2m or more) from a masonry wall; and *base crucks* in which the blades do not join but instead are linked by a tie-beam or wall-plate.

Whilst the use of crucks was not confined to timber-framed buildings, their construction, however simple, belongs to the timber-framed tradition just as a medieval timber roof on a masonry church does. Their individual timbers can be studied in the same way. Nevertheless they are very different in design terms to what could be called the 'standard' forms of timber-framed construction — the '*post and truss*' and '*box frame*' — with which most of the rest of this section is concerned.

45 *A medieval cruck-framed building in Weobley, Herefordshire. This decayed market town has one of the most interesting and varied collections of timber-framed buildings in England, and a fine stone church. It is well worth a visit*

46 *By the sixteenth and seventeenth centuries the framing in south-eastern England, especially in East Anglia, used much thinner timbers than the western counties, presumably because of the available supply of building materials. These typical examples are in Lavenham, Suffolk, and may well have been completely rendered originally*

A timber-framed building is, as its name suggests, made up of frames of timber that fit together to form a basic structural carcass. For their strength they rely on the quality of the design and the carpentry techniques used, rather than on the sheer massive strength of stone or brick walls. Theoretically, a well-made timber-framed building could be lifted bodily from its plinth and rolled over without falling apart. In recent years the removal of timber-framed buildings in their entirety a few hundred yards to avoid, for example, a new road scheme occasionally makes the news, but is not a new phenomenon.

In cruck buildings the structure forms natural units, or *bays*, marked by the crucks. Thus a very small cruck structure with just two cruck frames, one in each end wall, would be a single bay building. Add a third cruck and associated purlins and the building is now of two bays, add a fourth and it is of three, and so on. This basic principle also applies to the more common type of framing, but instead of the crucks it is the more substantial cross-frames which mark the divisions between the bays, whether these are partition frames or not.

Terminology for timber-framing, as in everything else, has changed over the centuries and there is still no universally accepted dictionary of terms. The glossary of terms in the appendix gives at least a reasonable introduction to current usage. Usually, any vertical timber running the full height of a frame is called a *post,* and the posts flanking the cross-frames are for obvious reasons called *bay posts*; those between bays are called *intermediate posts*. Lesser vertical timbers are usually called *studs*. The bottom beam of a frame is called a *sill* or *sole plate*, and the top one, the *wall plate*. The long beams at the upper floor levels are called *girding beams* and most other horizontal timbers in the framing are called *rails*. Braces are either *curved* or *straight* and *up* or *down* depending on how they relate to the posts to which they are joined.

Generally the timbers for the individual frames would be measured and cut in the carpenter's yard, sometimes close to the building site and sometimes a fair distance away. They obviously needed to be joined together and this required properly designed joints; nails, whilst used in medieval times for fixing laths and lesser timbers, were not used for significant structural purposes until well into the post-medieval period.

The importance of studying the development and diversity of joints and carpentry techniques in general has been demonstrated only fairly recently by pioneering experts such as Cecil Hewitt but the subject is too vast to go into in detail. In general there are two main types of joints: the *open* or *half-lapped* and the *mortise and tenon*. Broadly speaking the half-lapped joints tend to predate the more sophisticated mortise and tenon ones but for several centuries the two were being used at the same time, often on the same building.

It is still possible to see the *setting out marks* on timbers that have not been exposed to the weather. These were usually shallow scratches cut by the carpenter to mark the position and size of the necessary cuts or mortises that needed to be cut or to ensure that adjoining timbers were properly aligned. These are not to be confused with *carpenters' marks*.

Once all the pieces of an individual frame were ready they would be loosely slotted together, virtually all joints being variants of mortise and tenons usually stiffened by pegs. At this stage the pegs would not be driven home. Once the carpenter was satisfied, the frame would be dismantled and the individual pieces carted or dragged to the site for

47 *Good examples of carpenters' marks and assembly scratches are literally the key to understanding the way timber-framed buildings were erected. These knife cut marks are in the fifteenth-century gatehouse of Lower Brockhampton, Herefordshire*

assembly. To ensure that the right pieces were put up in the right order it was usually to mark the individual joints in the yard beforehand in numerical sequences. These number sequences — usually but not always a debased form of Roman numerals — are generally called *carpenter's marks*. This is a term that some experts disagree with, arguing that they should really be called *assembly marks*. However they have been called carpenters marks for a long time and it seems pointless to change.

Carpenter's marks are too often ignored or underestimated but often they are the key to understanding an historic timber frame because they are, quite literally, the instructions to erecting the frames. Identifying a sequence of marks can help the archaeologist in understanding how a building was erected and how much it has subsequently been altered. Their design varied over the centuries but the sheer amount of regional variations and the often conservative nature of the carpenters makes dating by their design rather dangerous, unless there are many other similar local examples.

In general, the earliest marks in the highest status building have sometimes been quite complex early Arabic numbers but the majority of medieval and post-medieval marks have been Roman. Again, in general, the earlier marks tend to be quite long and knife or scribe cut, whilst later ones were often cut by a chisel or curved gouge. One variant, found for example in some buildings in Warwickshire, consists of circular marks. Arabic numbers as we know them are fairly uncommon — mainly because they were much more complicated to cut than the straight lines of the Roman numerals — and tend to date to the later seventeenth century and after.

The way in which the marks were used varied enormously. In most examples the number sequences may only go up to the 20s, but there are others that reach into far higher numbers. For example there was a fashion in the Shropshire and south Cheshire area in the early seventeenth century for very large numerals indeed — with one example, Rowley's House, Shrewsbury, having numbers up to the high 80s all cut in a single design of crossed 'X's, 'V's, and I's that look initially like incomprehensible hieroglyphs. Incidentally because of the way the numbers were to be used it was very unusual to use the proper Roman system for numbers ending in 4 or 9 — an IV or IX could too easily be confused with a VI (6) or XI (11), especially as the 'V's were not always cut the right way up. 4s tended to be IIII and 9s, VIIII. Similarly, the numerals 'M' and 'C' were not used.

48 Builders making mistakes are not a twentieth-century phenomenon; it has happened throughout time. In this early sixteenth-century timber-framed building in Warwick the carpenter started to saw the stud in the wrong place before realising the error — hence the parallel cut to the angle of the brace

It was important in many buildings to distinguish between individual frames, sides of frames, or storey heights and in such cases the individual carpenter's marks would be given special *frame tags* or *differencing marks*. In the simplest form these would consist of a simple diagonal tick attached to the last digit of the number — to distinguish left from right, for example. More complex forms included the use of the curved gouge to cut circle segments; the late medieval framing of Sinai Park, Staffordshire, had *frame tags* that included quarter circles, semicircles, three-quarter circles, full circles, and 'V's formed by two quarter circles. This later proved invaluable in identifying reused timbers from this phase in later parts of the complex. Carpenters' marks were not confined to the main frame members and in some buildings every single common rafter or floor joist may be numbered.

Once the individual frames had been reassembled at the building site the joints would be fixed by timber pegs hammered home through holes already drilled through the timbers. It was quite common to slightly offset the hole through the tenon so that when the peg was rammed home it would pull it into the mortise as tight as possible. Depending on where the frame was to end up the ends of the peg would then be trimmed. However, it was normal to leave the pegs uncut if they were to be out of sight — in a roofspace for example. By identifying the direction pegs were hammered home, which will normally be from the same side as the carpenters' marks, it should be possible to see which side of the timber lay uppermost when the framing was laid out prior to being assembled. This can often help in working out the sequence of the assembly of the individual frames. Some frames could be reared in their entirety and others assembled section by section, and close study of joints and carpenters' marks can assist in working out which methods were used.

During construction it would be normal for a frame to require propping as other sections were raised. In the outer face of some timbers there is often an angled and apparently redundant open notch. This would have taken the head of a temporary raking shore either during initial assembly or, in some cases, later repairs. As the main frames were being erected so the floor structures and other internal structures would be fitted

49 The decayed plaster of this panel infill has exposed the manner of its construction. This is typical early seventeenth-century work

50 Typical early seventeenth-century lath-and-plaster (or daub) infill between close-studding

into place, completing the main timber carcass of the building.

Most floors were designed as integral parts of the structure, and their beams and joists helped to tie the main frame skeleton together. In usually later and lesser buildings floors may simply be supported on fairly thin beams pegged or nailed to the inner side of the framing. Similarly, roofs of timber-framed buildings were mainly integral and the main trusses formed the upper sections of the main cross-frames. Recently this technique has been called '*post-and-truss*' construction to distinguish it from '*box-frame*' construction in which the trusses (if any) and rafters of the roof may not align with the main framing. Instead these are simply supported by the wall-plates forming the tops of the wall frames; the main framing in this case simply creates a timber-framed 'box' on which the roof sits.

A variant of both types of construction is the *jetty*. This is where one or more of the upper floor wall frames projects further than that of the floor immediately below. The jettied frame is of a completely separate construction and is supported by the ends of the floor joists, which oversail the lower wall-frame. The sill of the jettied frame is called the *bressumer* and either sits directly on top of the jetty joists, or these are tenoned into the back of it. In some of the first type a moulded *fascia* would be added to the ends of the joists beneath the true bressumer. In general, medieval bressumers tended to be plain or simply moulded whilst richer moulding became more common in the late sixteenth century.

Jetties could be used on one or more sides of a timber-framed building. Because of the way in which the joists supported the jettied frames, matters became complicated at the corners if two or more sides of a building were jettied. The joists had to run at right-angles

51 One of the more unusual panel
    infills — alabaster slips fixed in
    between close-studding at Sinai
    Park, Staffordshire, of c.1500.
    The lower Trent valley was
    well known for its alabaster
    production, so such infills were
    presumably a useful by-product

52 Brick nogging could take
    several different forms. The
    narrow spaces between the
    close-studding of this frame
    meant that a herring-bone
    pattern of bricks had to be used

to the bressumers on both sides. This was accommodated by the use of a main diagonal
beam in the floor structure running to the corner and called a *dragon beam*. The inward
ends of jetty joists of diminishing length were tenoned into this beam allowing their outer
ends to support the bressumers in the usual way.

Jetties appear to have originally been mainly an urban feature and were well established
by the fourteenth century. One obvious benefit of having jettied upper floors in crowded
towns where space was at a premium was the additional floor space they created. It has
also been suggested that the design reduced the effect of sagging in the main beams of a
building by altering the weight distribution within the framing. Whilst this has been
disputed one structural aspect that may have been of some relevance is the fact that this
method of construction allowed for taller buildings without the need for long and
expensive main posts on the jettied sides.

Although possibly beginning in towns, jetties were also common in the countryside
where space was not at a premium; this was presumably simply a matter of architectural
fashion. Gradually, and also possibly in part for fashionable reasons, the character of jetties
changed from the medieval to the post-medieval period. Fairly plain jetties with broad
overhangs were gradually superseded by more decorative but shallower jetties — and in
some seventeenth century examples the 'jetty' was not a true jetty at all. The shallow jetty
was simply achieved by a *mock bressumer* — a particularly thick girding beam in the framing
that was cut to have the lower wall frame members tenoned into its inward side and the

upper ones into its outward side, created just enough displacement in profile to suggest a fashionable jettied elevation.

Two much rarer forms of jettying should be mentioned. The side walls of the two upper floors of Rowley's House, Shrewsbury, actually a large warehouse built in the early seventeenth century, are jettied. However, all the joists run axially (that is, along the length of the building), and so could not support the jetties. Instead, the main floor beams oversail the wall plate of each floor level and support the bressumers instead. The joists are tenoned between these beams and so take the flooring in the jettied sections and addition 'cornice' joists were used to fill any gaps between the side frames and floor structure under the jettied sections. In this case the jetties were certainly used to increase the available floor space and the unusual design to cater with the heavy loadings on the jettied floors.

Composite forms of jettying, in which a timber-framed upper section is jettied beyond a lower wall of stone, may once have been more common than they are now in Britain. One recently rediscovered example is at Astley Castle, Warwickshire, where the early seventeenth-century jettied upper frame survives largely intact (though no longer as an external wall), but most of the stone ground floor wall below it has been removed. The main archaeological clue is in the return façade, which is entirely of stone; a full height construction break follows the original profile of the jettied elevation. In the south-east of England in the later eighteenth and early nineteenth century composite construction of this type was revived, usually for vernacular buildings. Typically these would have a brick ground floor and a timber-framed first floor, its framing either rendered or covered with weatherboarding.

The design of the framing pattern, or panelling, of the walls of a timber-framed building mainly fell into two separate categories. The first was the rectangular, or square panel, efficient and economical in the use of timber; by and large the size of the panels gradually decreased from the medieval period and in some areas, particularly the western Midlands, a rich tradition of introducing decorative timbers into the smaller panels evolved.

The second, usually used for display, was *close studding*, a series of closely set uprights, structurally unnecessary and lavish in the use of timber. The cost of such studding mean that it was usually confined to the show fronts of the building, the rest of which would be square panelled. Both types of framing could be augmented by curved or straight bracing, usually structurally desirable and often an excuse for decoration.

Generally the openings for the required doors and windows of the building would be incorporated into the pattern of its framing. Often these openings would be decorated by anything from a simple chamfer to splendidly ornate moulding, but from the early seventeenth century it became more common for the door or window to have a separate frame nailed into the gap in the framing. The other gaps between the timbers - the panels - obviously needed to be infilled and there were many different ways of doing this. In square framing by far the most common, up until the start of the eighteenth century, was by the use of 'wattle-and-daub'.

The 'wattles' are usually horizontal twigs of hazel, willow or other pliable tree or cleft narrow pieces of oak. These are wound around thicker vertical staves - usually of oak -

between the top and bottom of the panel. At their top these were commonly tapered and slotted into a drilled *stave hole* in the underside of the top rail of the panel. The base of the stave would then be bent inwards and sprung into a shallow narrow groove cut into the top of the bottom rail. In the large early medieval panels some of these staves were virtually structural. Once the wattling was in place it was daubed with a wet and variable mix of clay, mud, dung and any other available material, the mix sometimes stiffened by the addition of straw or horsehair. Finally, once that had dried, a thin skim layer of plaster would be spread and smoothed flush with the timber-framing.

This type of panel infill leaves evidence in the timbers even after it has been removed, or the framing has been radically altered. A sequence of widely spaced stave holes in the soffit of a timber, and a matching groove in the top of the one below it usually show where such a panel infill has been. Conversely, if there are occasional sections in the same frame that do not have these fossilised features, it is generally safe to suggest that these may relate to original window or door positions.

As usual in studying old buildings, a degree of caution is needed. Sometimes, though rarely, the wattles were simply sprung tightly into place without the need to drill holes or cut grooves for their staves. Once the original fills have been removed then the evidence left for them in the fabric is very limited.

The second most common form of infilling to square-panelled framing is brick, known as *brick nogging*. Most of the brick nogging found in buildings earlier than the late-seventeenth century is secondary, replacing original wattle-and-daub panelling either for reasons of fashion or necessary repair. Fashion is often the real reason, as well-maintained wattle-and-daub panels are extremely long lasting. The earliest buildings that incorporate primary brick panel infills are difficult to identify and were probably few in number until the start of the eighteenth century. One early example is the much-restored Horseshoe Cloister in Windsor Castle, built around 1480, but generally the use was vernacular.

From the start of the eighteenth century onwards brick-nogged timber-framed buildings — mainly cottages and farm buildings — became more and more common as a compromise between a well-established and relatively cheap way of building, and the increasingly fashionable brick. In the past other 'hard' building materials, such as stone and flint, were used occasionally and in recent years it is not that unusual to see materials such as breeze-block or concrete used to fill the panels of ancient timber-framing.

Other infills for square panels include varieties mainly designed for agricultural buildings where a degree of ventilation was desirable. Split oak wattles with no daub covering, wound around oak staves in the usual manner, were often used for granaries. Close-set horizontal timber planks slotted into grooves in the sides of the panels were also used for both external and internal use. In other cases, decorated timber sections could be added into the panel but these were usually purely for decoration.

There was as much variation in the infills of the much narrower but taller gaps in close-studded framing. The most common form consisted of short horizontal lengths of split oak or other suitable material sprung into vertical grooves cut into the sides of the adjacent studs. These would then be covered in daub and plaster. One alternate way of fixing the split oak included having them spaced further apart, fixing one pointed end into a stave hole and the other sprung into a groove, and threading wattling through them; the

53 *This internal wall in an early eighteenth-century brick house in Chester is of poor quality, using quite thin timbers and a single leaf of brick nogging. Amazingly, it is structural, and supports the first and attic floor joists*

normal design in square panelling rotated 90 degrees. Another, less sophisticated, way was simply to wedge the staves in place and apply the daub directly to them.

Vertical planks were sometimes slotted in the gaps, held in place by grooves cut into the sides of the studs. This was more common in internal partitions, especially in the later medieval period, and is called *plank and muntin* framing; this was often carefully decorated. Externally, plank infills were rarer and seem generally to have been used for lesser buildings. The granary at Tusmore, Oxfordshire, has external close-studding with this type of infill.

In some parts of the country it was possible to obtain thin lengths of stone that could be used to infill the close-studding. Slips of alabaster waste were used at Sinai Park, Staffordshire, for example, soon after 1500 and were then daubed over. Examples of roof tile used in a similar way have also been identified. In each of these methods the grooves required tended to be wider, deeper and of a more open section than the normal 'V' shape required to slot the cleft oak pieces into. As in square panelled buildings, brick nogging could be used to replace older forms of infill, often laid in a herringbone fashion.

Towards the end of the main timber-framed era simpler forms of making frames weatherproof evolved that did not require the infilling of individual frames. The various forms of *cladding* simply covered up the exterior of the framing, and the interior was usually hidden by a lath-and-plaster covering as well. As early as the start of the

54 *Removal of some of the original render cover of this building in Newtown, Powys, has exposed its brick-nogged ephemeral timber-framed carcass, which probably dates to the late eighteenth century. It was never meant to be seen*

seventeenth century some internal timber frames were being lath-and-plastered on both sides. Most forms of external cladding were far more popular in the south-east of England although they were used elsewhere.

The simplest, and possibly oldest, form of external cladding was of horizontal timber boards nailed directly to the framing and usually called *weatherboarding*. Relatively cheap in materials and certainly in labour, this technique was mainly used for farm buildings and the planking was usually fairly crude. Its origins may be much older than generally realised, and possibly medieval. In some areas more carefully cut weatherboarding was used for post-medieval and mainly vernacular houses.

By the later eighteenth century timber-framed buildings were seen as unfashionable in comparison to those in brick or stone, and many fine buildings had their frames hidden as a result, especially in towns. Those that could afford to do so actually built real brick skins on the facades of timber-framed buildings, whilst the less wealthy just covered the frames with lath-and-plaster. Plaster covering to frames was a much older tradition, particularly in Essex and Suffolk where even by the late sixteenth century an increasing number of timber-framed buildings were designed to be rendered and where, subsequently, the decorative possibilities of moulded plaster were appreciated. This *pargetting* was never particularly widespread in the rest of Britain. Other ways of hiding or cladding timber-framed building in the eighteenth and nineteenth centuries included the use of tile or slat hanging or the more sophisticated '*mathematical tiles*'.

Iron and Steel Framing

A direct modern equivalent to timber-framing is the use of iron or steel framing in construction. Whilst this has its origins at the end of the eighteenth century, iron has been used in construction for a surprisingly long time, and in Britain from the Roman occupation onwards. Whilst its use was mainly confined to fixtures and fittings, most obviously in the form of the humble nail, iron was occasionally used for important structural purposes from the medieval period onwards.

There are two traditional forms of iron, *wrought* and *cast*. Of these, wrought is by far the older. It is almost pure, with a very low carbon content, and by hammering on the hearth, and later through rolling, could be easily shaped. It is good in tension and if properly made resists corrosion well; it has a fibrous texture because of the way it is made; and if it does eventually rust it tends to 'flake' rather than pit.

Cast iron, as its name suggests, can be poured into moulds. The temperatures required to melt it are much higher than those used in the manufacture of wrought iron and led to the development of the blast furnace. Cast iron has a higher carbon content and is crystalline, making it rather brittle and poor in tension. It is, however, very strong in compression and also fairly rust-free.

Wrought iron tie-rods were used in the vaulting of the chapter house of Westminster Abbey in the thirteenth century, and the internal ties of the great soaring spire of Salisbury cathedral are also made of iron. Many more spires have hand-wrought vertical armatures of iron in their upper parts, often ending in the weather vane. All this type of work was hand wrought by the blacksmith, and the joins where individual *billets* of iron have been butt-welded together are usually quite obvious. Iron was also used in the stanchions and glazing bars of windows, the framing of opening casements, and for a variety of door furniture.

Until the later eighteenth century the two most common types of ironwork in building construction were nails and cramps. Nails were hand-forged and relatively expensive until the development of the rolling and slitting mills, and even after a degree of automation was introduced they still had to be hand finished until the mid-nineteenth century. By that time several different types had evolved for different purposes. Most were flat-sectioned because of the way they were made, and this had the advantage of not splitting the wood when in use. Some had small heads and others, particularly those used for deal, had none; L or J-shaped nails were used for fixing things to timber, such as hinges to door; and double-ended nails were used in the late Georgian period instead of lateral wooden dowels to fix together the floorboards of higher status houses.

Cramps were needed to hold masonry together, especially on parapets and gable ends. Usually they were 'run' in lead. Shallow recesses were cut into each of the stones to be joined, often with a 'dovetail' plan. These were made larger than the iron cramp itself, which was usually a piece of flat iron with the ends bent downwards. Molten lead was poured into the recess at the same time as the cramp and, once hardened, provided a reasonably tight and long-lasting joint. Another form of cramp was used to tie the facework of a stone building back to the rubble core, a feature that became more and more common as the facework became thinner and thinner, so much so that in some early nineteenth-century buildings virtually every facing stone would be cramped back to the rubble core.

55 Charles Bage was a pioneer of fireproof factories and the flax mill he designed at Ditherington, Shrewsbury, in 1797 is now accepted as being the first iron-framed buildings in the world. Its external walls are still of load-bearing brick, but the crossbeams and pillars are all of iron and support the brick 'jack-arches' of the floors. This photograph was taken in 1987 when it was still a maltings

The use of iron to support masonry was mirrored in the use of iron in timber structures, mainly from the early eighteenth century onwards. Elongated wrought-iron bolts were used to stiffen mortise and tenon joints, particularly in king-post roof structures where such bolts were often used to support the junction between the tie-beam and the king-post; typically a slot was cut into the post to allow a nut on the bolt to be turned to adjust the tension in the joint. An alternate form was the use of iron stirrups.

Inevitably the innovations being made in the iron industry in the mid-eighteenth century led to some fundamental changes in the way in which iron was used for building. Documenting the first significant structural use of iron is difficult as the evidence has not always survived because of the scrap value of the material. This was demonstrated as recently as 1987 at Newdale, Shropshire, identified at the last minute as a surviving pair of iron foundry buildings of *c.*1759, built but seldom used by the Coalbrookdale Company. Preliminary study of the buildings, subsequently reinforced, suggested that both double-pile buildings were open-plan inside and that the valleys had once been supported by cast-iron columns, one of which was thought to have survived, moved and reused, as a drainpipe. Just before industrial archaeologists moved onto the site this evidence was stolen — presumably for scrap — and the buildings have now been demolished.

Not far away, and built by the same company, is the first internationally significant use of iron as a structural material: the famous iron bridge of 1769-71 over the River Severn that gave its name to the small town that grew up nearby. Both Abraham Darby of the Company and the local architect Thomas Farnolls Pritchard had a say in its design, and its main span was built of cast iron. The cast iron was used in a fairly unsophisticated manner

56 By the time J U Rastrick's elegant bridge had been built over the tidal Wye at Chepstow, Gwent, in 1815-6, the use of iron for major civil engineering works had become well established. Its use would increase rapidly a generation later in the railway age, but the elegance of the early works tended to disappear

but the sheer size of the bridge and the strength and durability of the new technology had an enormous effect.

One of the rapidly growing industries of the later eighteenth century, textiles, required large multi-storey mills and these were prone to being destroyed by fire. Various methods were tried to make these expensive buildings fireproof, including sheeting timbers with iron. Cast-iron columns were also introduced to support the main timber floor beams by mill owners such as William Strutt, who used them in his Derby calico mill of 1793. The most fundamental innovation came in 1796-7 in Ditherington, a suburb of Shrewsbury and only 14 miles or so from Ironbridge. Charles Bage's new flax mill had brick external walls but an internal structure based on cast-iron beams supported by cast-iron columns; the beams supported brick 'jack-arches' forming the floors. No structural timbers were used in what was, in effect, a prototype iron-framed building.

This form of construction spread rapidly in the textile mills of the early nineteenth century, though generally the framing was used inside external load-bearing walls of traditional materials. The designs benefited from the fact that cast-iron was cast: this allowed decoration to be introduced without any great expense on a huge variety of differently profiled columns and beams. Some mill roofs were also made of cast-iron but were found to be rather heavy.

By the mid-nineteenth century the possibilities of iron seemed to be endless and many

57 *Delicate ironwork in the piers and trusses of Charles Hollis' St. John's church, Windsor, opened in 1822, suit the vaguely Tudor Gothic revival style of the building. Rapid advances in the technology of cast-iron allowed such designs to be developed (Ken Hoverd/Archive)*

58 *Simple but effective smith-worked wrought-iron decoration, forlornly rusting away above the doorway of a derelict chapel at Invergowrie, Perth & Kinross; this photograph was taken in 1978*

59 (left) Cast iron is a versatile material because as well as being used structurally it could also be used decoratively. The molten metal could be poured into intricately carved moulds to mass-produce architectural features such as this lamp-standard base on the seafront at Margate, Kent

60 (below) Various mid-twentieth-century uses of iron at Monmouth cattle market in Gwent. The main shed is steel-framed and covered with corrugated iron sheeting. The stanchions of the stalls are made up of typical 'I' section RSJs — rolled steel joists — and the rails are of tubular steel. Most of the gates are of tubular steel as well, with braces of 'L' section iron

61 Lead was an important commodity in building, its main use being in the form of sheets for roofing — hence the term 'leads' often used for the roof top walks loved by the owners of sixteenth and seventeenth century mansions. This is the flat roof over the Long Gallery of Aston Hall, Birmingham, built between 1618 and 1635

of the structures of the time are still impressive today. Paxton's pre-fabricated Crystal Palace of 1851 has gone but the more utilitarian Boathouse in Sheerness Docks survives. Finished in 1860 and designed by Godfrey Greene it has a complete frame of I-sectioned iron and is sheeted in corrugated iron; it is claimed to be the oldest surviving multi-storey iron-framed building in the world. Other iron masterpieces remain, such as William Barlow's train-shed at St Pancras' station, London of 1868, 74m wide and 33.5m at the apex of its slightly pointed arch. The platforms are well above ground level and at track level there was an overall iron deck that also served as a collar tie for the great wrought-iron arches supporting the roof. On a much smaller scale, iron also became more commonly used in building construction in the form of cast or wrought-iron lintels and load-bearing girders.

Steel had been used in very small and specialist applications for many years — mainly associated with swords and sharp tools — but could not be produced cheaply enough for building until the introduction of Henry Bessemer's 'Convertor' in 1856, and then William Siemens 'Open Hearth' method of the 1860s. The resultant mild steel soon supplanted both wrought and cast iron for most structural purposes and led to the development and use of the ubiquitous RSJ (the rolled steel joist), and, inevitably, to the steel-framed building.

The steel-framed multi-storey building developed in Chicago, USA, the pioneering 'first' generally accepted as the Home Insurance Building of 1883-5. Britain lagged behind slightly, mainly because of Government restrictions on its use. Nevertheless, by the first decade of the twentieth century the larger new buildings in major towns were mainly steel-framed structures faced with more traditional materials in their non-load-bearing screen walls. Improving technology and design allowed for more storeys than before and the development of new trussed girder forms, such as the 'Pratt' and 'Warren' trusses, originally developed in part for railway bridges, allowing far greater clear spans that were particularly important in industrial use. Structurally, despite this technology, these new buildings mirrored the timber-frames of the medieval period, although the pegged mortise-and-tenon joint had given way to the bolt, the nut, and the fish-plate.

Not all of the new iron or steel framed buildings were large or prestigious. The use of lightweight corrugated iron sheeting for roof and wall claddings, developed in the later nineteenth century, meant that cheap prefabricated framed buildings of lightweight timber or steel framing were possible. Several designs for 'instant' churches or chapels, known affectionately at the time as 'tin tabernacles', were used and hundreds built at the start of the twentieth century. Other typical buildings of this type up until the 1950s were village halls, sports pavilions and garages. Another very important and numerous type of structure using corrugated iron in this way were the thousands of prefabricated steel-framed Dutch barns for agriculture, again mainly dating from the first half of the twentieth century and built by a few specialist companies, such as WH Smith of Shropshire.

Reinforced Concrete

At virtually the same time that true iron and steel frames were being developed, pioneers were working on using frames of reinforced concrete. Like iron, the various forms of concrete and cement used in building work also have a remarkably ancient lineage; *concrete*, a mix of aggregates and a suitable binding agent, or *cement*, were utilised by the Romans as early as the first century AD. Around Rome builders were fortunate to be able to use a locally-derived natural volcanic cement called *pozzolana* which was used to bind aggregates of stone or brick rubble. Concrete was used extensively for footings, vaults, and the cores of masonry walls. Much of the port of Caesarea was built using 50 ton blocks of concrete formed in wooden crates sunk into the sea. In this form of concrete the strength of the material depended on its sheer mass.

The development of artificial cements, as opposed to the natural binding agents such as lime mortars, was only seriously begun in the early nineteenth century. The first of these is attributed to Louis Vicat in about 1820, but the most significant was the patenting in 1824 of Portland Cement by Joseph Aspdin. Cements of this type are formed by burning chalk or limestone and shale or clay together. After firing, the mix is ground down to a fine powder and this, when mixed with water, then sets hard and binds any materials laid in it. By mixing this artificial cement with aggregates a cheap and simple form of concrete became readily available, although one of the earliest uses for Portland cement was in the stucco facing of buildings. Another was within the vaults and some types of floor construction in fireproof buildings.

Most subsequent developments in concrete in the nineteenth century took place in

62 *Early twentieth-*
   century warehouses in
   Bristol; Redcliffe
   Wharf in the
   foreground is part
   concrete framed, and at
   the time this form of
   construction was
   mainly used for
   industrial and
   commercial buildings
   rather than, as it was
   later, for flats and
   housing

France. In the late 1840s, François Coignet used shuttered concrete for walls, effectively updating the earlier pisé or shuttered earth techniques. At the same time Joseph Monier, a gardener, had begun to use ironwork in the construction of concrete water basins, and in England W.B. Wilkinson patented an improved version using wire rope in the concrete. The first significant structural use for this new material, *reinforced concrete*, was in fireproof floors, usually within buildings constructed of other materials, either traditional brickwork or the equally innovative iron or steel frames.

During the latter part of the nineteenth century there were several pioneering attempts to develop whole structural frames of reinforced concrete. The most successful were undertaken by another Frenchman, François Hennébique, who substituted steel for iron reinforcing rods or wire, and designed new form of connections between them including the 'stirrup beam', patented in 1892. The use of reinforcing transformed the structural nature of concrete, as it introduced a tensile strength it hitherto lacked. This, combined with the inherent compressive strength of the concrete, produced an extremely rigid and strong frame in which all the horizontal and vertical members shared the load.

Hennébique opened an office in London in 1897, and most early reinforced concrete framed buildings in Britain were based on his methods. The first large building was the seven-storey Weaver's Mill, Swansea of 1898, since demolished. In the first decade of the twentieth century the technique began to become more widespread. Most of these new buildings were designed for industrial or warehousing use, utilising the inherent strength of the reinforced concrete framing. More prestigious buildings soon followed, one of the first being the Liver Building in Liverpool of 1908-10, designed by W. Aubrey Thomas. In such buildings it is often difficult to see the concrete framing because of the cladding of the main elevations in other materials, such as brick or stone.

Reinforced concrete was not confined to buildings and quickly proved an excellent and versatile material for civil engineering projects. Early examples of sizeable bridges of reinforced concrete included two over the River Severn, the recently demolished Jackfield Free Bridge of 1909 and the still extant Cressage bridge of 1913. Both were built by L.G. Mouchell and Partners under licence from Hennebique's company.

63 Only the decay on the balustrade betrays the fact that this graceful bridge over the Severn at Cressage, Shropshire, is not made of stone. The decay was caused by the rusting of the iron reinforcing of the concrete structure

The use of concrete for solid walling and structures was relatively limited in Britain, although Robert MacAlpine, nicknamed 'Concrete Bob' by his peers, used shuttered concrete for the otherwise conventional looking viaducts of the West Highland Railway opened in 1901. Shuttered concrete walls of often massive thickness were also used for military works, particularly pill-boxes and gun emplacements.

Variants of the now ubiquitous concrete blocks were also well developed by this time and have, since the end of the Second World War, become a fairly basic building material that is both cheaper in terms of cost and labour than conventional brickwork. Another form of concrete was pre-cast panels that were made in a factory and then transported to the building site. This was also developed to a much greater extent in the second half of the twentieth century, but amongst the earlier examples were those designed by John Brodie for Liverpool Corporation, including a three storey tenement block (1904) and stables in Walton (1907). The combination of reinforced and pre-cast, and later pre-stressed, concrete was a vital factor in the development of modern architecture, and the work of its early luminaries such as Le Corbusier, Erich Mendelsohn and Frank Lloyd Wright.

3 External wall coverings

DIRECTLY APPLIED SURFACES

The covering over of the outside of walls for architectural effect, or more pragmatically for weatherproofing, has been practised for centuries and several different approaches were developed depending on the availability of materials, regional needs, and changes in fashion. Some types of construction, such as cob, relied on an external covering of plaster or limewash whilst the richly moulded pargetting of the eastern counties of England was mainly for show.

The earliest material for rendering a building was undoubtedly clay, simply spread over the wall surface to fill in any gaps between stones or the cruder forms of framing. Daub such as this, stiffened with animal hair or straw, mixed with dung, and covered with lime-wash, was virtually identical to that used to cover the wattle infills of timber framed buildings.

One long lasting external covering that is still in vogue, albeit in a debased form today,

64 Render and colourwash hides all sorts of construction techniques. This building in Saffren Walden, Essex, is a late-medieval 'Walden' house, but dating it without being able to study the frame is difficult

65 *Primary rendering of buildings of poor quality stone is surprisingly common. One of the houses in this nineteenth-century terrace in Caernarfon, Gwynedd, was being repaired in 1990 and the rubblestone of the front wall was temporarily exposed*

are the variants of *roughcasting* and *pebbledash*. Roughcast, also called *harling* in some parts of the country and *wet dash* in others, consisted of a variety of mixes, generally of lime, sand, small gravel aggregates and water trowelled onto a still wet lime and sand 'undercoat' applied onto the wall. It usually resulted in a fairly rough surface texture and was particularly common in much of Scotland. Typically buildings covered in harling were built of rubblestone but their window and door openings, and often corners, were of better quality worked stones that were left on show. To achieve this these stones were usually built slightly 'proud' of the rest of the true wall surface; the extent of this projection would determine the depth of the harling. Where the harling of such a building has since been removed, the survival of these projecting features provides the evidence for its former existence.

An updated and more sophisticated version developed at the end of the eighteenth century, but became more popular in the nineteenth and — in some often hideous examples — very popular in the twentieth. In pebbledashing, small washed pebbles were mixed with a cement and thrown against a still wet cement coating on the wall. Strawberry Hill, Middlesex, built in stages during the mid-eighteenth century, is a very early example and unusual in being one of high status.

The introduction of gypsum based plasters — formed from burning and crushing gypsum and then mixing the powder with water — from France in the mid-thirteenth century had a tremendous effect on wall coverings in general. Originally called 'plaster of Paris', indigenous sources of gypsum were soon being exploited, particularly the alabaster of the lower Trent valley area of England. The Staffordshire writer Plott described in the seventeenth century how the waste alabaster from the quarries was piled onto a load of wood (sometimes augmented with coal) and then fired. This broke up the alabaster, made it brittle, and then it needed 'only thrashing to reduce it to powder'. The powder was then sieved, and the larger pieces used for floors and the finest for ceiling and walls. The result was both stronger and less malodorous than daub, Plott remarking that not only did 'the walls of their houses [endure] like stone, if the plaister fall not out from between the

66 *Render by the Regency period was used as a matter of course for most speculative building, especially in the expanding resort towns. This is part of Brunswick Terrace in Hove, West Sussex, built of fairly mediocre brick but superbly gilded with stucco facing and decorated pilasters. It was built in the mid-1820s and designed by Charles Busby and Amon Wilds*

Timbers', they had 'nothing of the ill smell of those made with lime and hair'.

In the sixteenth century, decorative plasterwork for interiors of the grander buildings became fashionable, but in parts of England the exteriors were treated in a similar manner. The craft of what is now termed pargeting reached the height of its popularity towards the end of the seventeenth century, particularly in East Anglia. Sometimes used to revitalise a much older timber-framed building, when used on a new one it generally hid a fairly skinny and poorly designed frame that was never intended to be seen. Both plain plaster 'rendering' and decorative pargeting were used for this purpose from at least the end of the sixteenth century. The mix for the plaster used in pargeting varied greatly, but typically the ingredients would be mixed to a stiff paste in water and included lime, sand, animal hair or straw, and dung and urine. Patterns would be formed by moulds, outline moulds and hand modelling, and the better quality work would usually have been coloured. Centuries of utilitarian limewash layers have generally eliminated any colour and unintentionally blurred the once crisp workmanship of the decorators.

Although some buildings had previously been rendered with lime or gypsum based plasters and cements, it was the development of several 'patent' cements in the later eighteenth century, including ones by a Dr Higgins in 1779 said to be harder than Portland stone, and the more famous Parker's Roman Cement of 1796, that led to the popularity of facing buildings in *stucco*. The later patenting of Portland cement in 1824 further strengthened, literally, its grip on architectural fashion until there was a Victorian backlash against what was perceived as a 'dishonest' material.

Historically, the word 'stucco' also applied to decorative internal plasterwork, but in Britain is usually associated with smooth external cement lined to resemble masonry. Originally the stucco would be painted to resemble the stone it was meant to imitate, but a fashion developed for painting walls white, and this has continued. It did allow perfectly ordinary houses, generally in towns, to achieve a superficial grandeur that they would otherwise have lacked, and it also allowed architects and developers to built terraces in many towns of dubious structural quality. Stucco became synonymous with the Regency terraces of the seaside and spa towns of Britain.

As with most architectural fashions in the past it was also used to bring older buildings up-to-date, so that many perfectly fine brick or timber framed houses were faced with stucco. Since the start of the twentieth century there has been a growing wish to see the 'real' faces of such buildings, but the result of removing stucco can be disappointing. Sometimes the damage done to the original walling to provide a good enough 'key' for the stucco has destroyed its character. Where stucco has been removed its former existence can usually be seen in deliberate 'hacking' of brickwork or timber, or in traces of render between joints or under window sills and string courses.

Cladding

Varieties of what can rather clumsily be called 'cladding' differ in applied surfaces in being physically separate to the main wall surface and simply attached to it, usually by timber laths or directly by nails, for example. Weatherboarding and corrugated sheeting have already been mentioned in the sections on timber-framing and iron-framing, and are both common examples of this type of wall covering.

Plain roof tiles were one of the main forms of wall cladding, and this is usually referred to as *weathertiling* or *tilehanging*. Whilst in many cases the tile cladding was added to a traditional timber-framed building that may have required repairs to its infill panels, or an architectural updating, by the early eighteenth century it seems to have been an integral part of the original design, particularly in the south-east of England. The tiles protect the walls from the weather, hence their name.

The technique was very simple in either case. Riven laths and, later, sawn battens, were nailed horizontally onto the outside of the timber frame and the tiles were hung in the same way as they would be on a roof. As the walls were vertical, there was a greater need to nail each individual tile. Tile hanging could be enlivened by using rows of specially produced tiles with shaped edges, and, with just a few different designs, quite intricate patterns could be introduced into otherwise quite plain tile-faced walls.

One of the great admirers of the visual effect of tile hanging was the late Sir Alec Clifton-Taylor who, in his marvellous book *The Pattern of English Building*, declared that 'a good tile-hung wall is a creation of infinite subtlety, an agglomeration of shallow and slightly irregular convexities, seemingly held in place.....by a fine mesh of shadow'. A much rarer form was to use wooden shingles instead of clay tile.

A logical evolution from the weather tile was the *mathematical* or *brick tile*. Confusingly,

67 External cladding, old
and new; the barn, in
Shropshire, possibly of
eighteenth-century date,
is timber-framed and the
weatherboarding is
probably original. The
corrugated sheeting is an
early twentieth-century
replacement

68 Machine-sawn
weatherboarding on
Hambledon Mill, by the
Thames on the
Buckinghamshire
boundary. (Mark
Twiselton)

69 *A rather spectacular example of plain tile hanging on an early seventeenth-century jettied timber-framed building in Salisbury, Wiltshire. The tiles in this case only date to 1972, having replaced earlier slates. (Ken Hoverd/Archive)*

these were, in the eighteenth century, also sometimes referred to as *weather tiles*, indicating their humble origins. These tiles were specially formed to resemble bricks and would be used either on a new timber-framed building or as a way of 'improving' an old one. Contrary to popular belief these were not introduced as a way of avoiding the Brick Tax of 1784; the earliest dated example, in Surrey, is from 1724 and the tiles were, in any case, clearly subject to the tax.

The development of the mathematical tile had more to do with architectural fashion. One of the recurring themes throughout the centuries has been the wish to keep buildings up to date. By the start of the eighteenth century, brick was the most fashionable material for all but the wealthiest. At the same time, uniformity and symmetry replaced the multi-gabled diversity of the past. The brick tile offered a way of updating buildings at a stroke without having to demolish them completely, going to the extent of building a completely new brick shell or facade, or having to make do with an unsatisfactory lath-and-plaster makeover.

In particular, because they were lightweight, they could cope with the overhanging jetties of timber-framed buildings. By building up a proper brick wall beneath the jetty and continuing the line of it by mathematical tiles on the floor above, the illusion of a new vertical brick wall could be created whilst improving the stability of the house. Where the jetty could not be underbuilt because of problems with street widths, many owners happily clad each overhanging storey with mathematical tile anyway.

Not all mathematical tiles were used simply to 'improve' an old timber-framed building. There are examples of older brick buildings being treated in this manner as well. More importantly, there are many examples of new timber-framed buildings of late eighteenth- and early nineteenth-century date designed to be covered with mathematical tile, particularly in Kent and Sussex. It was a cheaper form of construction than brick or stone but one that still looked fashionable. In some cases there were structural

70 *Mathematical tiles, when used well, can easily look like solid brickwork; the medieval timber-framed origins of this building in the ancient port of Faversham, Kent, are, however, quite obvious*

considerations, such as when a lightweight wall was needed that could nevertheless resemble brick.

The method of fixing mathematical tiles to buildings was not usually as simple as that for plain tile hanging, although some examples of them being laid in the same manner have been found. Usually they would be nailed to horizontal softwood boarding or set in a soft lime putty. The tiles evolved into a fairly standard cranked shape that allowed them to overhang each other sufficiently to keep out the weather. The projecting face of the bottom of each tile then looked just like an individual brick, and as 'stretchers', 'headers' and 'closers' were produced, a reasonably convincing 'bond' could be created. In both main methods of fixing, the tight 'joints' between the bricks were given added realism by being pointed.

The main problems occurred at the angles and the openings. Although special 'return' bricks were produced for corners, it was cheaper to simply tidy the corners with timber. This could simply be vertical timber board or more elaborately shaped woodwork designed to imitate rusticated stone quoins. In any case, most buildings faced with mathematical tiles were in towns and most only had their street front treated in this way. Around the openings, timber frames could also hide the edges of the tile work. Decorative false lintels were sometimes, but by no means always, added in imitation of brick or stone.

Identifying a building faced with mathematical tile purely from its facade can be difficult, especially if it has been well maintained. If a tile or patch of tiles has slipped, the deception becomes obvious. If not, there are some clues: the treatment of corners; the window heads; the manner in which the windows are virtually flush with the wall face; and subtle differences in colour or texture between the solid brick underbuild and mathematical-tile-hung upper floor of a jettied building help. By far the easiest way to check is to look around the back.

Mathematical tiles were mainly popular between the mid-eighteenth and early nineteenth centuries; their colour and texture largely following the same changes and tastes in fashion as contemporary brick. They were largely confined to the same area of England as tile hanging, that is the south-eastern part of England. The most surviving examples are found in Sussex and eastern Kent, with clusters in Surrey, Hampshire and

71 *Slate hanging was popular in areas where the material was easier to come by than tiles. These late Georgian buildings in Tenby, Dyfed, are built of stone but the slates help to protect them from the Atlantic winds*

Wiltshire, and isolated examples in other counties. Most are found in towns, especially in Canterbury, Faversham and Lewes.

Another standard roofing material, slate, was also used to face walls. Sometimes this would be in the same way as normal tile-hanging, where slates fixed to battens would be added to hide a timber-framed wall. More commonly, however, slate-hanging was used to protect masonry walls, and particularly ones built of poor quality rubble.

No one developed *mathematical* slates directly comparable to mathematical tiles, but the innovative architect Samuel Wyatt did invent something even more sophisticated. Wyatt and others of his family — a veritable architectural dynasty between the later eighteenth and mid-nineteenth century — made great use of slate for roofs and other things such as the shelves in wine cellars. This may have been due in no small measure to the fact that his brother Benjamin happened to be the land agent for the Penrhyn slate quarries in north Wales.

For a few of his most prestigious houses Wyatt used slate in a very different way. The slates were cut to resemble blocks of ashlar and then fixed to battens that were in turn fixed to the brick wall of the building. Once in place the slates would be 'drenched' with fine sand and painted the appropriate stone colour and, even from close up, it was virtually impossible to distinguish the slate-faced wall from one built of real ashlar. One drawback quickly identified was the problem of water penetration and rot affecting the timber battens; at Shugborough, Staffordshire, this eventually led to the removal of the slates, although the columns of the portico are actually fillets of slate surrounding tree trunks. At Soho House, built for the industrialist Matthew Boulton, Wyatt improved the fixing by replacing the timber with slate off-cuts. Despite the undoubted architectural success of the technique it did not become widespread, probably because stucco facing was far cheaper.

72 *(above) Soho House, Birmingham, a fascinating and deceptively complex building, is also slate clad, although less obviously so. The home of Matthew Boulton was never really finished. Its present appearance was the work of Samuel Wyatt who fixed slate slabs resembling blocks of ashlar to the brick walls; the slates were then drenched in sand and paint to complete the illusion. Since this 1990 photograph the house has been restored and is now one of the city's museums*

73 *(below)A different form of cladding; the mock timber-framing of the former George Hotel in Winchcombe, Gloucestershire hides the genuine early sixteenth century frame of the guest house built by the nearby abbey. Since this 1989 photograph the hotel has been converted into apartments*

4 Roofs and roof covering

ROOF STRUCTURE

Excluding those of the grandest of stone-vaulted ecclesiastical buildings, virtually all roofs up until the end of the eighteenth century were fabricated out of timber. The carpentry techniques and setting out of a typical roof structure differed little in essence from the construction of a timber frame and can be studied in much the same way.

In a cruck or post-and-truss timber-framed structure the trusses were integral parts of the roof structure and supported the purlins. In box-framed and masonry buildings the roof structure was supported by the side walls. Roofs can generally be divided simply into single and double roofs. Single roofs mainly consist of trussed pairs of common rafters all of the same size whilst double roofs have larger pairs of principal rafters at bay intervals, forming trusses that take most of the weight of the purlins which in turn support the lesser 'common' rafters.

In a single rafter roof there is either no purlin or a collar purlin. In its simplest form a trussed rafter roof consists only of the rafter pairs. These usually have one or more collars and some braces, but no tie beam at the level of the wall tops. To help alleviate the structural problems associated with this, it was usual for there to be two or more occasional tie-beams from wall-plate to the wall-plate, typically at either end of the roof and in the middle.

The most sophisticated form of a trussed rafter roof is actually not a single roof, but a double one: the crown-post roof. In this the tie-beams are at closer intervals and support a central vertical post — the crown or, in older text books, king post. This supports a central *collar plate* or *collar purlin* which supports the collars of the trussed rafters. The crown post and the collar purlin are usually braced as well. This form of roof was popular in the fourteenth century in buildings of note, but its survival after then varied from region to region. In the Midlands of England it was supplanted by side purlin roofs but continued in the south-east and the north for much longer.

In a side purlin roof the trusses carry one or more *tiers* of purlins in each slope, and these in turn provide support for the *common rafters*. Side purlins, like collar purlins, could be braced, but this bracing was in the plain of the roof slope and the bracing timbers are called *wind-braces*. Where large roofs were open to their apex rather than ceiled, wind-braces were often superbly carved to form decorative shapes. To accommodate even wider spans, the *hammer-beam* roof evolved for the grandest spaces, such as Westminster Hall. In this design, the thrusts of the roof structure were diverted away from the wall top and down to the upper part of the side of the wall through the horizontal cantilevered

74 *Crown-post roofs are not particularly common in the western Midlands of England, and the rediscovery of this fine early fourteenth-century example in Hereford in the late-1980s — hidden behind an inserted ceiling for nearly four hundred years — was a major architectural 'find'. The ceiling was removed and the first-floor hall restored to its medieval grandeur*

'hammer' beam, its vertical wall posts and the brace between them.

For most side purlin roofs from the fifteenth century onwards, two main types of roof trusses evolved. In one, the trusses have one or more horizontal timbers between their *principal rafters* called *collars*. These will be supported by vertical posts now generally called *queen struts*. Sometimes these are still called *queen post* trusses but most modern writers use that term to describe a variation of this type of truss in which two vertical posts from the tie beam are used to support the purlins directly. The queen strut type of roof was the most common of side-purlin types until the mid-eighteenth century.

In the eighteenth century a different basic type of truss began to be more popular, although it had been in use for at least two centuries beforehand. In this the truss has a central post (the *king-post*) from the tie-beam to the apex instead of collars. The head of the post was usually swollen to take the tops of the principal rafters and the foot was swollen to take paired braces supporting the rafters lower down. In earlier roofs the foot of the post had a simple mortise and tenon junction with the tie-beam, and later in the eighteenth and nineteenth century this joint was stiffened either with an iron stirrup or a vertical bolt.

From the start of the nineteenth century more ironwork began to be introduced into the design of roofs, though early cast-iron trusses proved to be quite heavy. As a result, experiments were made in combining cast and wrought iron, utilising the compressive

75 *Some medieval carpentry simply astonishes by its virtuosity and effect — and has proven difficult for the architectural historians to neatly categorise. This amazing roof structure is in Queen Street, Salisbury, Wiltshire and dates to the start of the fourteenth century (Ken Hoverd/Archive)*

76 *Other roofs are more mundane. This is a king-post roof over an eighteenth-century barn in south Lancashire with two tiers of trenched purlins. The structure is utilitarian and the timbers either freshly cut 'waney edged' pieces of poor quality or, like the left-hand strut of the truss in the foreground, reused from elsewhere*

77 *The liggers and stays at the ridge and eaves of these pleasant cottages on the Isle of Wight, indicate
that they were roofed with long straw thatch when this photograph was taken in 1978*

strength of the one and the tensile strength of the other. Amongst the main pioneers of
this were Charles Fairbairn, who typically used wrought bar iron for the tie-beams and
vertical tension rods, and cast iron for the principal rafters and diagonal braces. Several
examples of his mill roofs survive in Lancashire and Yorkshire. Fairbairn also realised the
limitations of the cast-iron beam and developed a stronger wrought-iron box beam made
up of many separate sections bolted together and capable of quite wide spans. Other
examples of early nineteenth century iron trussed roofs include the former Warwickshire
Asylum at Hatton and the Riding School of *c.*1830 in the grounds of Syon House,
Middlesex. A century later, more sophisticated trussed girder roofs could be
manufactured that had even wider clear spans.

Roof Covering

As in most matters relating to building, the roof coverings can be divided into two main
kinds, natural and man-made. Of the former, the two most important are vegetable —
thatch — and mineral — stones and slates.

Thatch

Thatch is one of the most ancient of roof coverings and was once also the most prevalent,
used widely from Cornwall to Caithness and beyond. Its name is derived from the Old
English word *thæc*, which simply meant the cover of any roof. Presumably because so

78 A newly thatched house in Toddington, Bedfordshire, in 2000. Norfolk reed needs no fixing at the eaves but does need a sedge or, in this case, straw, ridge. The ogee decoration is rather attractive

many roofs were covered in reed or straw in the medieval period the term became more specific. In Welsh too, the word for thatch, *to*, also means roof covering, and whilst it is sometimes suffixed with *gwellt*, meaning 'grass' or 'straw', the word for thatcher is simply *towr*.

Although now seen as an attractive and traditional part of the rural vernacular scene, confined mainly to picturesque cottages and farm buildings, thatch was, up until the end of the thirteenth century, almost universal. The majority of town houses were thatched, including those of major cities like London, as were thousands of churches and even buildings inside castle walls. One of the earliest references to thatch was by the Venerable Bede, writing in the seventh century about a new church on Lindisfarne built 'of hewn oak thatched with reeds after the Scottish manner'.

Thatch is a lightweight but bulky material that can be laid on quite flimsy roof structures supported on equally flimsy walls. It could thus be used on even the poorest cottage or hovel. Partly because of the way in which air is trapped in the vegetable matter it is naturally well-insulated, keeping heat in during the winter and letting heat out during the summer. Laid properly it is also efficient at coping with most types of weather. The raw materials for making it were also readily available and relatively cheap.

Whatever the cost-effectiveness and weatherproofing capabilities of the thatched roof, one inherent drawback sometimes proved, literally, disastrous. Thatch, once completely dried out, was flammable. In crowded towns where there was a large concentration of

1   The buildings behind the facade are generally far more interesting, archaeologically, than the facade itself. This is the fairly regular and stuccoed neo-classical frontage of the Green Dragon Hotel, Hereford, seen from Broad Street

2   Seen from the top of a nearby church spire the true complexity of the site is obvious. This apparently haphazard collection of buildings reflects centuries of changing property boundaries, changes of use, and developments in both construction techniques and architectural fashions

3   *The variety in the types of dates of buildings that can be studied archaeologically is enormous, and almost infinite. These caves cut into the sandstone cliff by the Severn at Bridgnorth, Shropshire, were lived in until the twentieth century. Scars of roof lines and joist sockets can be seen but accurate surveys can be difficult*

4   *At the opposite end of the archaeological spectrum is this former hospital at Rochford, near Southend-on-Sea, Essex, begun at the end of the 1930s and not properly finished until after the Second World War. It is a particularly fine pre-NHS building and had been little altered. The county's planning authority quite rightly requested an archaeological and architectural survey and analysis before it was converted to housing in the mid-1990s*

5-6 *The spirit of a place, the* genius loci, *has a bearing on its architectural character. Although often difficult to define, it is something that needs to be taken into consideration by the buildings archaeologist — providing it does not affect objectivity. The no-nonsense granite built fishing port of Stonehaven, Grampian (above), is very different to the decayed and mainly timber-framed Suffolk market town of Lavenham (below)*

7   Stone varies considerable throughout Britain. There is a little more consistency, in colour if not in type or texture, in Scotland and Wales than there is in England. Stone provided the main building materials for all but the poorest peasant buildings in Scotland until the late arrival of brick. This is Kellie Castle, Fife, mainly built at the start of the seventeenth century but restored in the nineteenth

8   A lion carved from Grinshill stone, a Shropshire stone much sought after in the region because of its combination of durability and ease of carving. This one guards Lord Hill's column on the outskirts of Shrewsbury

9   *An elegant quarter of Stamford, Lincolnshire, towards the northern end of the broad sweep of the Cotswold limestone belt across England. The honey-toned oolitic stone was used both for the medieval church and the eighteenth-century town houses; Stamford was the first English town to have a conservation area*

10 *Barrington Court in Somerset is one of the best examples of a mid-sixteenth-century 'E-plan' house in the country. The gold stone for its walls came from the Ham Hill quarries, providers of the most consistent liassitic limestones*

11 *Crediton's Holy Cross church was mainly remodelled in the Perpendicular style and is built of russet red sandstone quarried locally. The clerestory is not a feature found often in the county but this, and the fact that the church is unusually large, is due it being collegiate until the Reformation*

12 *Not far from Crediton, but on the edge of Dartmoor, Lutyen's made spectacular use of another Devonshire stone — granite — for his early twentieth-century masterpiece, Castle Drogo, near Drewsteignton. Normally such a hard stone that it is difficult to work with, modern methods have made it more manageable*

13 *Yorkshire grit, a typical Pennine milltown scene. This is Holmfirth, with nineteenth-century houses and paving of Millstone Grit clinging to the steep valley sides of a river*

14 Flint is a difficult material to work with but in some parts of south-eastern England the only stone available. The ruined parish church of Ayot St. Lawrence, Hertfordshire, is mainly built of it. A major campaign of repairs — preceded by archaeological recording — has just been completed

15 Flint, decorated with ashlared stone, is called 'flushwork'. The gateway to St John's Abbey, Colchester, Essex, was built in the fifteenth century. It is mainly of brick but the main elevation boast particularly fine flushwork

16 *Brick-making died out in Britain after the departure of the Romans but their cities made convenient quarries for later builders. The tile-like bricks used in the west front of another Colchester priory, St. Botolph's, by early Norman builders came from the Roman walls and ruins of the town*

17 *Aston Hall, near Birmingham, is one of the finest yet probably most overlooked brick mansions of the early seventeenth century. Not only is it a very fine house in its own right, and well presented, it has also been subject to conservation repairs since the early nineteenth century when it first saved by James Watt junior, the son of the great engineer*

18 The versatility of brick as a building material is shown in this interior view of the dome of the eighteenth-century ice house in Kew Gardens, London

19 Fiery Ruabon red brick, plain or moulded, and terracotta decoration became relative cheap in the later nineteenth century. This chap guards a corner of the former Eye, Ear & Throat Hospital in Shrewsbury, now awaiting redevelopment

20 *The former Guildhall in Thaxted, Essex, dates to the mid-fifteenth century. It has a massive central post and dragonbeams for jetties on three sides. Hips replaced gables on the roof early eighteenth and it was then rendered. When it was enthusiastically restored to its 'original' condition in 1911, mistakes were made and medieval material lost in the process*

21 *Little Hall, Lavenham, Suffolk, has also been restored but presents a good example of a typical medieval timber-framed open hall house, with cross-wings. It has a good crown-post roof as well*

22 *Lower Brockhampton, Herefordshire, is one of the most picturesque properties of the National Trust. As with most historic buildings, changes and repairs have led to alterations and when an archaeological survey was undertaken it was found that only the roofs of the main ranges were medieval. The gatehouse, however, is virtually intact.*

23 *Pargetting — the decorative plasterwork on mostly timber-framed buildings — was only really popular in the south-eastern counties of England. This exuberant example is on the Sun Inn, Saffron Walden, Essex and was added in the later seventeenth century to medieval buildings*

24 *The fine timber roof of Rotherwas Chapel, Herefordshire is dated 1589, surprisingly late for the design. This may have been due to the fact it was to all intents and purposes the chapel of the nearby but long demolished mansion*

25 The complex tilestoned roof structure of the main hall range of Stokesay Castle, Shropshire, built in the thirteenth century

26 An evocative mixture of Cotswold stone and Norfolk reed thatch, complete with roses round the door. Note how easily thatch can cope with dormer windows. This house is in Barnack, home of the famous quarries, in modern Cambridgeshire; it was the home of the artist Wilfred Wood

27 *Innovations in structural ironwork, pioneered in late eighteenth-century Shropshire, led quite quickly to very ambitious projects such as the glorious Palm House in Kew Gardens, begun in 1844. It was designed by the architect Decimus Burton and an ironmaster, Richard Turner*

28 *The huge twin sheds at Cardington, Bedfordshire, each cover over four acres. Iron framed and covered with corrugated steel sheeting, they were built as airship hangers. No.1 shed was started in 1916 and enlarged ten years later when No.2 shed was also built. The ill-fated R101 was built here*

29 *A face from the past — a wall-painting, probably of St. Margaret, in the private chapel of Astley Castle, Shropshire, a fortified fourteenth-century house only just rescued in time from complete ruin. Derelict, and dismissed as being of no real importance, it was finally surveyed archaeologically in 1989 and its true importance became clear. The site has since been converted to apartments*

30 *It is impossible to know what our successors will think about the architectural legacy that we are leaving them — or how much will survive. Dundee is a friendly city of great character occupying one of the finest natural sites in Europe, but has few great buildings. How many of the ugly high-rises and shopping centres of the 1960s and '70s will survive to be 'recorded' — and how much alteration can be made to the reinforced concrete piers and box-girder spans of the Tay Road Bridge to warrant recording in a hundred years or so?*

closely-packed timber-framed buildings, a single spark from an open hearth landing unseen on a thatched roof could start a serious conflagration. With only the most primitive and disorganised of fire-fighting techniques available, it was difficult to stop fire spreading from thatched roof to thatched roof, and soon a whole street could be aflame.

In a single year, 1161, the cities of Canterbury, Exeter, London and Winchester were all badly damaged by fire, almost certainly caused or aggravated by thatch taking light. London had suffered so many serious fires that by the end of the twelfth century William Fitzstephen considered that the only two inconveniences of the city were 'the immoderate drinking of foolish persons, and the frequent fires'. The increasing use of wattle-and-daub and then brick chimneys rarely solved the problem. Nantwich was badly burnt in 1583 and Stratford-upon-Avon suffered major fires in 1594, 1595, 1612 and 1641, which according to a local chronicler 'had their beginnings in poore Tenements and Cottages wch were thatched with strawe'.

Legislation was introduced by most towns in the medieval period to combat the threat of fire, following the Draconian example set by London in 1212. At the Assizes it was ordered that thatch would not be allowed on any new building unless plastered, and that all existing thatched roofs had to be plastered within eight days or be demolished. Some towns lagged behind the rest: Wareham, in Dorset, only banned thatch roofs in 1762 after another major fire. Nevertheless, by the seventeenth century the thatched roof had become generally regarded as a feature of the countryside rather than of the town, and of the cottage rather than the farmhouse.

The increased availability and decreasing costs of other longer-lasting roof materials, even in country areas, from the eighteenth century onwards led to an accelerating decline in the popularity of thatch for all but the humblest of dwellings. Not only did the percentage of new buildings with thatched roofs fall rapidly, but tens of thousands of houses that were originally thatched were re-roofed with tile or slate. By the start of the twentieth century building regulations in many districts also discouraged the use of thatch to such an extent that P.H. Ditchfield, writing in 1910, was convinced that 'Thatch as a roofing material will soon have altogether vanished'.

Thatch has, however, proved remarkably resilient. This was due partly to economics but partly a result of the various Picturesque strands in British architecture from the end of the eighteenth century onwards, attempting to evoke a rustic and well-ordered Golden Age that never existed. Thatched cottages appeared in countless pattern books and real ones were built by renowned architects in model villages such as Milton Abbas, Dorset (*c*.1780), John Nash's Blaise Hamlet, near Bristol (*c*.1810), and John Loudon's Great Tew, Oxfordshire, of about the same date. These were still built for the labouring classes, of course, although a few thatched follies were built on larger estates purely for the pleasure of the upper classes. As late as 1934 Lutyens designed the thatched Drum Inn in Cockington, Devon.

The picturesque appeal of the rustic thatched cottage has increased in the twentieth century in line with increasing mobility and wholesale changes in demographic and social patterns. Few of the estimated 50,000 historic thatched buildings in Britain today are inhabited by the farmers or farm labourers for whom they were built. Most will now be well-maintained and re-thatched when necessary, and this has led to a revival in the thatcher's art. No modern successful substitutes have been found for genuine thatch; mock panels of plastic thatch tried in the 1970s were as about as convincing as the average toupee.

There is no doubt that thatching is an art, and a very skilful one at that. It is also a craft that has been little altered by the technical advances of the past five hundred years or more, simply because it is virtually impossible to improve. New materials can help, especially in the different types of tools and fixings now available, but by and large the skill of the thatcher is all important. The modern world has, however, had a great impact on the thatcher's raw materials.

In general the pitch of a thatch roof is steeper than that of more substantial roofs designed to take slate or tile. Typically it will have an angle nearer to 50 degrees than 45. This allowed for a more rapid run-off of rain or snow, both of which, if allowed to lie for too long, could badly affect the thatch. However, just because a roof is steeply pitched does not mean it was necessarily once thatched, and the evidence for an earlier thatch cover can be very elusive. Many different species of plant have been used for thatching in the past, but the two most important raw materials for thatch have been reed and straw.

Reed, often called *Norfolk Reed* simply because so much of it is grown in that county, is generally grown in saltwater estuaries or marshes. When properly cultivated it can grow quite straight and well over 2m tall. It is also grown in parts of Essex, Suffolk, and Cambridgeshire, as well as in Dorset, particularly around Abbotsbury, and in South Wales. The reed is usually harvested in the winter and always used to be cut by hand. More recently a mechanical cutter has been developed.

On the roof, the overlapping bundles of reeds are laid in rows and vertical *lanes*, with the thatcher usually working from right to left but in a variety of regional or personal ways. Some will work up the lanes one by one, whilst others will stagger the work. In all cases the laying begins at the eaves which overhang the side walls. At the foot of the slope there is usually a *tilting fillet* of wood that helps to fix or tension the slightly upward tilting angle of the lowest bundle.

As each vertical lane of overlapping bundles is fixed in place the cut ends of the reeds are carefully *dressed* with a special tool called a *leggat*. This ensures that only the ends of the reeds show, giving the surface a tight bristle-like texture not dissimilar to the bottom of a yard brush. The bundles are then fixed in place by horizontal wooden battens, traditionally made of hazel or willow and called *sways*. These are usually held in place by bent hazel staples called *spars* or *buckles* but could also be tied to the roof battens by rope or twine, called in some areas *ropeyyarn*. In modern thatch the sways are sometimes replaced by mild steel bars and the spars by steel hooks. These fixings, and the iron hooks fixed into the rafters, are hidden by the next bundle of reed above.

Reeds cannot be bent easily, so that at the ridge a different material, usually sedge or rush, is needed to complete the roof cover. This was held in place by a series of longer horizontal hazel battens called *liggers*, secured in turn by more spars. Similar liggers were also used at the vulnerable eaves and verges of the roof to reduce the risk of wind damage. A good reed roof can last for over half a century, although the less sturdy sedge ridge would need replacing before then.

Because of the difficulties of obtaining good quality thatching straw, reed thatch is gradually becoming predominant. In many cases, a long-straw roof will be rethatched with reed. Even so, the number of commercially cropped reed beds in this country has fallen to such an extent that around half of the reed used in the thatching of British buildings is now imported. It comes from countries as diverse as France, Turkey, and Poland.

Straw thatch is divided into two types, *long straw* and the so-called *Devon reed*, or *combed wheat straw*. Long straw thatching utilises the straw left over after the grain has been separated during threshing. Today the most common source of the straw is wheat but, up until the Second World War, rye, which has a stronger and more flexible straw, was generally considered preferable. This was not always the case. In his early eighteenth-century building guide, Richard Neve considered the best source was 'Helm, that is long and stiff Wheat-Straw (with the Ears cut off,) bound up in Bundles unbruis'd; which well laid, lies thin, lasts long, and is much neater than the common way'. Both barley and oat straw were also used, but were not as strong or as supple.

The long straw needs to be *yelmed* and *drawn* before it can be used; as with most crafts, terminology varies from region to region. Yelming is the slight dampening of the cropped straw to make it pliable, and drawing consists of combing the straw into tight bundles of straw known as *yealms*.

Generally working from right to left and up from the eaves, these bundles of straw are fixed to the widely set battens of the roof slope, each overlapping the other until the ridge is reached. Special attention is paid to the eaves, verges and ridge of the roof to ensure that the weather cannot get beneath the thatch and generally more liggers are required than on a reed roof; these can often be decorative. In a long straw roof the strands of straw lie lengthways down the line of the slope, giving the roof a soft undulating texture that is quite different from other forms of thatch.

The other form of wheat straw thatching is called *Combed Wheat Reed* or, more commonly though less accurately, *Devon Reed*. Neither term has anything to do with true reed, but this method of thatching is very similar to true reed thatching, and became very popular in the south-west of England, hence its name. This method is usually thought to have evolved at the start of the nineteenth century. The wheat straw was originally combed with an iron-toothed hand tool, but later in the century successful experiments were made with adding mechanical combs to the new-fangled threshing machines. This allowed for more regular and well-sorted bundles of cut straw that could be used to form the same type of bristle-cut surface as Norfolk reed. Laying the thatch was also similar, but its pliability meant that the ridges could be of the same material.

Neither type of straw thatch is as durable as Norfolk reed. Long straw has a typical life span of 15-25 years, and combed wheat of 20-45 years. This is reflected as much in the relative price of thatching as it was nearly 300 years ago when Richard Neve noted that 'common' wheat thatching cost between 2s 6d per hundred square feet as opposed to 4s for reed thatch.

The mechanical harvesting methods first introduced at the end of the nineteenth century became universal by the middle of the twentieth. Unfortunately the machines tend to crush the straw, reducing its waterproof qualities. In addition, most modern wheat varieties are also shorter stemmed than older ones. Despite some areas of older longer-stemmed varieties being set aside for manual harvesting, long-straw thatching is gradually becoming rarer. However, modern thatchers can also add some of the traditional features of long-straw roofs to combed wheat straw ones, thus retaining some of the regional traditions in a longer-lasting roof.

Over the centuries many different plants other than reed or straw have been used in the thatching of buildings, either completely or in conjunction with other materials. This was particularly so for the roof coverings of the poorer cottages and hovels which the majority of the population lived in. One of the most widespread of these lesser materials was the common *Heather*, or *ling*, a durable roofing material widely used in moorland areas where there were no other readily available or affordable materials. Thus, in England, it was used in upland areas in the Yorkshire Dales, parts of Northumbria and Cumberland, and the uplands of Sussex and Devon. In the Scottish Highlands it was almost universal and there are still some examples of crofters cottages, or more often their outhouses, roofed with it. Two well-preserved examples have been restored by the National Trust for Scotland on Culloden Moor near Inverness. Some of the cottages of upland Wales were also roofed with this material.

The use of heather thatch has also been occasionally identified elsewhere, including Oxfordshire and Hampshire, and it was also used as the original roof covering of the late eighteenth-century cob houses in the model village of Milton Abbas, Dorset. It enjoyed a brief revival of sorts from the late nineteenth to early twentieth centuries along with other traditional materials. The quality of roofs on which heather was used varied and it could also be used in conjunction with other materials such as straw or turf used for the ridges. Typically the heather would be cut whilst still in flower in the early autumn. It was then simply laid directly on the roof structure with the roots uppermost and crudely stitched together; then it was trimmed. As it dried out and died the heather would turn black and match the remaining soil clinging to it. Whenever it rained, soil within the roots must always have seeped out and ended on the floor beyond the overhanging eaves of the roof.

In some areas, particularly in the more exposed parts of northern Scotland and its offshore islands, the heather would be tied down by a series of ropes or netting weighted down with stones literally hanging from the eaves or tied around deliberately projecting stones of the walls.

Rush was once a very common thatching material, having similar attributes to reed and straw. Its use was particularly widespread in the Fens where it was known as *fenstraw* and *fenthakke* in the medieval period. Rush, like reed, was also found growing around estuaries and so was used, for example, to roof buildings in north-western Kent and in coastal areas of Sussex. In the north of England, rush was used in some areas of Cumbria, mainly around Penrith, up until the nineteenth century. Examples of rush thatch have also been found in parts of central Wales, where the ridge was often covered with turf.

Other less common materials used for the poorer sort of dwellings included *broom* and *bracken*, mainly in the Scottish Highlands but also in parts of upland England including the Lake District. Like heather, it was cropped in the autumn and simply laid on the roof with the roots exposed; it apparently only lasted for a few years before needing to be replaced. The common *fern* is known to have been used in parts of northern Lancashire at the end of the eighteenth century and *sedge*, a grass-like marsh plant, is still used in the ridges of reed thatched roofs. In the Fens, it was used to thatch entire roofs and has the advantage of being very pliable when green and easily handled at most times of the year. In some areas it can grow to nearly 2m high, and it can last up to 30 years before needing to be replaced.

Turf

Turf was a fairly common roofing material until quite recently for smaller cottages in parts of Scotland and Ireland, and was also used across most of the north of England from Cumbria to Northumberland. It is possible that turf roofing in England was once more widespread. In the late seventeenth century, Robert Plot noted turf being used for ridges of straw-thatched roofs and, in some of the meaner cottages in the north Staffordshire moorlands, for complete roofs. Throughout much of the rest of the country, many labourers lived in fairly squalid and poorly built hovels well into the nineteenth century, and whilst many of these were almost certainly roofed with turf, their remains are scanty.

Turf would usually be cut in as long a strip as possible to avoid too many joints and potential gaps between them as they were laid, grass side up, on the roof. Turf was also used as ridging for more traditional thatched roofs in parts of the Welsh Marches, and conversely, there is some evidence in the northern counties of England that turfs were laid on roofs as a base on which thatch could be pinned.

In the lowlands of northern Cumbria it was fairly common to use a technique called *stapple thatching* using a mixture of turf and straw thatch on the roof. The turf sods, faced grass-side downwards, were fixed to the battens and interleaved with small bunches, or *stapples*, of straw. This technique may also once have been a little more widespread.

Tile

Tiles, although initially far more expensive than thatch and necessarily requiring a better roof structure to support their weight, had the very real advantage in the medieval period of being far less prone to fire. The two main materials for tiles were some types of stone or ones manufactured from suitable clays. There was a third, now virtually unheard of in this country but still used in other parts of the world. This was wood — generally cleft oak — and the tiles made of wood were called *shingles*. In the medieval period they were in common use even on the most prestigious of buildings such as castles and cathedrals. In a damp climate they needed to be replaced quite regularly and were also not fire resistant. The rapid decline in their use was probably related to the availability of more durable materials, and in particular to the ceramic tile from the later thirteenth century onwards.

Stone, a natural roofing material, has been used for roofs since the Roman period. Certain varieties of sedimentary rock could be cut to reasonably thin flat section tiles, though the most common material is slate. After plain tile, slate is the most common of today's roofing materials, but this has only been the case since the later nineteenth century.

Several varieties of laminated stone were capable of being cut quite thinly along their bedding planes. The capacity of some stones to be split in this way was obviously useful for roofing in many areas of Britain and the percentage of grander buildings with stone

79 Tilestones and a medieval ceramic ridge tile — a fairly rare survival — await to be put back onto a Shrewsbury roof

80 Tilestones were usually graded in size, with the largest at the base and each course gradually diminishing in height towards the ridge. This is a recently relaid tilestone roof on a late medieval timber-framed granary in Oxfordshire

covered roofs was certainly greater than it is now. These stone tiles were, and sometimes still are, confusingly called stone slates. A more logical term should be *tilestones*. The use of such stone was not confined only to roof covering; for example, the louvers in the great tower of Pershore Abbey, Worcestershire, are made not of wood but flat squares of limestone.

Limestones provided the best tilestones and are seen to their best in the broad Cotswolds belt of England, and the best of these are claimed to be those from around the aptly named Stonesfield, near Woodstock, Oxfordshire. Further east, in Northamptonshire, the tilestones from the Collyweston area are arguably as good if not better. Sandstone tilestones were also spread over many parts of the country and varied greatly in size and texture. This fact also means that it is impossible to say just by its pitch if a roof was once covered in tilestones. Generally, large tilestones required a fairly substantial and low pitched roof, but the smaller tilestones used in parts of the Cotswolds and in Shropshire can be laid on quite steeply pitched ones, countering the argument. Tilestones, like thatch, gradually gave way to plain tiles and Welsh slate in the nineteenth century, and the craft of making them almost died out. In 1910, P.H. Ditchfield lamented in his *Vanishing England* that, in Sussex, 'If you want to have a roof of Horsham stone, you can only accomplish your purpose by pulling down an old cottage and carrying off the slabs'.

Slate, a metamorphic rock, has already been discussed as a wall-cladding material.

81 Medieval ceramic roof tile fragments found in excavations at Kilpeck, Herefordshire, in 1989

82 Machine-made plain and decorated tiles at Hamstall Ridgeware, Staffordshire, typical of the later nineteenth century.

Because of its fissile nature it is much more useful as a roof covering as it can be split quite thinly and laid in a similar fashion to ceramic tiles. There are several local varieties each with their own distinct characteristics, ranging from the bluey schist slates of Devon and Cornwall to the granular greeny slates of Cumbria, the lovely Swithland slate of Leicestershire, and the well-known smooth slate of north-west Wales. Slates were transported quite long distances by land and water and were light enough to make this relatively easy, but local colour and texture remained significant until the end of the eighteenth century.

The dominance of the Welsh slate really began with the improvements of transport effected by the canals in the later eighteenth century, and the massive exploitation of the quarries around Penrhyn and Blaneau Ffestiniog. The fact that Lord Penrhyn's agent at the quarries was Benjamin Wyatt, brother of two of the most famous architects of the day, James and Samuel, helped. Samuel Wyatt even invented a different form of laying slate — his 'patent slating' method. Instead of overlapping slates in the manner of tiles, the slates in each course were butted together so that all the joints running up the slope were in line and the slates were fixed directly to the rafters; the joints were then covered in thin slithers of lead, fixed in a cement putty, giving a distinct ridged appearance. It was not particularly successful but a handful of examples survive. After the Wyatts, it was really the development of first the canals and then, in the second half of the nineteenth century, the railways, that opened up all of Britain to the Welsh quarries. As a result their thin steel-grey slate became almost ubiquitous in urban architecture.

For practical reasons, in both slate and tilestone roofs it was common to 'grade' the individual pieces so that the larger ones were used in the lower courses and the smaller ones higher up. They were obviously laid so that all joints between them were covered by the courses above and below. The head of each slate or tile would usually be pierced with one or more small holes to allow a small timber dowel or bone to be tightly fitted through that would hook it to the split timber batten nailed onto the rafters. Because of the uneven nature of the materials, there would inevitably be gaps through which the wind and weather could penetrate. One way of trying to prevent this was to encourage moss growth by ramming moss into the gaps and allowing it to grow. Later and more advanced forms of this *torching* included bedding the feet of one course of tiles into a lime mortar or moss mix laid onto the heads of the tiles on the course below. At the ridge, special bonnet or ridge tiles were needed, often simply 'V' or 'U' sections laid upside down and mortared into place. Suitable stone could be cut to this profile, but where no such stone was available, ceramic ridges were used instead.

Ceramic tiles and bricks have a common heritage and their historic development in Britain has been on parallel lines. The Romans used some tile for their buildings but it was only in the twelfth century that ceramic tile appears in the documentary and archaeological evidence. The term *'baked tile'* appears in an ordinance of 1189 in London, and in 1212 *tile* was one of the roof coverings allowed to replace thatch. Despite a few early isolated examples, tile only seems to have become into normal use in the south-east of England by the thirteenth century, and slightly later elsewhere.

On the available evidence these early roof tiles seem to have been quite large and were subsequently replaced by the mid-fourteenth century by smaller tiles not dissimilar in size to those used today. This mirrors the change from the medieval 'Great Brick' to the smaller 'Flemish' brick. Quality and size of tile continued to vary until a statute of Edward IV in 1477. To ensure that every tile should be 'good, seasonable and sufficient', it was also decreed that 'the earth whereof it shall be made shall be digged and cast up before the first of November, and stirred and turned before the first of February, and not wrought before the first of March'. The size was decreed to be $10\frac{1}{2}$ in long, $6\frac{1}{4}$ in wide and $\frac{5}{8}$ in thick. The last pre-metric British Standard size was virtually identical: $10\frac{1}{2}$ in long, $6\frac{1}{4}$ in wide and 3 or $\frac{5}{8}$ in thick. As with brick sizes, this was an ideal compromise between portability during making and use and the amount of area covered, so once a size had been established it made little sense to change it.

Most handmade tiles have a very slight concave profile in both sections, partly as the result of the way they are formed. Tiles could be fired in clamps or kilns, but in contrast to brick, kilns seem always to have been the preferred option even from the early medieval period. Because of their thinness and weatherproofing functions, tiles had to be of the best clays and fired more in the kiln.

The basic principle of tiling has altered little since the medieval period. Split laths, or since the later nineteenth century sawn battens, are nailed to the common rafters. The tiles are hung from these either by a nib moulded below the top edge of tile before firing, or by a wooden or bone peg fixed through a hole in the tile. Examples of both have been found in medieval contexts but the latter method seems to have been more common for

83 Pantiles on 'Mansard' roofs of a working-class terrace in the suburbs of Bath. The city is noted
  for its fine Georgian houses and public buildings but its planners allowed far too many of the
  'lesser' buildings to be demolished in the 1960s and early 70s, unbalancing its architectural
  hierarchy

most of the post-medieval period, up until nibs were revived at the end of the nineteenth
century. At the same time, the cheapness of mass-produced nails allowed a bib-and-braces
approach, with some courses of tiles being nailed to as well as being lipped over the
battens.

The normal roofing tile is now called a *plain tile*; an alternate name up until the
eighteenth century was a *thack tile*, harking back to the same Old English word from which
thatch is derived. Each course of plain tiles overlaps the one below it, but the courses have
to be staggered to ensure that a full tile always overlaps a joint between tiles on the course
below. The overlap also has to be long enough to cover the top of that joint, so that it will
in effect just overlap the next course of tiles as well.

Obviously, plain tiles meeting at the apex of a pitched roof will have a gap between
them. This has to be covered by a different type of tile, usually called *ridge* or *bonnet* tiles,
though other terms such as *crest* or *crease tile* have been used in the past. These are typically
triangular or segmental in profile, moulded on a wooden *former* before firing and then laid

along the ridge. Medieval bonnet tiles were often given a hand-formed decorative serrated ridge before firing. Bonnet tiles could be of the same continuous profile and then overlapped as they are laid, or, in more sophisticated forms, be slightly narrower at one end and interlinked. *Hip* or *corner* tiles are similar to bonnet tiles and are laid on the angles of hipped roofs, and *gutter* tiles are the opposite, laid in the valleys between roofs.

A different form of tile is the *pantile,* probably introduced to Britain during the seventeenth century as an import from the Netherlands; the name, however, is thought to be derived from the French *pente,* or bent. British made pantiles were well established by the start of the eighteenth century when they were also known as *crooked* or *Flemish* tiles. An edict of George I decreed that their size should be $13\frac{1}{2}$ in long, $9\frac{1}{2}$ in wide and $\frac{1}{2}$ in thick, a British Standard that continued until metrication. These usually have a shallow 'S' section and can be laid more economically than plain tile. In each course, each tile overlaps its neighbour and the shape of the tile means that there is no need for the courses to be staggered, and less tiles are needed.

Pantiles had two disadvantages over plain tiles, other than cost. One was the difficulty of moulding or cutting them to fit into the valleys of intersecting roofs or at the angles of hipped ones, so they tended to be used on plain or coped gabled roofs. The other was the need to fill the gaps left between overlapping pantiles, and between pantiles and the ridge tiles. This particular form of *torching* was usually done with mortar rather than moss, as was the case with tilestones. Pantiles are mainly found in the east of England but there are also areas in the south-west, around Bridgewater and in the valley of the Avon between Bristol and Bath. Pantiles occur also in parts of east Scotland, particularly in the Lothians and the Kingdom of Fife. Different forms of pantiles, such as the *Roman* or *Spanish,* never seem to have become popular, although in the Bridgewater region in the late nineteenth century there were tiles called the *Patent Roman* and *Double Roman* that were used in the Somerset and Gloucestershire area in particular and are occasionally found elsewhere.

Great changes in the manufacture and distribution of ceramic tiles, mirroring those associated with brick, were made from the mid-nineteenth century onwards, and machine-made tiles began to dominate the construction industry. Local variants tended to give way to mass-produced products from large manufactories concentrated in areas where there was good clay, good coal, and good transport. Mass production coupled with machine moulding also led to the introduction of cheap decorated tiles with scalloped edges, for example, or ridge-tiles with ornate crestings; most of these lack the subtlety of the hand-crafted article.

Lead

Lead has been a significant building material since at least the Roman period, and until recently those who worked with lead were called *plumbers* — from the Latin word for lead. England, in particular, had significant and widely spread lead deposits that were worked nearly 2000 years ago by the Romans, as evidenced by a stamped pig of the material found in the west Shropshire leadfield. Roman use of lead seems mainly to have been associated with plumbing, but sheet lead was used for a few Saxon churches.

Lead was easily worked, having a relatively low melting point that allowed it to be cast easily and, once cast, it was sufficiently malleable to be worked without heat, unlike iron, for example. Most of the lead used in buildings was cast in the form of sheets for roof covering, for forming valley gutters, or for ridge covers. Lead was also needed for the related rainwater goods — hopper heads and down-pipes, as well as for a variety of smaller but equally important uses such as the fixing of iron cramps into masonry and the U-sectioned lead *cames* that held glass *quarries* in *leaded light* glazing.

Up until the advent of *milled* lead towards the latter part of the seventeenth century, most cast lead was distinguished by being relatively thick and having a textured finish produced by the sand onto which the molten lead had been poured. Milled, or *rolled*, lead is much smoother and thinner. Lead sheets could be used on virtually any pitch or profile of roof, as shown by the covering of some of the decorative ogee topped towers of Jacobean mansions, for example.

Generally the roof pitches originally covered by lead sheets were quite shallow and in some cases, virtually flat. This attribute meant that such roofs could actually be walked on without too much trouble, and this was extremely useful in medieval castles and, later, on the roofs of grand mansions of the sixteenth and seventeenth centuries when 'walking the leads' became an important part of fashionable exercise. Many of the great houses of this time had roofs deliberately designed to be used for open air recreation and as a viewpoint; the more extravagant, such as Hardwick New Hall, Derbyshire, had banqueting suites reached from the roof as well.

While most of the lead used in rainwater goods is fairly utilitarian, in the seventeenth and eighteenth century there was a fashion for decorative cast lead hopper heads. These varied from simple designs, sometimes with a date and initials, to more elaborate ones including coats of arms, crests, or just decoration for the sake of decoration. Dates on hopper heads, incidentally, should be looked at with a degree of caution; hopper heads were easy to transport from one building to another. The real glories of decorative leadwork are only tenuously connected with buildings through the superb statuary and fountains in the gardens of stately homes.

Copper and zinc have similar structural attributes to lead and have been used for sheeting roofs and for rainwater goods, though have never been as common. Waste products of both, and of iron, have produced some of the odder building materials, used to a limited extent in the vicinity of smelting works. Slag blocks — created by skimming off the scum floating on the molten metal and casting it into solid blocks — could be used in wall construction. One of the more elaborate uses was in a huge statue of Poseidon in the middle of an ornamental lake by Richard Champion's late eighteenth century zinc works at Warmley, near Bristol. The lake has since been drained and the remains now loom incongruously overlooking a caravan park.

5 Floors

Buildings obviously needed floors; the simplest and earliest were probably little more than the scraped earth. In the medieval period, compressed earth floors could achieve a very fine smooth surface and this was almost certainly a more common form of flooring than is generally recognised, and few examples survive intact.

Pebbles and stone laid into early earth floors for additional strength and water resistance evolved into well-made cobbled floors; in the medieval period floors were usually covered with rushes or other grasses so that the undulating surface of the cobbling was of no import. The use of stone tiled flooring was initially of a much higher status and a wide range of building stones were used for this purpose. By the start of the eighteenth century, stone floors with plain decorated patterns were the height of fashion, typically contrasting the main paving stones with smaller dark rectangles at their junctions. In contrast, the relative decrease in the price of stone allowed the homes of the poorer — and outbuildings and farmsteads — to be paved with more utilitarian stone slabs or flags.

Stone floors were not confined to the ground floors or cellars of buildings. Where a cellar or undercroft was vaulted there were few problems in providing a stone floor to the room above. Where the undercroft was not vaulted, the floor above would usually be of timber, but examples of stone floors supported on a series of necessarily substantial timber joists have been identified in several parts of the country.

One of the less known uses for plaster was in floor construction, and in 1611 John Speed wrote that in Nottinghamshire the soft alabaster, when burnt, 'maketh a Plaister harder than that of Paris; wherewith they flower their upper roomes'. Flooring with plaster was quite simple. Floor joists were laid in the normal manner and reed, or sometimes straw, was laid across them. The wetted plaster was either laid straight onto the reed or onto an underseal of lime that evened up some of the irregularities. Normally it was around two inches thick and could easily be flattened when still wet. In some cases, riven timber laths would be used instead of the reed. Once set, the plaster would be extremely hard and long-lasting.

Although used extensively in cottages and farm buildings, it was also used in some buildings in the eastern Midlands of England, as architecturally important as Robert Smythson's Hardwick Hall, built at the end of the sixteenth century, and the stables of Kedleston Hall designed by Robert Adam and Samuel Wyatt in the 1760s. It continued in use well into the nineteenth century, often used for the second floors of the standard three-storey brick farmhouses of the Tame and Trent valleys. Later on, plaster floors — sometimes also called 'lime ash' or 'cinder ash' floors because of the many impurities found in them as coal became the more important fuel for firing — were largely supplanted by cheap imported timber from the Baltic.

Floors paved with ceramic tiles were known in Roman Britain but then died out before being revived in the medieval period. Decorated tile *pavements* are well preserved in many churches, but relatively few have survived in domestic buildings. To cope with the greater wear and tear on a floor tile (compared to a roof tile) they were generally thicker, smaller, and the clay would be mixed with sand. Decoration for *encaustic tiles* was generally by impressed designs into the still wet clay, filled with a slip of a different material prior to firing and glazing. These patterns range from religious subjects to heraldry, and from individual tile designs to composite designs using many different tiles. Tiles were often moved and relaid. Many were removed during the dissolution of the monastic houses in the late 1530s, some finding their way to churches and others to homes. Encaustic tiles enjoyed a revival in the nineteenth century in parallel with the Gothic Revival in church architecture. A cheaper version of the floor tile in the eighteenth and nineteenth century was the ubiquitous red or yellow 'quarry tile'.

Most upper floors, and many ground floors, were of timber. Timber floors have a simple design, being made up of closely set floorboards laid onto joists. In smaller rooms the joists could run from wall to wall (or, in a framed building, from frame to frame), but usually there was a need to introduce one or more larger beams at right angles to the joists. If these run across a building they are usually called *cross beams* or *bridging beams*. If they run along the axis of a building they are usually called *axial beams* or *spine beams*. The development of jointing techniques in floor construction was the same as that for general carpentry and timber framing, and in one sense the basic floor structure below the floorboards can be seen as an horizontal timber-frame.

The methods of fixing this floor frame to the walls of a building depended on the nature of those walls. In a timber-framed building the floor formed part of an integrated whole with the external walls, and this was also the case in more recent times in iron and reinforced concrete frame structures. In masonry or brick buildings the junction of floor and wall was always a potential weak point in the design, and as a result was sometimes deliberately over engineered.

Typically the main beams of the floor would be embedded in the masonry as the building was built, the end or *bearing* being embedded in a pocket in the masonry. This was the case in both stone and brick buildings. Sometimes the bearing would be supported by a horizontal timber beam fixed into the wall, theoretically helping to spread the loading on it. One common practice was to deliberately position a window under a beam end so that the window lintel would also act as an added support. Timber *bearing pieces* were important in solid mud walls where bearing pockets were of little structural use.

An alternate form of floor support in some masonry buildings was to lodge the beams onto, or tenon their ends into, a horizontal plate running along the inside of the wall. This could simply rest on a set-back in the wall or, in higher status medieval buildings, be supported on a series of stone corbels. When the timbers of a floor have long gone, the evidence for the different types of construction is usually fairly clear.

Once the joists were in place the floorboards were laid. Early ones tended to be of oak but other woods were also used; common deals later became fairly widespread. The boards were usually nailed directly to the joists, but the way in which they were joined to their neighbours changed over time in higher status buildings. The earliest means of horizontal fixing was by timber dowels. Nails were later used, generally hammered home on the diagonal. One form used in the late eighteenth and early nineteenth century was the double-ended nail; this would be hammered into the first board and the next board would be hammered home onto the projecting nail ends. The development of interlocking 'tongue-and-groove' floorboarding is considerably older than would be expected, with half-lapped variants in use in the sixteenth century. Since the end of the nineteenth century, various modern materials have been used in floor construction and surfacing, ranging from iron to concrete.

The ceilings of the earliest buildings were simply the floors of the rooms above, and if of sufficiently high status, the joists and beams would be decorated with mouldings or plain chamfers. Usually all the timbers would be limewashed to maximise the available light, and the 'black-and-white' beamed ceiling so popular with estate agents has no historic precedents.

In high status buildings from the sixteenth century onwards, the fashion was to hide the floor structure and to introduce a lath-and-plaster flush ceiling, often richly decorated. The joists for floor and ceiling were now generally fixed into the same main beam though the latter were of a smaller scantling. Flush ceilings also allowed the use of *pugging* beneath the floorboards; this was designed to reduce the transmission of sound and smell between floors. There were different methods of achieving this: one of the most common was a simple lath-and-plaster infill between the floor joists, sometimes with sand added on top. Despite the widespread desire for smooth plaster ceilings, old fashioned 'beamed' ceilings continued in vernacular buildings to the end of the nineteenth century.

6   Glass and glazing

In about AD675, French glassmakers came to Wearmouth to make the windows of the new church, because it was said that the process was unknown in Britain. In fact it was a craft that had been forgotten, as there is evidence that the Romans had glazed windows in some of their buildings in England. Even so, window glass did not become common in even comparatively high status buildings until the late sixteenth century, being confined until then mainly to the church and the houses of the very rich.

Although glass was being manufactured in England on a small commercial scale by the early thirteenth century, a great deal of the glass used was also imported, particularly from France. In the 1560s and '70s, however, French glassmakers appear to have revitalised a small domestic glassmaking industry in the Weald and, later, in Staffordshire and as far north as Yorkshire. Their improvements in the quality of window glass coincided with a growing secular market for the product. Twenty years later William Harrison noted that 'glass is come to be so plentiful and within a very little so good cheap', remembering that, 'Of old time, our country houses, instead of glass, did make much use of lattice, and that made either of wicker or fine rifts of oak in chequerwise'. This latticework in the windows was usually filled with greased paper or fine linen rather than glass and, in the better quality buildings, the windows would have shutters.

Medieval glass was made mainly in small wood-fired furnaces. The development of larger and more efficient coal-fired reverberatory furnaces in England in the seventeenth century meant that glass became cheaper still, and the quality of domestic window glass continued to improve. The manufacture of glass tended to be concentrated into certain areas of the country where raw materials, particularly coal for fuel, were available, and in the early eighteenth century each area produced a slightly different type of product.

From the late seventeenth century the cheapest seems to have been *Newcastle Glass*, which was shipped down the east coast and commonly used in London as well. According to Neve it was 'a kind of an Ash-colour', and despite its specks and blemishes was the most widely used in England. Other types included *Staffordshire* and *Bristol*, but the best was considered to be either *Lambeth* or *Ratcliffe* crown glass. By the end of the eighteenth century, there were also important glassmaking centres in south Yorkshire, Lancashire, and Clackmannanshire.

The traditional methods of making glass, up until the nineteenth century, were simple. To make what we now call *Crown glass*, a blob of molten glass was taken by the glassmaker from the furnace on the end of a long hollow *blowing iron*, and blown into a hollow sphere. This would be transferred to a solid iron rod called a *pontil* that the glassmaker rotated at speed. Centrifugal motion converted the sphere into a flattened disc which, depending on the amount of glass and the height of the glassmaker, could be up to 5ft or more in

84 *Surviving medieval shop windows are rare. In Shrewsbury the Abbots House, dating to the late 1450s, has a series of them. Recent stripping of layers of black paint allowed these to be closely examined and it was found that most were original*

85 *A late sixteenth-century mullioned and transommed window at Dolbelidr, Denbighshire. It has survived remarkably intact and the future of this important but derelict house has recently been assured by being leased by the Landmark Trust*

86 *A four-light window in an early seventeenth-century timber-framed building in Ludlow, Shropshire. The thinner vertical bars are the glazing stanchions. This example was well preserved because it was blocked and hidden from view for well over two centuries*

87 An early eighteenth-century sash window with segmental head and decorated frame surround. This building, in Warwick, is probably by the town's famous architect Francis Smith

diameter. After annealing, it could be cut up into individual squares ready for sale; the thick 'bulls' eyes' so beloved of Tudor-style theme pubs and suburban houses were the point at which the pontil was connected to the glass, and usually rejected or sometimes sold as third-rate glass. Finally, glasscutters produced the *quarries* of glass ready for the window. An alternative form, *cylinder glass*, was similar, only the glass maker worked by blowing the molten glass into a cylindrical mould, and as the glass was cooled this was split along one side and carefully unwound until it was completely flat.

Until casement and sash windows with wooden glazing bars came into general use in the later seventeenth century, the most common method of glazing windows involved fixing the small individual quarries of glass into thin H-sectioned lead *calms* or *cames*. A complete pattern of leaded cames was thus created ready to be fixed into the wooden frame in the window aperture. Often the pattern would be framed in timber or iron for additional strength; the whole assembly was then fitted into a rebate in the window frame and tied in position. The fixing was usually to iron bars, either horizontally set *saddle bars* or *glazing bars*, vertical set *stanchions*, or both. The cames would be fixed to the ironwork by twists of soldered copper or lead.

This simple method was still in use in the early nineteenth century when most window frames were of timber. Typically such frames will have shallow rebates on their outer faces for the framed 'leaded lights' to fit into. Where such windows have been

88 Winchester is noted, amongst many other things, for its Georgian bow windows and few are better than these examples on Kingsgate Street

modernised, it may still be possible to identify these external rebates and the redundant holes or scars for the stanchions or glazing bars.

Changes in fashion led to the development of the sash window — or, more correctly, the balanced sash window — from the late seventeenth century onwards; in many medium- and large-sized houses earlier casements were replaced with the more fashionable sashes. In this type of window the glazing bars and the glass panes are integral parts of the same design and are raised or lowered by the action of weights and pulleys connected by the sash cord in the *sash boxes* on either side of the window. Generally, the earlier sashes have thicker glazing bars, or *astragals*, often only moulded on the inside. Towards the end of the Georgian period glazing bars became increasingly thinner. More primitive sashes dispensed with sash cords and were simply held open by iron or wooden pegs; a horizontally sliding sash, or 'Yorkshire sash' was also fairly widespread in vernacular buildings.

Cast-iron windows were being made in some parts of the country, notably Coalbrookdale in Shropshire, by the end of the eighteenth century. Initially these were seen as an inferior product and were seldom used on any building of pretension. Workers cottages in some areas did have them, as did nonconformist chapels.

Cast or *plate* glass was developed in France at the end of the seventeenth century but not made in England until 1773 and not widely adopted until the start of the following century. That coincided with the improvements to *cylinder* glass, developed from the crown glass method but capable of producing larger and cheaper sheets with fewer imperfections. This in turn led to a change in the character of window glazing, as larger and larger panes could be used.

The manufacture of stained glass, most commonly used in churches, was well established by the twelfth century. Coloured glass was also found in excavations at Monkwearmouth, suggesting that the French glaziers brought over in the seventh century were well versed in the technique. The colours were mainly achieved by adding metallic oxides to the glass during firing: cobalt for blue, copper for green, manganese for purple, gold or selinium or copper for red, etc. Much of the multicoloured magnificence of our great medieval churches was destroyed during the Reformation; stained and painted glass was only revived during the nineteenth century.

One of the many myths of building history relates to windows and to the idea that any blocked window is the result of the various window taxes levied between 1694 and 1851. Whilst some windows were certainly blocked up, many such windows were deliberately designed to be 'blind' from the start. This was usually because they were needed to complete a symmetrical facade, rather than the internal arrangements of the house. Sometimes the recessed 'window' was left undecorated; sometimes a painted window would be added; and in the most expensive houses, a fully glazed window would be added in front of the black-painted brick blocking to complete the illusion. The degree by which a window is flush or recessed with or to the outer wall face sometimes relates to the materials used, sometimes to fashion, and in some areas — particular in London — to local bye laws. As most fashions originated in the capital, the results of the bye laws generally spread further afield, though there was often a time lag.

PART III:
RECORDING THE EVIDENCE

89 Where time and money allow, surveying is best done in a single phase on site. This archaeologist is perched nearly 200 feet up on the spire of All Saints' church, Hereford (note the skinny facet drawings). Checking for errors back on the site if a two-stage strategy was being used would not have been very popular

7 Surveying

Much has been written about how to survey or 'record' historic buildings, but surprisingly little about the rather more fundamental issue of why a particular building deserves to be recorded and the amount of detail required. Apart from its educational and training value, recording for recording's sake in the professional field is both wasteful in resources and does little to enhance the reputation of building archaeology. The type and level of an historic building survey should simply be dictated by what is actually needed. Ideally, before any decisions are made, the reason for the archaeologist's involvement in the project in the first place needs to be looked at, followed by the building itself. Only then can sensible decisions be made about the appropriate approach to the recording of it.

There is a misconception amongst some building archaeologists that the greater the detail and the larger the scale, the better the survey. This has also influenced, to a degree, some of the official conservation strategies for historic buildings. The underlying reasons for this are partly due to the influence of the more traditional field of excavation archaeology — and of excavation archaeologists. This is dealt with in more detail in the following section on interpretation.

There are two main archaeological reasons for surveying a building. One is the 'preservation by record' already mentioned in respect of excavations, though in this case more usually (but not exclusively) confined to the existing visible structure rather than each uncovered layer of it. Thus, if a building is to be pulled down and is considered to be of sufficient historic value, it will be recorded for posterity. Also included within this category is the recording of small parts of buildings that are to be changed irrevocably, even though the rest of the building will survive; for example, a section of masonry that needed to be refaced, or part of a timber frame that needed to be replaced.

The second, and more common, reason is to assist in the understanding of the building and its structural development. The old dictum that a picture is worth a thousand words is as true in the field of building archaeology as it is in any other. A long written description of any building and an interpretative text outlining its historical development is almost impossible to produce in a meaningful form without the aid of some form of illustration. The information from a good archaeological survey can be used in many ways other than a simple representation of the building: it can be used to highlight, amongst other things, particular types of building materials, changes in construction techniques, or areas of different types of mortar. Perhaps most usefully the information can present, graphically, the various phases of the building and be manipulated to produce objective reconstructions. The uses are wide ranging.

In either category, the degree and detail of the survey should be carefully thought out in advance and respect the need, rather than be led by any other criteria. A complex medieval masonry structure of several obviously significant phases will need to be recorded in far more detail than a simple and regularly coursed brick building that is clearly of only a single phase. Even in a complex structure, some thought should be given to whether every stone should be recorded, or whether just recording the main construction breaks and adjacent masonry and supplementing the drawn survey with a detailed photograph would suffice. Understanding the evolution of a timber-framed — or indeed, steel- or concrete-framed — structure is different again, and a basic survey of its frame carcass alone will be of far more use than fully detailed elevations on which surface finishes and later additions obscure the clarity of the design.

All of this may sound sensible, but in practice it is not always possible. Sometimes the money is simply not available to fund the degree of recording that is necessary. At other times, and particularly for the professional archaeologist, the recording strategies are dictated by the client's brief for the work, which in turn is usually dictated directly by the relevant planning authority or heritage body.

Because of the increasingly heavy workload on conservation officers and the inspectors of organisations like English Heritage and CADW, it is virtually impossible for them to have anywhere near the amount of time to properly assess the degree of recording needed for the many planning applications that land on their desks, and most briefs tend to be the result of simply altering a standard *pro forma*. As a result there are cases where too little or too much information is requested. Both cause problems: too little recording means that potentially vital information is lost; too much means that the clients are funding unnecessary research and archaeology, and for that matter, planning, is placed in a bad light and could lead to a lack of cooperation on future projects.

Survey Drawings

There are three basic types of survey drawings — plans, elevations, and sections — and all are two-dimensional. Plans are horizontal slithers through a building, usually at each floor level; elevations are the drawings of the walls, usually external but occasionally internal as well; and sections are vertical slices through the building. Sections across the width of the building are usually called cross-sections or transverse sections, whilst those down its length are long or axial sections. From these two-dimensional surveys it is possible to produce three-dimensional drawings, which can be useful in aiding the interpretative text on a building.

A photograph is, in itself, a form of survey, and a grasp of good photographic techniques is something that a building archaeologist should master. The more usual surveys are those measured scaled drawings produced by hand-taping or, more and more commonly, by advanced computer-aided digital techniques. Specialist tools have evolved and continue to rapidly improve that can provide highly accurate and detailed surveys in a very short space of time, such as the EDM (Electronic Distance Meter), and use sophisticated computer-aided design (CAD) software to print and manipulate the measurements that they gather. This is sophisticated and expensive hardware that requires specialist training in its use and is thus usually out of the reach of most of those involved in historic buildings.

Nevertheless, these are still only tools and, as with all tools, it is not the ability of the equipment that matters but the ability of the person using it. There has been a growing tendency in this computer age to allow many disciplines to become technology led. A new and more advanced piece of equipment comes onto the market place and uses have to be found for it; at times it becomes too evident that the basic principles that underlie this modern technology have been forgotten and that the reliance on it has become total. This then sets a dangerous precedent and it is sometimes necessary to 'go back to basics'. Indeed, one thing that the mechanical survey equipment cannot do is get a 'feel' for the building.

At the risk of sounding very unscientific, literally having a 'hands-on' approach to a building does give the archaeologist a unique opportunity to study subtle differences in the texture of stones, or the manner in which a piece of wood has been worked. A tactile approach can also allow the fingers to feel residual features, such as well-worn carpenters' or masons' marks, that are invisible to the naked (or digital) eye. Conversely, if a surveyor is working on a building for a long enough time he or she may notice a feature in a certain light when the sun moves round that an EDM would miss. For example, on one Gloucestershire building recently the rays of the lowering sun picked out, for an instance, shadows on a plaque on a stone building. Suddenly this ceased to be read as a Cromwellian coat of arms and became instead a date of over half a century later; as a result the building ceased to be interpreted as a former court house and became instead a slightly less remarkable barn.

Basic Surveying Techniques

The perfect survey is a myth. No survey technique can achieve 100% dimensional accuracy no matter what technology is being used. Survey drawings attempt to translate parts of the real three-dimensional full-sized world into a much reduced two-dimensional form. In this, as in all translations, there is unlimited scope for error. Good surveying technique is about maximising the amount of relevant information recorded and minimising the amount of error in doing so.

Fortunately, the 100% accurate survey is not as vitally important in the interpretation or recording of historic buildings as many seem to think, although attempting to achieve it is. To place matters into perspective, when a building is surveyed by hand, measurements are usually made to the nearest centimetre. This means that there is an inherent potential inaccuracy of just under half a centimetre for every measurement on a survey drawn up at a scale of 1:20 — the largest of the standard scales in use on site. At a scale of 1:50, this will increase to nearly 25mm, or about 1in. Similarly, on a scale drawing, lines drawn with one of the standard pen sizes, 0.5mm, will be 10mm, or 1cm, thick at 1:20 and 25mm thick at 1:50; on 1:100 site plans this will increase to 50mm, or nearly 2in. None of this takes into account the action of drawing itself, even by the best and most steady-handed of surveyors, or the fact that the various building planes will not be exactly flat.

The choice of scale depends on the project. If the purpose is to record a complex piece of masonry that is to be altered or demolished, or a section in which subtle complexities need to be seen to properly interpret it, then the larger the scale the better, and a 1:20 scale would normally suit. Larger scales, such as 1:10, are usually too large for recording of areas of a building but can sometimes be used for recording specific features. For less intense surveys, or of very large buildings, a 1:50 scale should suffice. Some details, such as moulding profiles, will often need to be produced at a life-size scale of 1:1, though this is often done by using specialist thin-tined profile gauges rather than by measurement.

The metric system

Virtually all surveying is now done in this country using the metric system of measurement. Some have argued for the retention of the old Imperial standards, partly out of innate conservatism but partly out of the more sensible belief that historic buildings were built by people in this country using feet and inches rather than metres and centimetres. Whilst there is merit in that argument, it does not take into account that, until the eighteenth century at least, one region's feet and inches were not necessarily the same as another's, or that many of the older measurements have been obsolete for centuries. Nor does it take into account that, since the 1970s, the education system has been metric and that any potential surveyor from the late twentieth century onwards would have to learn an archaic and superficially illogical system of measurement before being able to use it.

The old Imperial system should not, however, be completely discounted during a building survey. It is quite possible in structures clearly built using the later standard Imperial measurements that an understanding of them may be of great value in their interpretation. A specific feature, such as a blocked window or a series of floor joists, may be a specific Imperial measurement apart, and being aware of these distances could help in locating the present or former positions of other similar features either obscured or removed. The system of measurements used in a building, whether standard Imperial or antiquated but empirically logical medieval, should be treated as another potential source of the archaeological evidence.

The modern metric system was officially introduced to revolutionary France in 1799; the standard metre was calculated to be 1/10,000,000th of the distance between the North Pole and the Equator on a quadrant passing through Paris. For the technically minded it was redefined in 1960 as being equal to 1,650,763.73 wavelengths in vacuum of the orange radiation ($2P_{10}$ - $5d_5$) of a krypton atom of mass 86. In real life, the metric system offers a logical, versatile, and universally accepted system of measurement.

In Britain there is still a slight reluctance to wholeheartedly accept metric measurements, where journeys and fuel consumption are still worked out in miles and gallons, and people still buy their food in pounds and ounces. The situation is gradually changing but, where this is relevant to the buildings archaeologist, the building trade is often still caught in two separate systems, where terms like 'about 12 metres of 3 by 2 (i.e. 3" x 2")', or 'I want a trench 10 metres long and about a foot deep', are common.

Generally, the buildings' archaeologist can cheerfully ignore all but three of the standard linear units of metric measurement. There is usually little need for the kilometre, and certainly no need for the hectometre (100m), decametre (10m) or decimetre (0.1m). Just the metre (1m) and the millimetre (0.001m) are adequate for most purposes, and the use of the centimetre (0.01m) is more down to personal taste.

Simple survey equipment

With modern technology there is a bewildering array of new and highly sophisticated survey equipment available, much of it incredibly expensive and sometimes difficult to master. Fortunately, the majority of archaeological surveys can be carried out using quite basic tools such as tape measures, string, line levels, plumb-bobs, sharp pencils, scale rule, compasses, drafting film, and common sense. Ordinary builders' retractable hand-tapes are perfectly adequate for most surveying work, with the 5m and 8m length ones being more useful than anything shorter. Also needed on most sites will be a larger roll tape, typically of 30m. Line levels, string, nails, chalk, and other tools can also be bought at builders' merchants and the telescopic vertical measure — or 'big stick' — is a more expensive, but very worthwhile, luxury.

For work on site it is recommended that all drawings be produced on good drafting film, even if a two-stage survey process has been chosen. Drafting film will retain its size and shape in all weathers without the risk of shrinking in ordinary paper and tracing paper and can be used in the wet. Obviously any distortion of the drawn image will reduce its degree of accuracy.

An expensive specialist drawing board on site is not really necessary and a simple piece of board — preferably slightly soft and fairly light like the ones used for pin boards — will suffice. Usually this will be covered with metric graph paper on the top side, simply held in place with masking tape. The drafting film is then fixed with the same type of tape on top of that. Generally it is recommended that the film is cut slightly larger than the board and that the 'extra' is folded onto its back before being fixed. This will allow a greater area of film, avoid 'rucking' the taped edges, and prevent rain getting under the drawing.

A good HB pencil, traditional or retractable according to taste, is cheap enough to buy and it makes sense to have several on site. Many surveyors prefer the traditional lead pencils because with a bit of practice they can be sharpened to a needle point. The retractable pencils have the benefit of a consistent size (usually 5mm) but their leads do have an annoying tendency to snap in use, especially in the cold.

Finally, a large transparent set-square, an architects' scale ruler (with at least 1:20, 1:50 and 1:100 scales), a decent compass and an eraser complete the basic drawing tools usually needed. Other basic equipment is needed to set up the all important data to which the drawing will be related, and this will include a builders' level, some builders' string, nails, and a hammer.

In an ideal world a good surveying team would consist of three people. For tape measurements one would hold the start of the tape, another do the measurements, and a third plot the results. Elsewhere, if a theodolite or EDM is being used, three is again a useful number. In the real world, archaeologists usually have to make do with teams of two or even one.

Survey basics

One rather obvious surveying rule, surprisingly often flouted, is to measure horizontal distances from left to right. This is, after all, the way that the tapes read, and it is much easier to read them the right way up. In practical terms this means that internal walls are surveyed in a clockwise direction around the room or building, and external ones, in the opposite, anticlockwise, direction.

As far as possible, *running measurements* are infinitely preferable to short single measurements, though this can cause difficulties for a solo surveyor. If single measurements are made along a whole length of wall, from corner to door jamb, width of door, jamb to window jamb, *etc.,* the potential cumulative inaccuracy can be quite large. Each measurement will usually be to the nearest centimetre, and the potential inherent error of just under 50mm for each single measurement will be multiplied by the number of separate measurements needed along the wall. If there are ten such measurements along a 5m long wall, the potential inaccuracy is just under 0.5m: 10%. Any sensible surveyor will automatically compensate for this, but nevertheless the use of running measures for as long as possible will help to cut down on the potential error.

In a running measurement, the zero end of the tape is fixed or held in place, usually by an assistant or by a nail, and the tape is gradually unwound along the length of the elevation. All measurements are then read off from the tape until the end of the wall or section of wall is reached. Even though these will still be to the nearest centimetre, so will the full length of the wall and all the features in it and there should be no major discrepancies in the resulting survey drawing. Where features, such as projecting chimney breasts or, externally, bow windows, disrupt the running tape, individual measurements may have to be used to measure those until a second set of running measurements can be set up on the other side of the obstruction.

To avoid other cumulative errors that might creep into a drawing, it is advisable with any type of drawing to measure the overall parameters first — the outline of a plan, for example — and then add the main features such as doorways and windows, and only after that the more detailed measurements. If the survey is simply started at one end and drawn up bit by bit it is possible for just one unseen mistaken reading to cause an entire drawing to be redone.

Trigonometry

Trigonometry is a word that strikes fear into those of us who never got to grips with mathematics at school. Virtually all basic surveying is based on a very simple basic premise: the constancy of the triangle. From this evolved the ancient but incorruptible theories of trigonometry as used in surveying. When a triangle is enlarged or reduced the relative position of its three corners, its angles, and the lengths of its three sides remain the same. Providing enough of this information is known it is possible to recreate the real size triangle at any scale. This simple principle applied to surveying can be explained in the most basic and simplest exercise — the survey of the inside of a single, square-shaped room (see **91**).

The length of each wall could be measured in turn and drawn to scale, each being set out at right angles to form the square. This would not, however, necessarily produce an accurate scaled drawing of the room. Even if all four walls (AB, BC, CD, DA) are the same length, this does not mean that the room is definitely square; it could be a parallelogram. (Several nineteenth century churches and nonconformist chapels were built to a parallelogram plan for a variety of reasons usually associated with property boundaries.) The only way to check that the room is square is by introducing theoretical triangles into the equation. If the internal plan of the room is truly square then the two *diagonals* measured between the corners (AC and BD) will be of equal length. This is because they form the hypotenuse of two matching right-angled triangles (ABD and BCD). If they are of different lengths then the room cannot be square.

In theory there are two methods of plotting the results of the survey of this room at a set scale on paper; in practice, there is only really one. Assuming that the walls are straight, their lengths can be measured. This means, for example, that the distances between points A and B, and B and C, will be known. If the diagonal line between points A and C is measured as well, all the information is available to plot the three corners accurately.

To do so, simply draw a straight line representing the scaled distance between A and B. Then, take a compass, opened out to the scaled distance between B and C. With the foot of the compass on point B, draw an arc roughly in the area where C should be. Reset the compass to the distance between A and C, and with the foot on point A, draw a second arc to bisect the first. Because of the basic law of triangles, the place where the two arcs cross has to be the position of point C. The wall BC can now be drawn. Point D can now be plotted by the same method, either using two more arcs produced from either end of the line AB, or by one arc from point A and one from the newly found point C. This simple form of linear measurements using triangles is called *trilateration*.

The other method of plotting, without diagonals, requires instead that at least two of the angles of the triangle are known. Using a theodolite indoors is not to be recommended, and internal angles are thus difficult to obtain. However, there is an easy way of seeing if a corner is indeed at right angles. This also relies on trilateration, but in its most basic form. A triangle in which the two shorter sides and the hypotenuse have the numerical relationship 3/4/5 will be a right-angled one.

In practical terms, it is possible to measure from a corner with a hand tape 300mm in one direction, and 400mm in the other and if the diagonal distance between the two is 500mm, then the corner is a right angle. In the simple example in figure **91** this means that, if the angle at point B was checked in this way and found to be a right-angle, then a set-square could be used on the scaled drawing to find the position of C without any need of the diagonal AC. Nevertheless, it is recommended that diagonals are always taken wherever possible.

Expanding this very simple principal it is possible to measure not only quite complicated plans but also elevation drawings as well. In this case the horizontal datum forms one side of a theoretical right-angled triangle. Each of the main points will be measured at right-angles to the datum (either above or below it) forming the second side of the triangle; the third side is generally irrelevant but it can be used to check the dimensional accuracy of the elevation in much the same way as diagonals on a plan.

One- or two-stage?
One other basic decision has to be made before a survey starts, and this depends upon several criteria, not least of which is the time available on site. Surveys can be one- or two-stage. In the first, the drawings are measured and drawn on site; in the second, they are measured on site and drawn up in the warmth of the office. In the first method, the measurements made can be translated directly to a pencil-drawn scale drawing on site.

This is then taken back to the office when complete and forms the basis for the final inked overlay drawn on a fresh sheet of drafting film. In the second, only a sketch is made on site, onto which the measurements are noted; this is then taken back to the office and the scale drawing is produced.

Despite the obvious attractions of the latter approach, especially in the winter, experience shows that it is not usually the most effective method of the two. Mistakes will inevitably crop up in survey drawings and if they are being produced on site then they can be corrected as soon as they become apparent. If they only become evident back in the office, a trip back to the site may be needed and if the site is some distance away this can become expensive. If there had been a delay in processing the sketch measurements, the worse scenario is that the part of the building in question — or even the building itself — had gone by the time the mistake was spotted. Sometimes the measured sketch drawing can be used and the final drawing based on it can be drawn up on or near site. This offers the best of both worlds but is only possible when the site circumstances allow it.

Where measurements are going to be properly plotted later, whether on site or back in the office, it is important to ensure not only that every necessary measurement and cross-check has been made, but that they are also legible and make sense. They should be based on a sketch plan or elevation. Some recommend that these sketch drawings should be drawn as near to scale as possible on graph paper, but this can cause problems, particularly where small areas of detail need to be measured. Instead, it is usually easier to exaggerate details such as doors, windows and fireplaces, *etc.* on the sketch to allow more space for the relevant measurements.

On the field sketch plan, it is important to distinguish between single and running measurements. Different ways of doing this are possible and there are personal preferences. Normally, individual measurements are marked above a line with arrows at each end, whilst running measurements have an arrow at one end and a dot or bar at the other signifying that these are measurements from a fixed point. Sometimes very small details, even if exaggerated, will need a slightly different way of being marked, such as having the measurement between two inverted arrows; this would be the case for a wall thickness, for example.

Ultimately, the method of indicating measurements on a sketch plan is down to common sense and personal taste, but clarity is vital; there is nothing more frustrating than sitting at a drawing board trying to read figures mixed up in what seems to be pencilled spaghetti. The methods used for annotating site plans and elevations are usually different. On plans, lines between the points measured are used in the normal method. On elevation drawings this can sometimes be confusing, and another, clearer, method is to mark the position of the relevant points, such as a corner of a window or base of a door, by a spot or 'X'. Each of these is then numbered, logically if possible, and that number listed in a site notebook; the relative position of each 'spot' to the horizontal and vertical data are then noted next to the number in the site notebook for later reference.

The site plan

A measured site plan will usually be needed if a group of buildings is being studied; for example, in an industrial, agricultural or religious complex. Sometimes, even if just one

90 *Typical site drawing for a survey plan. The main top section has been produced in the most common way using mainly running meaurements along walls with a series of check diagonals. In the lower section a running straight line has been plotted and triangulated offsets to the relevant points taken from it. These drawings are not meant to be works of art but clarity is essential; leaving a space for a few detailed sections can be useful*

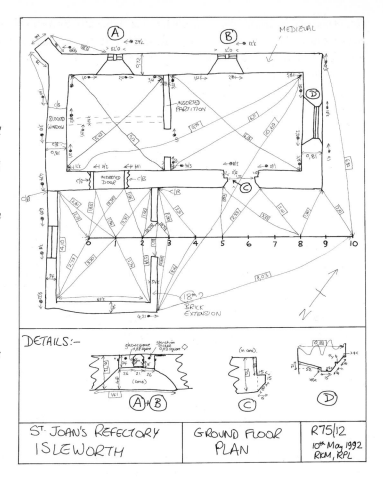

building is to be surveyed, its relationship with other structures around it may need to be established. As with all survey drawings the scope and detail of the site plan should depend on the needs of the individual project. There is no point in producing a superbly detailed site plan if it adds nothing to the interpretation of the building in question. It is also worth checking that no suitable plan has already been produced or if there is a suitable Ordnance Survey map that could be used or enlarged, bearing in mind the copyright laws.

Site plans can be outline or detailed or anywhere in between. In an outline plan, literally just the outlines of the buildings and other features will be depicted. A detailed plan, particularly on a complex site, could show complete ground floor plans of all the buildings as well as boundary walls, ditches, embankments, water features, etc.

There are several different survey techniques that can be used to create a site plan, ranging from the simple to the sophisticated. In most cases a good site plan can be produced without the need of expensive survey equipment such as an EDM or theodolite. All that is needed is a long tape measure; the quality and consistency of the modern tape means that the old surveying chain is now a thing of the past.

As with all survey drawings, it is important to decide on the scale before setting up.

Usually site plans tend, for obvious reasons, to be drawn to a fairly small scale — usually no more than 1:100. If, as recommended, the site survey is going to be carried out and drawn up in the field, the size of the hand-held drawing board will to a certain extent dictate the scale. If all the required data will be easily seen on an A3 drawing, then use a scale that will fit an A3 drawing board. For general work, any drawing board over A2 size will prove unwieldy and cumbersome on site.

The simplest form of base line is literally a suitably sited straight line marked out by a tape. To ensure that the line is actually straight, the simplest method needs just two ranging rods and two, or preferably three, people. One person stands or kneels at the start of the line; another holds a ranging rod vertically at the end of it. The third person takes another ranging rod and at a selection of places along the line holds it vertically, the point touching the tape. If, looking directly along the line, the first person can see the end ranging rod, then the line cannot be straight and the tape needs to be adjusted. Once the line is set the tape can either be fixed in place, by steel tent pegs if possible, or, if nothing else is available, by bricks or stones. It is, however, important to keep checking that the tape has not moved. The one advantage that the old measuring chains did have was their ability to stay fixed in one place.

If a theodolite or dumpy level is available these can save time. Simply set up the equipment at a suitable spot over one end of the intended line and look through the sight to the other. An assistant with a ranging rod can then walk between, occasionally standing the rod on the tape. Providing the vertically held rod remains aligned with the sights centre bar of the theodolite, the accuracy of the line can be assured.

If only one long tape is available, or if it is felt that the line needs to be used for several days, it is possible to make it a more permanent feature. It can be set out in string, pegged in place, and preferably marked in some way at every metre length. It may, instead, be possible simply to hammer in wooden pegs, suitably marked at metre intervals along the line to act as fixed points from which to measure. In this case, the actual metre measure should be the head of a nail or similar object hammered into the top of the peg.

For convenience, where a theodolite is not being used, at least one end of the tape could be fixed at a significant point in the plan such as the corner of a building. If possible, the other end of the tape could be the corner of another building. The layout of a site may dictate that it will easier to have a line that has no direct connection with any building at all. In any case, the two ends of the line need to be fixed on the plan before any other surveying takes place.

Fixing the ends of the line on plan requires only simple trigonometry. If the tape end is free the easiest way is usually to measure from it to any two fixed points. Ideally these will be the corners at either end of an elevation of the nearest convenient (and straight-sided) building. The length of the two measurements from the building to the tape end (*a* and *b* on Fig.x), and the distance between the two points on the building (*c*), form the three sides of a triangle (*abc*). These can then be processed in the usual way.

A fourth measurement (*d*), from one of the points on the building to the other end of the tape will create a third triangle (*bdx*). In this example, its other two are one of the previous measurements (*b*) and the length of the tape (*x*). and thus plot that end of the tape as well. If that is not possible, variations on the same theme can be worked out. Once the base line is in place, all other points can be measured from it. If the survey is being drawn up on site, the line needs to be plotted onto the drawing board before these measurements are taken. Simple right-angled offsets are often used to measure from a base line but these are not necessarily accurate enough unless the distances are very short. Instead, it is better to create small individual triangles for each point to be measured.

The procedure is shown in Fig.xy. The distance to each feature is measured from two separate points on the base line, preferably from metre marks at least 3-4m apart, depending on the end scale of the survey. The resultant measured lengths (*a* and *b*) form two sides of a triangle, the third being the distance between them on the base line (*c*). Using the compass method already outlined, each point is then plotted. The advantage of using the metre marks on the base line is that every metre length can be marked on the scaled-down version plotted on the drawing board. As each point or feature is plotted, the scaled site plan gradually takes shape. Where the buildings are reasonably straight-sided, only their corners need to be plotted from the base line; all other features can be measured along the walls.

On larger and more complicated sites, more than one line will be required and thought must be given to the way additional lines are linked to the first. The separate base lines do not have to be joined physically. Once a base line has been set up, the ends of additional base lines can be plotted in the same way as any other point on the site.

If one or more of the buildings on a site has a fairly complicated plan it may be worth creating an entire *survey box* around it. Setting up a survey box by hand is relatively straightforward when the physical conditions are suitable. The first line can be set up in the same way as before and becomes one side of the box. Depending on the site, the next two sides can be formed using the 3/4/5 technique of finding a right angle at each end of the first line. These two perpendicular lines can then be continued for as long as required and then joined by the fourth and final side of the main box. Constant checking will ensure that the box is accurately set out. Once in place, the building can be planned using offsets from any one of the four sides of the survey box, and the box itself will be plotted into the overall site plan as any other line would be. If appropriate, the survey grids can be tied directly to internal survey grids used to create the ground-floor plans of individual buildings.

Occasionally, but only on the largest and best funded of projects, it is worth creating an entire grid system of squares that covers the entire site. Although this can be achieved

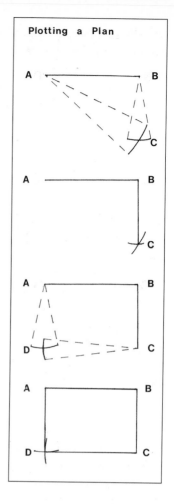

91 The basics of plotting a very simple plan

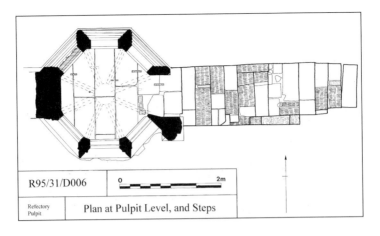

R95/31/D006   0   2m

Refectory
Pulpit   Plan at Pulpit Level, and Steps

92 A detailed plan will often include a great deal of information above and below the theoretical level that the plan is being made at. In this example there was no alternative, as it includes the steps leading up to the former Refectory pulpit of Shrewsbury Abbey. Shading of some treads indicates that they are of a particular type of stone which would have been explained in the main site key and the text

by hand, it is easier to set up using a theodolite. As with everything else in surveying, the site, the information required from it, and the equipment and personnel available, will dictate the manner in which it will be surveyed.

Another method of fixing the positions of features in a site plan swiftly and accurately is a variation on the old *plane table* method, but using a theodolite or EDM. The instrument needs to be set up in a convenient position; in a typical farmstead, for example, it could be in the middle of the foldyard, positioned so that any sight lines through gaps in the surrounding buildings can be used if necessary to fix buildings further away. Once it is set up and levelled, with an arbitrary zero degrees set on its horizontal reader, each significant point around the site, such as the corners of buildings, is viewed through the sight. The distance to it from the theodolite is measured and the angle read. These are then plotted on the drawing board to scale using a protractor and a scale rule and gradually the main plan is worked up into as detailed a site plan as necessary.

Building plans

A building plan is a horizontal slice through a building and one of the most basic but often most useful types of survey drawings. Plans are usually drawn at each of the floor levels of a building to give a complete picture of its internal layout. Plans can also be adapted to show such details as building materials, basic phasing and development, and room use.

In a standing structure plans are not usually drawn literally at floor level. This would be very inconvenient and also miss significant features, such as windows higher up the wall planes. Instead, plans are usually drawn at roughly shoulder level, allowing a convenient working height for taping and including most significant features. However, plans should not ignore features not exactly on their plane, and elements not on the plane line, such as ceiling beams, a particularly high or low window, or a hearth, should be included.

Plans can be drawn from measuring both inside and outside of a building, depending on circumstances. If the external walls are to be drawn, and a *datum level* has been set up on them, it makes sense to use that straight line as a basis for measuring along. Otherwise, it is important to try and ensure that the tape is held horizontal in use, though for basic surveys the slight discrepancies that might be produced if it is not perfectly level are fairly insignificant in most cases. Slight variations over the length of a building will not matter a great deal once drawn to a reduced scale.

Once one wall has been plotted to scale, the end of the walls adjoining it needs to be located by measurement and diagonal checks. In a simple room plan, just two measurements from opposing corners may be all that is needed, but in more complex buildings several others will be needed to ensure accuracy. This is particularly so when the walls are clearly not straight and the rooms are not square.

If it has been possible to complete a plan of the external walls of the building, then, providing there are suitable doorways and windows through which the wall thickness can be measured, it should be a relatively straightforward exercise to fit the individual room plans within the basic drawn shell. Additional longer diagonal check measures between rooms through internal doorways should then be used to eliminate any potential mistakes. Sometimes the exterior will be inaccessible in part and a more complex system of internal check diagonals and triangles will be needed to link the rooms.

On particularly complex or large buildings it is sometimes worth considering setting up a base line or even a grid in exactly the same way as could be used to create a site plan (see above). Before setting up a box or a grid it is well worth spending time thinking about the best way of aligning it. For example, see if it is possible to get one of the lines of the grid through or across the more significant buildings by siting lines through convenient doorways or windows. In a medieval site it could be worth trying to get a main line along the axis of the great hall; in a monastic site, along the axis of the nave of the church; and on an industrial site along the axis of a mill building. As these lines could later form the basis of measured sections, time spent in working out the grid is time well spent.

Elevations

Measurements taken for an elevation drawing are useless unless they are related to a known point, or *datum*. The ground level is not a suitable datum as it will not usually be completely level. A datum is a vertical or horizontal line, actual or theoretical. Usually the main *horizontal* datum is set at a convenient working level, just below shoulder height for example, whilst the *vertical* datum is set close to, but not necessarily on, the left hand end of whichever elevation is being surveyed.

There are several methods available to obtain a horizontal datum and the one chosen relies on the type of equipment available and the length of time the survey will take. It is worth remembering that in some more regularly constructed buildings the original builders probably tried to produce a level building. A simple check can be made with a level on brick or stone courses to see if they are truly horizontal. If one at a convenient height is seen to be level, it can be used as a datum and there is no point in creating a new and arbitrary one.

Unfortunately, such instances are rare and often 'horizontal' courses flatter to deceive. The simplest reliable method of getting a datum along the outside of a building is to use a *dumpy level*. A theodolite can also be used but is a little too complicated for the purpose. The cheapest dumpy levels are optical and basically consist of a tripod-mounted mini-telescope with sight lines in them. They are no longer particularly expensive to buy and they can also be hired by the day. Once properly set up and levelled on the tripod, a complete datum can be set up on the building simply by looking through the eyepiece.

Dumpy levels, like theodolites, have long-focus lenses and can be sited some distance from the wall in question. It is important to think about where to site the level for ease of use. On most projects more than one wall of a building will be surveyed or there may be more than one building. All measurements, nevertheless, should relate to the same main datum — usually referred to as the *site datum*. This can only be done by creating other horizontal secondary levels that relate to the main site level. The least number of times the dumpy level needs to be moved to create secondary levels the better, and time should be taken to chose the best place to set it up to create the first site datum. For example, on a typical rectangular building, set up the dumpy level where two complete sides can be seen, rather than just one.

A team of two is ideal for setting up a datum line, an observer and a marker. The observer looks through the dumpy level site, whilst the marker holds a piece of chalk or a pencil horizontally and slowly lowers or raises it close to the wall roughly at the level needed. As it comes into the dumpy level sight, the observer can get the marker to stop the pencil or chalk on the exact level and mark the spot. This exercise is repeated along the wall at appropriate intervals, with particular attention being paid to the position of any openings or other features.

The datum line then needs to be marked on the building, though the manner of doing this has to take account of many different criteria, including the state of the building, its archaeological or architectural sensitivity, the materials of which it is built, and the time that the datum line will be needed. A string line is by far the most convenient method providing no damage to the fabric occurs, and on large projects when the datum line may be needed for several days or even weeks, it is the only real option. Small nails are simply fixed to the wall on the marked datum line, preferably where they will not cause too much damage — in mortar or on the cracks between timber joints, for example. Thin parcel string is then taken along the wall and wound tightly around the nails, pulled taut, checked for sagging, and then tied off. If regularly checked for straightness, the string datum can be extremely accurate.

Where nailed string lines are not appropriate for whatever reason, chalk can be used instead, but care needs to be taken that it can be removed quickly afterwards. In many cases if chalk has to be used it need not be used as a continuous ruled line. Instead, it can simply be marked at every metre, or at critical points along the datum level, by window and door jambs, for example, or by distinct construction breaks or other architectural features. Once having created any datum line, in a string or in chalk, it is important afterwards to take them down again. There is more than one historic building in Britain that has in some remote part of it the rusting nails and rotting string that shows where building archaeologists once laboured.

Using the dumpy level or theodolite, the main site datum should, if possible, be related to the Ordnance Survey datum if there is a convenient benchmark handy. If not, it is nevertheless a good idea to fix the new site datum to a fixed point on the building. The main reason for this is if in the future more survey works are to be carried out. The temporary site datum created should have long gone and although the survey drawings should show it, a simple note that the datum was so many metres above a particular immovable feature, such as a step or a window sill, saves time.

If a dumpy level is not available, or if for various reasons it cannot be used (inside a room for example), an alternate way of creating a level is by using string and a string level, sometimes called a bricklayer's level. This is a lightweight bubble level that clips to the string. At one end the string is tied to a nail or tack fixed in the wall; it is stretched taught and level (checked by the bubble) and another nail position marked. Once that nail is fixed the string is wrapped around it a few times and then stretched taut again further along, and the process is repeated until the string line is finished. Obviously this depends on the use of potentially damaging nails or tacks and common sense will dictate if either should be used. Sometimes on more sensitive interior walls it is possible to use different fixings such as 'blu-tack', but the level of the string will need to be checked more often. An even simpler way, though one that needs more care and is not always suitable, is to simply go along the wall with a normal rigid builder's level and, making sure that the same level is used all along it, mark that level on the wall.

One datum is seldom enough for even the smallest building surveys. New datum lines will need to be created and will need to be related to the site datum. This is a fairly simple operation. For outside elevations, the tripod and dumpy will have to be moved to a new position for the new datum and the resultant heights will not be the same. The new level line in string or chalk is set up in the same way as the first. Usually, the 'break' between the two will be on the angle of a building. Once the second line is ready, the vertical distance between it and the first is simply measured and marked on the drawings. This process can then be repeated for any other secondary datum lines.

The easiest method of identifying the different datum lines is simply to call them D1, D2, D3, etc. On each working survey drawing the relevant datum lines will be labelled accordingly and only when the final drawings are being produced will a common datum need to be produced. On most buildings only one level line will be needed on each elevation, but taller buildings, especially those that are scaffolded at the time of the survey, will need two or more horizontal lines.

The vertical datum is generally set close to the left-hand side of the elevation being drawn. As already stated, it is easier to work from left-to-right when measuring, simply because that is the way all tape measures work. Sometimes the corner of the elevation can be used as the vertical datum, provided that it can be proven to be vertical, which is by no means always the case. If not, an arbitrary point, usually about 1m or so from the corner, can be marked on the horizontal datum to mark the position of the vertical one. A set-square, plumb-bob, or lightweight level can be used to ensure that the line is truly vertical.

Usually, all measurements from the vertical datum (y) are taken along the line of the

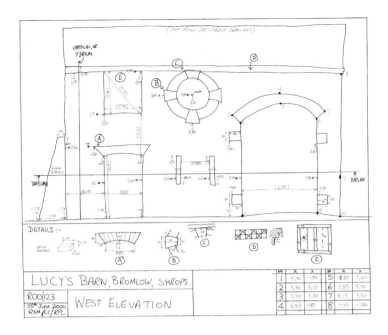

The table at the lower right of the drawing:

No	x	y	No	x	y
1	5,70	-1,92	5	8,83	3,60
2	5,70	3,10	6	7,95	3,10
3	8,50	3,30	7	8,15	3,30
4	6,83	3,85	8	7,95	-1,92

LUCY'S BARN, BROMLOW, SHROPS.

R001/23

WEST ELEVATION

25th June 2000
RKM /CC/ RPL

93 *Typical site drawing for an elevation survey. Most of the relevant points have been marked and their measurements from (and above, below, left or right of) the horizontal and vertical datums added directly onto the sketch. At the right hand, the alternate way of using numbered points has been used. The relevant 'x and y' measurements from the two datums are then marked next to the number in the table set out below the drawing*

horizontal datum (x), which is known to be level. Sometimes, a tape measure can be physically fixed in position along the datum, which certainly makes measuring faster and more efficient. In the simple example in figure **93**, the position of the lower left-hand corner of the window is being measured. The horizontal distance (x) is 2.3m and the vertical distance (y) is 1.2m. These figures can either be written onto the outline sketch for processing later, or transferred immediately onto the scale drawing. On that drawing, the horizontal and vertical data will already have been marked. By using a scale rule the appropriate scaled distances can be plotted and the relative position of the corner of the window fixed. By using the same technique, the other three corners of the window opening can be plotted and the jambs, lintel and sill drawn. As each desired point is measured, the whole elevation will take shape as it is plotted on the drafting film.

Where a very detailed stone-by-stone survey is needed it is obviously difficult to plot the corners of every single stone of a rubblestone wall using measurements from the two data. A different method is called for. Providing that the overall outline of the elevation has been plotted, it can be 'gridded out': that is, broken up into grid squares, usually of 1m by 1m, and based on the datum. Depending on the particular project, the grids can simply consist of chalked or nailed marks at metre intervals horizontally and vertically; in this case, each grid square becomes its own miniature datum, but one that is connected to the main datum by known measurements. Each stone within the grid can then be measured

134

94 Site drawing of a stone-by-stone elevation of a fairly complicated stone structure, using a grid system and, in one square, a planning frame. Although a certain degree of neatness is needed in such drawings it is always the best policy that the surveyor in the field is the one that inks up the final drawing in the office so minimise misunderstandings

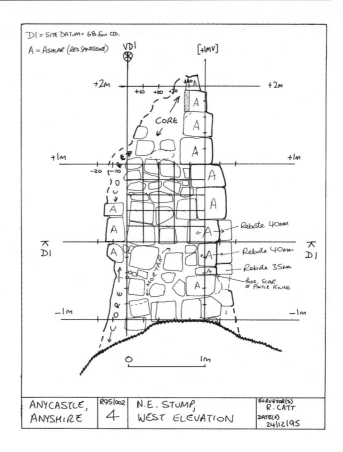

more easily by plotting its outlines using horizontal and vertical measurements from the sides of the grid. Once the outlines have been established the lesser details follow.

For the most detailed work these grids can be used to position one of the common tools of the excavating archaeologist: the planning frame. This consists of four pieces of straight timber fixed together to form a square, usually now with each internal side 1m long. Strings are nailed tautly at 100mm intervals from side to side in both directions, forming a more detailed grid inside the frame. The frame can then be fixed, usually by nails, directly onto the grid coordinates marked on the wall. The surveyor can then plot what he or she sees in each 100mm square of the planning frame to scale into the appropriate square of the survey drawing; this is obviously where the use of graph paper laid out under the drafting film is vital. With a little experience this can become a very quick and very accurate method of recording complex masonry, and one that archaeologists trained in excavations can adapt to very quickly.

Sections

Sections are usually produced, in part at least, by using the information generated by elevation and plan drawings; otherwise, to undertake a section through a building where there is no cross-wall or physical feature to measure between the two sides and the top and bottom of the drawing is difficult, simply because of the lack of a trustworthy datum to measure from. Usually, although the section is a slither through a building, it is useful to include, in outline at least, the features of the wall beyond the section line as well to place it more readily in context. Although generally not as detailed as elevation drawings, even a simple section is very useful in helping to understand how a building functioned, and can be vital when dealing with the processes and machinery in an industrial building.

Drawing in three dimensions

One of the undoubted benefits of CAD systems is the ability for the computer software to rapidly convert a series of two-dimensional plans and elevations into a three-dimensional drawing of the building. This can be very helpful in the interpretation of its development and in explaining that interpretation in the written report. The same type of drawing can be produced by hand, using special graph paper. Sometimes, even if resources are limited, a very simplified three-dimensional view of a building or buildings can be useful.

Drawing machinery

Industrial and agricultural buildings are recorded in the same way as any other buildings, but their specific functions can be of particular importance and sometimes require a slightly different form of survey to elucidate the way processes worked. If machinery is still intact then there may be a need to record it. The critical factor in such work is to understand as much as the mechanics of the machinery before attempting to measure.

Most of the machinery likely to be encountered involved movement, and assessing what type of movement was involved and the relationship between axles and cogs can avoid the need to measure everything in painstaking detail and still have no real idea of what the machine did. Often a basic outline measured sketch of interlocking axles and a good photograph will provide far more information that a detailed but misunderstood survey.

Some emergency survey techniques

There are various emergency survey techniques that can be used for different reasons, whether they be access, cost, lack of suitable equipment, or, above all, time. There are also many useful shortcuts. For example, if no means is available for measuring a tall brick building, this can be done by counting brick courses. This is not quite as daft as it sounds and is usually quite accurate. Once the courses are counted, simply measure a few that are accessible. Five courses should suffice, not forgetting to include the five separate bands of mortar. The number of brick courses in the elevation is divided by five and multiplied by the sampled height to give the total height.

In a less accurate manner, where no long tapes or no tapes at all are available, a regular stride pattern can be used in emergencies to pace out a plan, and the stride measured when a tape is obtained. Of the more comprehensive rapid survey techniques, two are probably the most useful. The first is rectified photography; the second, the rapid frame survey.

Rectified photography

Rectified photography is one of the most useful and cost-effective forms of rapid survey

95 A typical elevation drawing, in this case of the shaft wall of the mid-nineteenth-century engine house of the Ladywell lead mine in south-west Shropshire. All the bricks have been drawn but the assessment indicated that there was no need to draw the rubblestone in detail as it contained no construction breaks and was of one simple phase

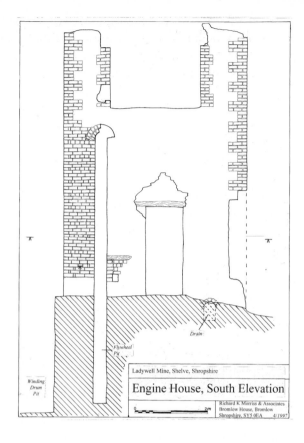

Ladywell Mine, Shelve, Shropshire

Engine House, South Elevation

Richard K Morriss & Associates
Bromlow House, Bromlow
Shropshire, SY5 0EA   4/1997

where circumstances permit or, in the case of a dangerous building, dictate. It relies on the most accurate photographic techniques and is best left to a skilled professional photographer experienced in this branch of architectural photography. Normally, large or medium format cameras are used, with 'rising fronts' that cut out vertical distortions.

The number of photographs needed on a particular elevation depends on the length and height of the elevation and the available viewpoints. Normally, a series of metre rods will be fixed to the plane of the elevation, so that when the photographer comes to print from the negative it is possible, with the use of a scale rule, to ensure that the desired scale is achieved. Another method is to get an outline survey of the elevation, consisting of little more than its basic parameters and main openings or other features such as string courses. This is then drawn up to scale and placed on the baseboard in the darkroom. The image can be projected onto this outline, enlarged until it fits exactly and then printed.

In both cases the end result is a rectified photographic print that should be sufficiently accurate to form the basis of a more detailed survey, achieved simply by drawing in as much detail as needed onto an overlay of draughting film placed on top. It is vital, however, that the drawing is done by someone who understands the archaeology of that particular building and who will go back to that building to check for any anomalies that may arise.

This basic principal underlies the far more sophisticated technique of *photogrammetry*

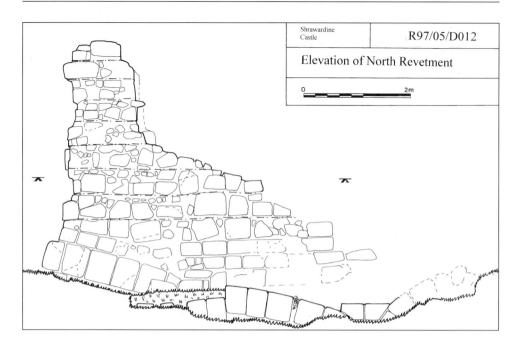

Shrawardine Castle	R97/05/D012
Elevation of North Revetment	
0 2m	

96 Usually it is pointless surveying corework. However, in this small fragment of Shrawardine Castle, Shropshire, the mortar of the core had fossilised the coursing of the robbed facework ashlar. Using a mixture of hand-tape survey and rectified photography a more detailed picture of the structure of the wall emerged. The reason why the masonry seems to hang in mid-air on the right-hand side is that it was partially buried in the bank of the motte

in which the photographs are processed and manipulated by a computer to produce a potentially very accurate and detailed record drawing. This process also allows a far more versatile integration with CAD systems and the ability to layer different types of information within the drawing — which, in turn, can produce instant drawings of a particular phase or of a particular type of architectural feature. However, it is still a specialist and expensive technology not readily available to most projects, and as it is only a tool, human error cannot be eliminated.

Rapid survey of timber frames

So logical were the original designs of most timber frames, it is possible to use a rapid survey technique in which the timber components become the effective datum of the drawing. In this type of survey, all of the timbers are drawn as if they are in their original alignments. Thus horizontal timbers are drawn horizontally and vertical ones, vertically.

The technique of this 'setting out' or 'assembly' survey method is simple, fast, and efficient. The best surviving and longest timbers are usually the wall-plates, so these are measured first. The length and height of the wall—plate is measured and plotted as horizontal onto the drawing. Then the spacings of the surviving posts or mortises for missing posts are measured along the wall-plate and plotted. The height of posts are then measured along their lengths rather than in the normal manner, and plotted vertically onto

97 *A frame survey of a late
seventeenth-century
building in the outskirts of
Hereford. The building
was built almost entirely of
reused material and the
documentary research
suggested that the suburb
was deliberately flattened to
improve Civil War lines of
fire. The timbers were
presumably stored and
were then available for
reuse once peace was
assured. (City of Hereford
Archaeology Unit)*

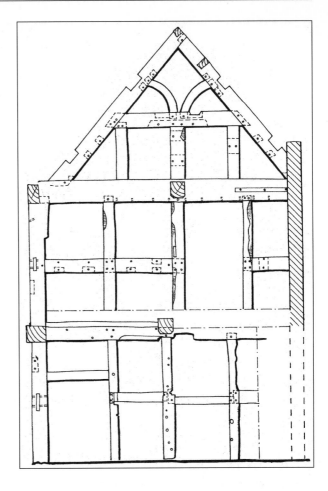

the drawing. Eventually each post will have been plotted onto the drawing along with the other vertical features, such as window jambs, and horizontal features, such as other horizontal timbers, lintels, and so forth. The end result will be a square frame drawing of the timber carcass as it was originally designed.

Once it is on paper, the missing timbers can be plotted too, using the evidence of mortises, etc. The beginning and ends of any curved timbers will be known from the frame survey and these can then be carefully added onto the survey drawing. Without resorting to expensive survey equipment or using up the most valuable of resources — time — a visual record of the frame design will have been produced quickly and cheaply and will be of far more use in understanding the evolution of the building than a complete, accurately levelled, detailed record of the building that includes all the various surface finishes that usually obscure the clarity of the frame. The rest of the information, useful as it is, can usually be recorded photographically and in an interpretative text.

The Archive Drawing

The end result of the survey work should be a final archive drawing that will be a permanent record of the building at the time of the survey. This should be deposited with

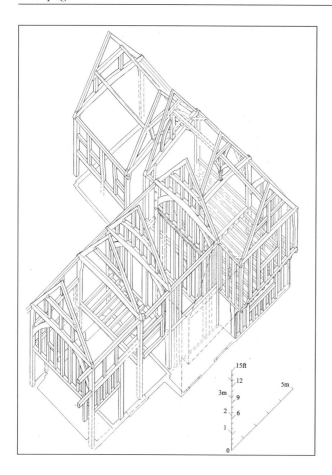

98 A good example of a detailed isometric drawing of a timber-framed house generated from the elevation surveys of individual frames and a site plan. The building is the heritage centre in Henley-in-Arden, Warwickshire, owned by the Shakespeare Birthplace Trust (Bob Meeson)

a suitable repository. The end of the twentieth century saw the start of the digital revolution and this has affected all forms of archaeology as it has done most other aspects of human endeavour.

There has been a growing call for the archaeological archive to be digitised, and this in turn has supported the arguments for a digitally based recording system based on EDMs and CAD. There is little doubt that both can be very useful, but at the same time a nagging doubt about the long-term stability of any digital technique remains, not because of the technology itself but because of the almost inevitable fact that any method used now will be obsolete within ten years. When this type of archive was first being mooted in archaeological circles in the mid-1980s the means was to be the 5.25" floppy disk; then later in the decade it was the 3.5" disk, and then the laser-disc; in the 1990s the recordable CD came and now is about to be replaced by the DVD and Zip-drive technology. Tomorrow it will be something else.

The old-fashioned ink drawing on draughting film still has a place and lacks such built-in obsolescence. Drawing techniques vary but the basics should be good clean draughtsmanship and clarity. Drawings should be done in permanent drawing ink using proper drawing pens of accurate nib widths, like those made by Faber-Castell or Rotring. They should be drawn on good quality draughting film.

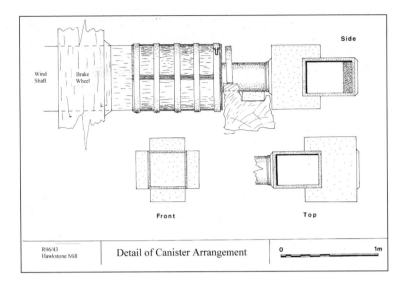

Side

Wind
Shaft

Brake
Wheel

Front

Top

| R96/43 Hawkstone Mill | Detail of Canister Arrangement | 0 | 1m |

*99 A detailed survey drawing of the 'canister' of the windmill at Hawkstone Park, Shropshire —
the piece to which the sails are connected to the main wind shaft. The conventions used in the
drawing are not 'standard', but were used to help illustrate the details. This is, incidentally, a rare
example of an oil mill and was one of the scenic set-pieces of the park*

Every drawing needs to have, at the very least, a title indicating the name of the site,
the code, if any, the part of the site being drawn, the date it was surveyed, and the scale.
Scales should be drawn out as a bar or line scale rather than just marked 1:20, for example.
In that way the scale bar can still work if the drawing is reproduced at a different size.
Plans should have north signs, and elevations and sections site datum bars and, preferably,
the adjacent ground-levels. Most of this is just common sense.

Drawing conventions continue to vary, despite, in England, at least, attempts by the
Royal Commission to develop a nationally agreed system. Whilst this certainly has merit
it has not been universally accepted, partly because of the differences between these
archaeologically based conventions and those used by architects. As a great deal of
interpretation of buildings is often done using architects' drawings, especially when there
is no way of funding new surveys, buildings' archaeologists will be using both basic
conventions.

In general the problems with conventions are more associated with plans rather than
elevations. Elevations are pictorial and conventions are seldom needed on them. Plans, as
theoretical two-dimensional slithers, need to differentiate between a window and a
doorway, for example, and the different types of windows and doorways. Overall,
differences in conventions are not a real issue providing that the information is clearly
presented. In some ways, the lack of a rigid drawing convention is a blessing in disguise.
It allows drawings to be produced in a way that best shows the particular elements or
aspects of a building being recorded, without shoehorning them into a way of drawing
that may be inappropriate.

8 Dendrochronology

There have been many technological advances that have made the role of the buildings' archaeologist easier. In surveying, the EDM and CAD systems have the potential to replace the tape-measure, theolodite and hand-inked drawings of draughting film, but their limitations have already been outlined. Improvements to computers have made access to, and distribution of, information incredibly easy compared to even ten years ago, and the potential of the digital camera, and video camera, have yet to be fully realised.

However, only one technological advance has really made a breakthrough in actually increasing our knowledge about the dates of buildings, and that is dendrochronology. Dendrochronology, or tree-ring analysis, is a highly technical specialist process that relies on powerful computer technology and skilled technicians. Only a handful of specialists can undertake it but it is, really, an important new type of 'survey', albeit a very minute examination of a specific part of a tree.

The complexities and scientific demands of dendrochronology, fortunately, do not matter to the average buildings' archaeologist. Whilst these are quite complex the basic principles are quite simple. Every year a tree will add another growing ring to its trunk or branches, and the width of that ring will depend on the climatic conditions. Good conditions will result in wide growth rings, bad conditions in narrow ones. As climate varies slightly from year to year, so will the thickness of these annual growth rings and a whole sequence of different ring thicknesses will result. By studying thousands of trees in different areas, an overall chronology of these tree ring sequences can be produced that spans several centuries. This master chronology can then be used as the basis against which to match the ring sequences of any new timbers to be sampled.

The timbers of an historic building can be cored, usually on site, by using a hollow drill bit. The hole produced is only small, generally around 1cm in diameter, and can either be left or capped; it is otherwise a non-destructive procedure. The resultant long cylindrical core will contain a complete sequence of the tree rings of the timber, and is then taken to the laboratory for processing.

After being sanded down the tree rings can be seen more clearly and are measured under a microscope. The measurements are then fed into a computer where the sequence of tree ring growth is compared against the master chronology. If there is enough information in the sample, a date range, or in some cases even a specific date, can be given for the felling of the tree from which the timber was cut. As most timber was used very soon after it was felled this will give a reasonably accurate date for the building in which it was used, providing, of course, that it was primary to it.

Surprisingly it is not the size of the timbers that dictates how successful the tree ring sampling results will be. It is, instead, the number of rings (around 70 or more is ideal) and, more critically, whether or not they were close to the edge of the growing tree. The edge of the tree was, of course, the bark, and sometimes timbers still with their bark on were used in buildings, especially in areas where they were not seen.

Bark was normally removed, as were the outer growing rings — the *sapwood*. This was partly because these parts of the tree were subject to insect attack, but more usually because the carpenters wanted squared timbers whether they were to be decorative or not. Nevertheless, the dendrochronologist can generally identify how close the outer rings of a sampled timber were to the outside of the tree, or to the important boundary between the main *heartwood* rings and those of the sapwood. Using a combination of objective analysis and professional experience, the dendrochronologist can usually provide a good idea of the felling date range of a tree even when the ring sequence is not complete.

If tree-ring dating is to be carried out on a building it is usually carried out with the full cooperation of the building archaeologist. It is up to the archaeologist to understand the basic phasing of the building and to identify which timbers are primary or secondary. The dendrochronologist can then assess which of these will be suitable for sampling.

In an ideal world, the results of the tree-ring dating will be ready before the production of the archaeological report, but this is seldom the case. Waiting for the 'dendro' dates to either match or contradict their own has become the unfortunate lot of building archaeologists. Despite this it has proven to be one of the most useful of all scientific innovations in the understanding of buildings. The relative cost of the procedure has been falling for some time and it is to be hoped that soon it will become cheap enough to be used on many more buildings than at present — but that will obviously rely on ensuring that there are enough dendrochronologists to go round.

9   Photography

A simple good quality photograph is one of the most cost-effective ways of surveying a building, but one that is often neglected by buildings' archaeologists. Sometimes, for example after a major fire, it may be the only way of recording a building if it has become structurally unsound and therefore dangerous. Much of the Royal Commission on Historic Buildings emergency recording is based on photographs and, if possible, rectified photography.

Unless it is rectified, a photograph will obviously not be dimensionally accurate, but the amount of information that it can convey is far more than even the most detailed of site surveys and an invaluable addition to the record. Photographs can simply be general views of a site or highly detailed rectified surveys from which large-scale stone-by-stone record drawings can be made.

Whilst there are a handful of professional photographers that specialise in photographing historic buildings, they are generally only used on major projects and the building archaeologist needs to master at least the rudiments of good camera technique. Rapid improvements in camera and film technology over the past twenty years or so have meant that equipment capable of producing excellent results is readily and cheaply available, and easy to use.

In the near future, improvements will obviously continue and the most significant of these will undoubtedly be the development of digital cameras. Their images can be transferred directly into computers, manipulated, resized and then stored or printed. The quality of their image is improving all the time and the most expensive ones are rapidly approaching the quality of traditional cameras. Such cameras are still comparatively costly and the potential problems of archiving the images for posterity have yet to be fully investigated. For the time being at least, the traditional process of film negative and print remains the only option for high quality historic buildings work — and for the archives.

Equipment

Camera film comes in several different sizes and film speeds. Generally, the bigger the film size, the better the result. On purely optical grounds the best quality photographs are taken on Large Format cameras with 'rising fronts' that eliminate the annoying vertical distortion seen on so many shots taken on smaller cameras. The degree of detail on prints produced from such cameras can be quite amazing, even when enlarged many times, and as an accurate photographic record they are unsurpassed. It only takes a detailed look at a 'full-plate' image taken a century or more ago to see just how good they are.

Regrettably, Large Format cameras, which take negatives of 4"x5" size and above, are also very heavy, unwieldy, cumbersome to carry (needing always to be mounted on a substantial

100   One of the dangers of recording tall buildings or smaller ones too close with wide angle lenses is that of vertical distortion, as shown in this otherwise perfectly acceptable photograph of Hardwick Hall, Derbyshire

tripod), difficult to use, expensive to buy, and expensive to use because of the cost of film and processing. Fortunately the improvements in film quality in the past twenty years means that for all practical purposes the quality between them and the modern Medium Format or 35mm cameras has diminished. While the differences in film size do become more apparent the larger the size of print produced, these are scarcely noticeable on a standard 10"x8" size photograph — a perfectly acceptable size for most record shots.

The so-called Medium Format cameras use 120mm roll film that produces negatives of 6x4.5cm, 6x6cm, or 7x6cm. They offer a good compromise between the quality of the Large Format cameras and the convenience of the 35mm cameras, but because they are very much in the minority, they are still relatively expensive to buy and use.

By far the most popular and most versatile cameras of all are those that take 35mm film, and they vary enormously in quality and cost. The small 'compact' cameras are ideal for snapshots of buildings and are light enough, small enough and cheap enough to be kept in a pocket or field bag. However, for survey work they have severe limitations as they generally have a fixed or small-range zoom lens and a fairly vague viewfinder.

Most archaeologists are capable of using the professional photographer's general workhorse: the standard 35mm SLR. Apart from cost, these versatile cameras (SLR stands for Single Lens Reflex) have two key advantages. Firstly, what you see through the viewfinder is the image that you will get on the film, and secondly, a single camera body can take a vast array of interchangeable lenses and other accessories.

Most modern SLRs automatically work out the correct *exposure* of each photograph. There are literally dozens of books and many magazines dedicated to photography, so this is not the place to go into great detail about technique. In essence, however, each exposure relies on the balance between the size of the *aperture* in the lens (the *f*-stop) and the speed of the *shutter*. The wider the aperture and the longer the shutter speed the more light is let in through the lens. However, a wide aperture also results in less *depth-of-field* — the zone in which things are in focus.

This can be very important in architectural photography. For example, where a long building, such as a factory, is being photographed on the angle, or where a shot of the interior of a cathedral is needed, a narrower aperture will be needed to ensure that each end is in focus. With the aperture narrowed down to an *f*-stop of something like *f*16 or *f*22, a longer shutter speed will be needed to let the right amount of light in through the lens to ensure a correct exposure. Unless the camera is on a tripod, or a flashgun is being used, longer shutter speeds also produce the possibility of camera shake and a poor photograph. In emergencies, a speed of 1/60th (or with practise, 1/30th) of a second is about the slowest that can be used hand-held to get high-quality results from a 35mm camera.

Modern cameras work out the required balance between aperture and shutter speed. Some are only *aperture priority,* in which the desired aperture is set on the lens and the camera then works out the right shutter speed. A rarer type, the *shutter priority*, works the other way round. The recent advances in technology now mean that many cameras can do both and also work out several different *programme* modes of their own depending on the type of photography required.

These cameras rely on built-in *light meters* that calculate the strength of the light reaching the film. Earlier meters simply took account of all the light and could be easily misled by large amounts of bright sky, for example, resulting in dark buildings. Modern cameras can offer one or more different types of *metering*, such as *centre-weighted*, or, more importantly for building photography, *spot metering*. A spot meter reading is taken from a very small area of the object being photographed and is not affected by anything else, resulting in a very accurate exposure.

Most modern SLR cameras are of the autofocus type, which is, for most purposes, very handy. For buildings this is one technical advance that is useful, but by no means essential. Buildings tend to be static subjects and speed of focusing is seldom a problem. The slightly longer time it takes for manual focusing is irrelevant. Indeed, in some cases, and particularly inside buildings, autofocusing occasionally has to be overruled and manual focus used instead. Earlier reservations about the reliability of these hi-tech cameras with their complex array of electronics and heavy reliance on batteries have largely been forgotten, and even hard-bitten professionals now happily use them.

In terms of quality, the more you pay the more you get. Whilst the differences in optical quality between the cheaper and most expensive cameras are now very slight, the more expensive cameras tend to be more sturdily built and will stand up to the often punishing treatment received in a dusty medieval roof space or a rain-swept farmyard. It is often better to buy a good second-hand example of a top brand camera than a brand new cheaper one for the same price.

This same rule applies to lenses. The top manufacturers lenses are built to last; some of the photographs in this book, for example, were taken on a favourite and now slightly battered Nikon lens, well over 30 years old but still in perfect working order. Changes in camera fashions also mean that second-hand equipment is often little used and in almost mint condition, offering tremendous bargains for those willing to shop around.

Choice of lenses is often down to personal preferences providing that they are capable of doing the job. Risking the wrath of the photographic enthusiast, in essence the longer the focal length of the lens the closer-up the view through it. Thus a 28mm lens on a 35mm SLR is a *wide angle* lens because it has a wide angle of view, and a 200mm lens is *telephoto* lens because it has a much narrower angle of view but what is seen through the viewfinder appears to be much closer. In practice, anything wider than 28mm is fairly useless for building survey work because of the degree of distortion.

The ideal lens for building recording is a PC, or Perspective Control, lens, usually of 28mm or 35mm length. These mirror the effect of the rising front of the Large Format cameras and eliminate vertical distortion. Because they are a fairly specialist tool they are also fairly expensive, but if a lot of architectural photography is envisaged then they are a good long-term investment. It is worth checking whether or not the type of camera being considered for purchase has a PC lens made for it; they tend to be made only for a handful of professional camera makes. Incidentally, a PC lens also makes accurate rectified photography that much easier.

Most archaeologists will make do with a small selection of lenses, typically one wide angle, normally a 28mm, one 'standard' lens, normally a 50mm, and one short telephoto, perhaps a 135mm. These *fixed* lenses offer high resolution and quality. Until the last ten years or so the alternative *zoom* lenses were considered to be not quite as good optically but this has changed. A zoom lens is capable of being used at an infinite variety of different focal lengths, thus obviating the need for several fixed lenses. A typical standard zoom will cover the 28-70mm range and a telephoto zoom, 75-210mm. Some zooms cover as wide a range as 28-200mm or more but tend to be unwieldy.

Perhaps the one item of equipment most overlooked by photographers is the tripod. Using a good quality tripod on site may be a little tiresome at times, but it does give a slight edge to the quality of the resultant photographs. A hand-held camera at all but the fastest shutter speeds is subject to a degree of camera shake, which will affect the resolution of the resultant photograph.

A good quality tripod-mounted camera operated by a cable release or its own self-timer is usually rock solid and all shake disappears. It also has the advantage of allowing very long shutter speeds, several minutes long if necessary, and this allows for smaller apertures and thus greater depths of field, particularly useful in interior shots of large buildings. If there is no tripod available, it is sometimes possible to prop the camera on a wall or piece of furniture, preferably on a small beanbag or even a jumper so that its base plate is not damaged and the camera can be set level.

Few building archaeologists will have access to sophisticated lighting for interior photography. If there is a reasonable amount of light then long exposures on tripod mounted cameras can be used. The camera's own light meter will need to be overruled as usually slightly greater exposure time is needed inside than the meter suggests, generally

*101   One solution to vertical distortion is to use a perspective control lens — as was used in this
fairly close-up view of the entrance to Chirk Castle, Clwyd*

about 20% more. Alternatively, a flash-gun will be used, though this is not of much use in
large interiors such as cathedrals or factories. Many SLRs have reasonably powerful 'pop-
up' flashes attached to them, but for best results a separate flashgun is necessary. These are
usually *dedicated* to a particular camera brand and become fully integrated with the cameras
automatic exposure system.

Other pieces of equipment include various *filters* that can be attached to the front of the
lenses for a variety of effects. A simple UV filter can help contrast and also serves to
protect the lens when in use. The more expensive *polarising* filter helps to eliminate
reflections, particularly useful when there is a lot of glass in view. A *lens hood* also helps to
reduce glare but must be the right size for the lens being used otherwise it can leave a
shadow around the edge of the image. A small and very cheap builder's or string level is
useful to place on top of the camera to make sure that it is level.

Photographic film is rated for its *speed*. The most common standard is the *ASA* in
which the higher the number the more sensitive, or 'faster', the film: thus 25 ASA is very
slow and 1000 ASA is very fast. On the other hand, the faster the film the larger the *grain*
in its composition and the less crisp its resolution and quality. Until recently a film speed
of 100 or 125 ASA was considered to be a good compromise between the quality of the
slower speeds and the convenience of the faster ones. Today, 400 ASA can be used with
confidence as a general purpose film.

Generally, survey photography uses black-and-white film stock. It is still considered to
be more stable than colour film, and colour print in particular is susceptible to fading.
Although debatable, the structural details on black-and-white prints are also thought to be
easier to read as colour can distract from the image. Colour photography can, of course,

102 Photographs of details, such as these floor joists, should if possible be accompanied by a simple scale bar

be useful sometimes — where there are subtle differences in shade of different stones in a masonry building, for example, or where colour schemes are an important element within the building. To counter the subjective colour shifts of different films, a colour chart should be used in photographs of important coloured details. Colour slides usually offer a more accurate rendering of colour and are obviously useful when presenting talks or presentations about a particular building.

The basic photographic survey

A typical photographic survey of a building or site is a matter of common sense and patience. One or two general shots of the building in its setting will make a useful introduction to the survey. If it is to be comprehensive, then all external elevations of the building need to be taken. If the sun is shining and parts of the buildings are in shadow, it makes sense just to assess whether that shadow will have moved later on in the day. If so, that particular elevation shot should wait until it has. The north sides of buildings can be particularly difficult because of the sun. A little time thinking about such matters, and about the best viewpoints, before even getting the photographic gear out of its bag is well worth spending.

The size of each elevation will determine the amount of photographs needed. On a typical small or medium-sized house, for example, one shot should cover each main side. On a long factory or church, several shots will be needed. Where this is the case, a more general 'three-quarter' shot is useful of the whole elevation to place the others into some kind of context. Sometimes such angled shots are all that can be achieved if true 'head-on' ones are impossible because of the terrain, vegetation or other buildings.

The interiors of buildings can cause more problems for the photographer, especially if there is a multitude of small rooms and the lighting is poor. Usually it is impossible to take full internal elevations of individual rooms, so most internal shots tend to be three-quarter views. Often several such photographs are required for each room. Roof spaces, often completely unlit and virtually inaccessible, provide even more problems but it can be quite surprising just how well a modern camera, good tripod, and a powerful flash can deal with the situation.

Incidentally, with all modern cameras (and, if necessary, flashguns) it is possible to artificially boost the amount of light available by using the camera's 'exposure compensation dial'. By overriding the normal controls in this way, the flashgun is effectively told that the film speed is much slower than it really is and the light output is increased accordingly. Usually one or two extra 'stops' are all that are needed.

In a full survey, specific close-ups of significant architectural details should be taken, sometimes requiring the use of a telephoto lens. These can include such things as date plaques, window heads, chamfers stops, ceiling decoration and wainscot; the list is endless. Indeed, the amount of photographs taken depends on the photographer, but it is worth remembering that 35mm film is quite cheap and not all negatives have to be printed up to large prints. It is far better to take too many photographs than too few, avoiding missing anything that might only later take on some significance. This is particularly the case if the building is going to be demolished or radically altered.

Unless the captions for each photograph are self-explanatory — such as 'west elevation', or 'Drawing room, looking south-east' — it is useful to use existing survey drawings (or if necessary, sketch plans) as a key to the photographs taken.

The use of scales in photographs depends largely on the purpose of the photographs. In general photography, a simple metre scale somewhere on an external shot may be of use, particularly if there are no survey drawings, but is not usually essential. For rectified photographs then scales are obviously crucial, and they are also useful to have on detailed shots of individual features. Simple metre scales can be created by painting thin lengths of timber, or cheap plastic metre rules, white with black tips 1m apart. For more detailed photographs, any rulers with clearly marked centimetre squares can be bought, or the squares can again be painted onto timber.

The photographic archive

Most archaeologists will not develop and print their films but leave this to a professional — either in a High Street outlet or through the mail. Once the film has been processed, it needs to be captioned and archived. The negatives are the real archive and require careful attention, as any number of prints can be produced from them. Each film needs to given an identification number or code related to the site's own code, if it has one, or a different Unit code if not. Individual exposures on the negatives have their own integral numbers and these can be simply incorporated into a typical photographic filing system.

Negatives need to be stored in dry conditions and in good quality negative sheets; these slot into purpose made ring-binders. For convenience, a *contact sheet* — basically a direct photographic print of all the negatives — can be added into the file next to the negative sheet. Prints to be made can then be more easily identified and marked than by squinting through the negative sheets. The final resting place of this photographic archive is down to the specific requirements of the archaeological brief; in an ideal world they should go to a suitable records office where they will be safely stored for posterity.

PART IV:
INTERPRETATION
OF THE EVIDENCE

*103   Buildings archaeology covers all structures, not just those with four walls and a roof. Potter
Heigham bridge, with a narrow clearance of just 2m, is not only a challenge to those navigating
the Norfolk Broads but also to the building archaeologist. Clearly it is substantially medieval, as
the outer arches and ashlar show; the main arch is post-medieval and the rest of the structure is of
brick from at least three different centuries*

10   Methodology

Understanding buildings is not something that can properly be taught by books. Whilst there are some basics techniques and tips that can be learnt from the written page, the only real way to learn how to understand our built heritage is through practical experience. This does not mean that a good buildings' archaeologist is necessarily an old one. Some are born with a definite but undefined 'knack' of understanding buildings that the rest of us can only envy. Even these lucky few, however, will need to have undertaken at least some fieldwork before being able to develop their skills.

As already stated several times, the role of the building archaeologist is a fairly simple one: it is to understand buildings. Unfortunately, it is also a role that has been confused by the type of ongoing debate that seems to plague all academic study. The main relevant debate within the archaeological profession is about the best means of interpreting buildings and it is one in which two apparently opposed approaches have been polarised.

On the one hand there are those who consider that buildings archaeology is a fairly new form of 'traditional' archaeology. In this argument there is no distinction between the material culture above and below ground. Therefore the same scientific techniques used in excavations should be adapted to the study of buildings along with the same detailed and inclusive recording methods.

On the other, there are those who are more willing to use any suitable means in order to understand a building's development whether they be 'archaeological' or not and to target recording accordingly. This line of thought is more in keeping with the origins of buildings archaeology as an adjunct of architectural history.

The first approach tends to deny that there are fundamental differences between excavations and buildings archaeology. At the risk of oversimplification, the excavator deals with the two-dimensional shadows of the past whilst the buildings' archaeologist studies the three-dimensional substance of the present. In an excavation, the principal method of interpretation is the study of the layers encountered and their relationships with each other. The process is called 'stratigraphy' and the layers and other features are termed 'contexts'.

This stratigraphical approach relies on the identification of separate contexts within the archaeological resource and the interrelationships between them. For convenience, the individual contexts are numbered chronologically as they are encountered and become the raw material for interpretative matrices. Because of the very nature of excavation archaeology, the surviving evidence is limited and often minute contexts hold the key to the interpretation of entire phases. The individual contexts are often so nebulous that numerical identification is the only logical means of discriminating between them.

Stratigraphy, a technique pioneered by nineteenth-century geologists, is thus an

*104   The original function of many buildings is easy to deduce from their design. This house in the
south Pennines, for example, has the typical continuous row of attic windows signifying the
existence of a weaving loft. It was built when the weaving part of woollen manufacture was still a
cottage industry, and before it became dominated by the factory system*

essential technique in archaeological excavations. It is also entirely appropriate with
contexts that have gradually formed different strata. It is usually the case that the higher
the layer, the newer it is; because of this, of course, the oldest layers are not encountered
until the very end of the excavation and no interpretation can be properly undertaken
until that point.

So how does this work in interpreting buildings? After all, stratigraphy is a pejorative
term, implying modelling in two-dimensions; buildings have three. It is argued by many
that buildings are actually made up of a series interconnected two-dimensional planes —
walls and floors and roof slopes — that can be treated individually using standard
stratigraphic techniques, combining the results to give an understanding of the whole.

It is true that in a complex masonry wall there will be many elements that can
conveniently be considered as contexts or separate phases of construction: windows,
doorways, patches of mortar, redundant beam sockets and their fills, patches of repair, etc.
On some buildings these can usefully be numbered, for ease of description and
interpretation, and the relationships between them used to interpret this particular part of
the building (see **109**). Unfortunately, many wonderfully detailed building surveys have
also been produced in which all such features have been carefully identified, numbered

105   *Other buildings, particularly industrial and commercial ones, are less easy to understand unless their context is known. This long brick shed could be virtually anything. It is, in fact, the bothy of the Pye Rod salmon netting station on the Tay estuary, a few miles from Perth, photographed in 1983. Two crews working alternately around the clock in the season live in the bunk rooms and there is also a kitchen and a fish store*

106   *Even after a building has been completely demolished there may be some clues as to its appearance fossilised in neighbouring structures. In this gable end in Brecon, Powys, there are wall stubs and joist sockets to show that the missing range was certainly narrower but probably taller than the existing building and that it had a pitched roof*

consecutively, labyrinthine matrices dutifully produced, and analyses made. But on closer examination, the same results could usually have been achieved without that level of recording and time.

The essential analysis of the relationships between the contexts is still an important part of the understanding of buildings but there is no need to confuse the issue by the use of irrelevant numerical sequences and convoluted site matrices. Contexts in buildings are usually fairly easy to identify: a window, a blocked doorway, a putlog hole, a row of infilled joist sockets, a patch of different masonry etc. If necessary, miniature matrices can be produced to understand more complex sections of a building, but this is seldom required. On copies of working survey drawings, liberal use of coloured felt tip pens to illustrate phases in the 'thinking' stage of any report writing are usually far easier and far more effective than any Harris matrix.

The nature of these relationships in a three-dimensional entity such as a building is quite different than in a broadly two-dimensional excavation, so much so that the word 'stratigraphy' is misleading. The individual contexts of a building are inevitably related to its historical and structural development, and because of the nature of standing buildings the identification of individual phases is far easier than it is in an excavation.

Explicitly or implicitly the study of the various 'contexts' has been used in building analysis for decades, if not for centuries, but only in the past couple of decades has it been confused by unnecessary academic debate. It now seems at last that the buildings' archaeologist can stop arguing and concentrate on simply trying to understand and record buildings using the most suitable methods available for the particular project in hand.

To understand the building's historic development the archaeologist needs to understand the changes to its fabric, form and function over time, and the relationships between them; in other words, to understand the main phases of its existence. When newly-built, in its first (or primary) phase, the fabric, form and function of any building will have a simple interrelated logic that is easily understood. As time progresses there will generally be changes to one or more of these elements, and usually all three. Improvements to military science, for example, may lead to changes in a castle's defences, changing architectural fashions to alterations to a church, and new aspirations to modifications of a house. For whatever reason, a new phase of work will have begun. If the building in question is adapted to cope, rather than being demolished and replaced, traces of all of the earlier phases of its existence should be fossilised within its present fabric.

At the ever-present risk of oversimplication, for the archaeologist the primary evidence is contained within the fabric and in the manner in which that has affected the form of the building. The architectural historian will usually first study the function, often through documentary sources, or the style of the decoration. The ultimate aim of both will be to understand the building, but the approaches are generally quite different, even though in practical terms many archaeologists have to take on the architectural historians role, and vice versa, for all but the best funded projects.

11   Site analysis

A common mistake made by archaeologists starting to study buildings for the first time is to rush in and start surveying any available wall surface in as much detail as possible. Before even emptying the site bag it is worth just walking around the individual building or site and thinking. From then on it is better to get a general idea of the building in question, and think how best to ask and answer the historical and archaeological questions it poses.

One of the first tasks must be to break the building or site down into its component parts. In a typical farmstead survey, for example, it is usually easy enough to separate the barn, cowsheds, hammels, and stables, and in a church, the nave, chancel, aisles and chapels. Each can then be studied in turn and the results later fed into an overall interpretation. Of course, there will be cases where it is obvious that the barn and cowshed are of the same build, and in that case they usually need to studied as a single entity. Sometimes a whole farmstead will be of one build, though in that case it will usually be easier to divide it up into separate sections for interpretative purposes. As in all aspects of building archaeology, common sense should prevail.

Even in a large single building such as a factory or a house, if there are several separate structural components they will usually be fairly obvious and need to be identified. Sometimes a little more understanding will be needed and some more thought spent, but eventually the various elements will become clearer. Typically, each can then be individually identified, either by a name, or by an alphabetical sequence, but usually by both. This could, for example, take the form of Building A: West Wing; Building B: Hall Wing; Building C: North Extension, and so on. From experience, the use of numbers to identify buildings can become confusing.

If a simple site plan exists, or can be produced, the parameters of each of the basic building components can be marked on it and this will become the backbone of the interpretation that follows. Each individual component can then be studied one at a time, always bearing in mind its position in relation to the others. This fragmentation of the building or site then helps the decisions to be made regarding the best way to record it.

Once the separate components have been identified, the next step is to assess the relative significance of its own various parts. Clearly all of the main walls will need to be looked at but the internal partitions need to be assessed to see if they are worth detailed study. Whilst all should be included on any plan, some, if they are found to be of relatively recent date, can be dealt with by a simple written description in the site notebook, and little more in the final report.

The manner of interpreting the various parts of the building depends on several factors, not least of which is accessibility. Ruins tend to be easier to study than buildings

107   *The wall of this barn in Merseyside appears to be complex, but closer analysis soon made sense*
       of it. Note the vertical construction breaks to either side of the left-hand doorway; these mark the
       position of the original threshing floor openings. The original phase included both stone, probably
       reused, and brick. Every other visible opening is a later insertion

in use, simply because more of the fabric is visible and there are no carpets or wallpaper
in the way. Most occupiers of houses or incumbents of churches have an understandable
reluctance to allow such surface finishes to be stripped away simply to please the yearnings
of the archaeologist. In many cases, there will be few unaltered and undecorated parts of
a building that can be studied in depth, often just the roof spaces and the cellar.
Nevertheless, just in such limited areas it is usually possible to at least glean some
information about the building and relate that to what is already known from the study of
the outside. Even an outline measured plan can be of use in interpretation as well,
especially if it can be linked to the roof structure, for example, or to possible separate
phases of components in the building.

Mass and framed construction are usually interpreted in slightly different ways. Mass
construction, typically stone, brick or mud, is usually the more difficult. The focus of
study will concentrate on identifying the fabric, form and function of each wall and its
individual phases and features. The key to this lies not just in the individual sections or
contexts of different fabric within the wall, but in the critical junctions between them —
the construction breaks.

On most outline elevation drawings the plotting of the construction breaks is crucial,
even if they are only sketched on. In more detailed work they should be plotted as
accurately as possible along with the adjacent masonry or brickwork to either side of the
join. In a complete 'stone-by-stone' survey these breaks may not always be plotted on the
main drawing, as the differences in materials should show anyway; however, they will

108 *There is an obvious staggered but basically vertical construction break in this ashlar built plinth. It will be up to the archaeologist, taking a much wider overview of the building and its site, to assess if this was due to levelling up courses during construction or the boundary between two completely separate phases of work.*
Accurately plotting such breaks is an important part of surveying at any level of detail

109 *There are times when a degree of 'contextual' recording is needed to interpret a particularly complex section of a building — and particularly masonry ones. This example shows a survey drawing and the interpretation of the evidence. The key and explanation will be in the text. This particular survey shed a great deal of light on the interpretation of the fine village church of Clifton Campville, Staffordshire (Bob Meeson)*

110   A basic knowledge of church
architecture is an obvious help when
studying churches. At Chepstow,
Monmouthsire, the blocked twelfth-
century openings in the side walls
can then be easily explained as the
aisle arcade at the bottom and the
triforium above. The aisle has long
gone; the surviving small clerestory
windows would have originally been
just above the top of its lean-to roof.
There is a third clerestory window,
now blocked, further to the left

111   The importance of understanding
the local and regional context of a
building cannot be expressed too
much. The farmhouse, farm
buildings, packhorse bridge and drystone walls at the head of
Longsleddale, Cumbria, can each be
interpreted archaeologically. Once
that has been done their relationship
with the landscape and local
architectural tradition needs to be
assessed; this will, in turn, help in a
greater understanding of the
buildings

112   Similarly, but in a much different setting, an independent archaeological interpretation of either
      the main cotton spinning mill, terraced houses or washhouse at Church Mayfield, Staffordshire,
      will be meaningless unless the inter-relationship of the whole site is understood. In this case, the
      site will then need to be compared to other purpose built ones in the region and to other less
      uniform ones.

113   Some regions or even smaller areas of the country have their own and virtually unique
      characteristics. The round, and so-called 'Flemish', external chimney stacks of Pembrokeshire is a
      typical example and the small village of St. Florence has several

114   Where there are different types of construction materials or techniques used in a building, such as in Aberconwy House, a fourteenth-century merchant's house in Conwy, a key question is whether or not they were used at the same time. In this case the line of corbels supporting the brackets of the jettied timber-framing seem to be original; clearly the ground-floor windows and doorway are not, because brackets have been removed to accommodate them

need to be used on the resultant interpretative drawing produced from it, usually by use of an overlay.

Some different contexts will be obvious. A fairly typical example would be something like a primary window in a stone wall blocked in brick. This will produce two identifiable contexts — the primary wall and the brick infill. The construction breaks are very simple and the interpretation is straightforward. Alternatively, a window may have been inserted into a stone wall. This will usually have resulted in new material tidying up the parameters of the new opening and, depending on how well it was done, the junction between old and new will be seen. In this case the renewed perimeter of the opening will be a separate context to the primary wall, but the window frame could be a later renewal and therefore a separate context.

Other changes may be more subtle. A new section of walling in a different material should be easy enough to identify, but if the new section was built in the same material as the old, matters can get more complicated. Flint walls and Bath stone, for example, are both notorious in this respect. As well as looking for subtle differences, such as in mortar texture, brick bonds, tooling techniques, or the degree of weathering, an overview of the development of the building as a whole needs to be kept in mind as well.

Gradually, as the elevation drawing is completed, there will be, depending on the complexity of the wall in question, a series of separate areas of masonry and features of

115   One of the basics of buildings archaeology is understanding building techniques. Usually these are hidden by decorative finishes and later changes, so Woodchester Park, Gloucestershire is quite remarkable. The mid-nineteenth-century Gothic pile was the work of Benjamin Bucknall, a friend of the French architect, Viollet-le-Duc; it was never finished and it has been left almost as if the builders had just left for the weekend (Ken Hoverd, Archive)

different dates. These and the breaks between should, if possible, be surveyed and plotted and the study of their relationships can then help to understand the building. In this respect they are akin to the different contexts identified in archaeological excavations, and they may even be given temporary context numbers if necessary, until their overall position in the development of the building can properly be identified.

Interpreting framed structures is more straightforward, and most of those studied by the buildings' archaeologist will be timber-framed, which are easier still — in theory. Even so, there have been some projects that have produced detailed spatial surveys of timber-frames with complex series of context numbers developed into Harris matrices, but the actual frame has not been understood at all; such cases of literally not seeing the wood for the trees are increasingly rare.

A timber-framed building is one of the most obvious cases in which the recording method should be targeted, and the target has to be, in most cases, the design of the frame. Usually the survey will produce drawings of each of the frames and cross-frames making up the building. Because of the nature of timber-framing, the positions of most missing

116   Fixtures and fittings are an important part of most buildings, whether functional or decorative, and need to be understood archaeologically. Dating different styles of decoration, however, can be less objective. In this case the fine wainscot and door of circa *1700 seem to be contemporary with the house but the chimneypiece — and the paint scheme — seem to be a generation or so later*

sections can be identified by the redundant mortises or peg holes and, on the survey drawing at least, they can be recreated. Carpenters' marks can also provide an extraordinarily useful source of information if they survive and are readily accessible. They were, after all, designed as the basic assembly instructions to illiterate craftsmen, and understanding their sequences and any 'differencing' or 'frame tags' can help the buildings' archaeologist several centuries on. With all this available information, later timbers, lost primary or later inserted openings, and other features can be identified in the surviving framework.

Close attention to the analysis of the fabric of the building provides much of the evidence for its form. The fabric necessarily gives shape to the form or configuration of the building because of the potential or limitations of the fabric used. By understanding the archaeology of the fabric it should be possible to then understand the development of the building's form. An inserted wall or window, for example, will be relatively easy to identify and will clearly have been a change to the form of the building.

At the same time it is possible to use the inherent structural logic of any period of the building's development to direct attention back to the fabric if there are gaps in the archaeological argument. If the interpretation suggests, for example, that the building was once longer than it is, or that a floor has been removed, the evidence could still be found in the fabric, either as redundant mortises in an end frame, for example, or an infilled row of joist sockets.

In assessing form, and implicitly, space, there will inevitably be a degree of supposition and several different ideas may have to be tested by the surviving archaeological evidence of the fabric. While the thought processes may be vague and subjective, the proof or otherwise has to be objective. Nevertheless, there is a great deal to be said for spending time thinking around a particular problem in this way rather than ignoring it completely. Indeed, most buildings' archaeologists will be thinking in three dimensions all the time they are surveying in two, and physically or theoretically testing each theory that evolves.

The final factor to be considered is the function of the building and the manner in which this may have affected the form. Specific functions require specific forms of buildings. A windmill is a prime example. There are only a handful of basic types of windmill — post, smock and tower — and all must conform more or less to type. The resultant structures therefore depend on the function of the building. However, this does not mean that they will not change and that there will be no archaeological evidence for change; it just means that identifying the basic function of the mill should help to determine how it was built and how it has subsequently been altered.

Most other industrial, and to a lesser extent agricultural, buildings have or had similarly distinct functions but others had a more flexible approach to their design in which the function is not always obvious. In such cases, a change of use did not necessarily mean a change in the fabric or form of the building. In these cases the importance of the documentary evidence becomes obvious.

The majority of buildings studied are, or in some cases, were, houses. In these it is identifying the function of individual rooms that matters the most. Changes in room use, and changes to the size and social status of the building, can usually be seen in its fabric and form. In the case of houses, the function is both obvious — they are to be lived in — and less easy to define. It is affected by general changes in the development of housing and architectural style, and with the changing aspirations of the occupier. A basic knowledge of all these variables is desirable to interpret the evidence that is left in the building. No building can be properly understood on the basis of its fabric and form alone.

12 Documentary research

It may seem odd to some readers that a section on documentary research is so near to the end of the book. This is deliberate. The archaeology of buildings is really about the study of the evidence of the buildings themselves. Indeed, it is often argued that documentary research is not really the job of the buildings' archaeologist and should be left to the building historian. Practicalities generally dictate that for most projects the archaeologist has to be the documentary researcher as well. Unless the building is of particular significance and money is available to pay for thorough archival research, the documentary side of things is seldom thorough.

This is due in part to the nature of that research. Whereas the amount of time spent on the survey and analysis of a building is usually reflected in the quantity and quality of the final report, days or weeks could be spent in looking through countless original deeds without any guarantee of finding anything relevant. Whilst this is not always a problem for the committed amateur with time on his or her hands, for the professional that time has to be funded, and most private clients are understandable reluctant to pay for more than they have to or can afford. There is also a shortage of good researchers with a knowledge of historic building terms and techniques. As a result, in all but the best funded projects, the historical research is usually limited to readily available secondary sources and locally available primary ones.

That is not the reason for the delay in introducing this subject, however. For most sites the documentary research required (or affordable) should not tax the buildings' archaeologist too greatly. The danger in undertaking documentary research before the survey and interpretation is that it can, at the risk of sounding priggish, affect the purity of the purely archaeological analysis. It can also lead to the idea that, because a particular building has been written about so many times and is well-known, that there is no benefit in further work at all. Worse still, it can lead to the compromising of the analytical process.

Conversely, documentary research can aid the archaeological work; it can point to specific areas that should be investigated with more care because of a known reference in the archives to a lost staircase, for example, or an earlier decorative scheme. The two studies are inexorably intertwined. Providing that a good understanding of the fabric of the building has already been established, the documentary material can then be assessed and used to aid the overall interpretation of the building.

Archaeologists do not necessarily make good historians, and usually need help. What follows is only a very brief outline of the more commonly available sources, but fortunately several good books have been written about researching local history that go into the subject in much more detail. If documentary research is needed, and it usually is even to a limited degree, the first thing to do is to ask the experts. The United Kingdom

117   An eighteenth-century view of 'Channery'; this is now called Fortrose, on the Black Isle in Ross & Cromarty, and has changed considerably. Perhaps the only surviving building from the engraving is the small medieval cathedral in the centre — then still partly roofed but now completely ruinous. Illustrations such as these vary in accuracy but can be invaluable for research

is blessed with an excellent network of local studies libraries and records offices, and most of the staff working in them are extremely helpful. Not only do they have the required archive skills to point people in the right direction, they will usually have an unrivalled knowledge of their own local sources and be able to unearth relevant material that would not normally have even been considered by just looking through the archive indices.

On a larger scale the main national archives will sometimes have to be visited as well, such as the Public Records Office and the new British Library in London, the National Library and Scottish Records Office in Edinburgh, and the National Library of Wales in Aberystwyth. Other major repositories include the library of the Royal Institute of British Architects in London and the House of Lords Records Office to name just two.

The main official national resource for buildings are the National Monuments Records (NMRs), formerly known as the National Buildings Records. These are run by the respective national Royal Commissions on Historical Monuments of England, Wales and Scotland, and collect photographs, drawings and other unpublished material on historic buildings within their countries. All have become far more 'user-friendly' in the past twenty years or so but they are not always conveniently close to researchers. New initiatives by these archives and the increasing expansion of the internet will make access into their records much easier in the future.

118   *The Buck brothers produced a remarkably comprehensive series of engravings of towns and individual buildings in a relatively short time in the first half of the eighteenth century. Reasonably, but not always, reliable, they provide an idea of the condition and extent of a building at a given time. This is Lindisfarne Priory on Holy Island, off the Northumbrian coast, drawn in 1728; compare this with the photograph taken 150 years or so later (see* **119***)*

On a more local level, each county or unitary authority has, theoretically, either its own or a shared *Sites & Monuments Record*. These are computer-based collections of information regarding buildings and archaeological sites within specific areas that can be accessed by the general public. The quality of the information is variable and is often rather dull, simply because of the present way it has to be presented as a computer printout. No doubt this will also improve, as will the overall quality of information, but much depends of the way that they are funded. Sometimes these 'SMRs' are housed in the local County Record Offices or Local Studies Libraries, but are sometimes tucked away in the local planning department.

All these varied archives are no longer to be feared and have knowledgeable staff. It would be unfair to rely totally on their help, of course, and a basic understanding of the main types of sources should be attempted. This will enable more preparation to be carried out before visiting the archive in question and allow more pertinent questions to be asked when there, saving time in the process.

There are two main categories of documentary sources, primary and secondary. Primary material is literally the original written word or illustration, deeds, wills, diaries, engravings, paintings, architects' plans etc. Secondary material is generally published, and will mainly be books and articles but also includes entries in the local Sites & Monuments Register and the statutory *Lists* of buildings of national importance. It is usually wiser to make use of these secondary sources first, especially as they will usually refer to potentially useful primary source material and save the researcher time as a result.

As many, if not most, of the buildings that will warrant the attentions of a buildings' archaeologist will be 'listed', their listing description is useful to read. Most of the lists have been updated within the past ten years or so but unfortunately they seem to have been slow in getting to record offices and libraries, many of which still have to make do with the older lists which were of extremely variable quality. Even the information in the latest lists is necessarily cryptic because of the time allowed for site visits and space allowed for text, and as yet they are not illustrated.

Most of the standard reference works are listed in the bibliographies and it is possible that the building being studied could be included or referred to in one of these. Over the years, there have been several gazetteers and descriptions of buildings on a county or nationwide scale, the most ambitious being the *Buildings of England* volumes produced by Nikolaus Pevsner beginning with *Cornwall* in 1951 and ending with *Staffordshire* in 1974. These are gradually being updated and similar series have been produced for Wales, Scotland and Northern Ireland. Whilst the entry for each building is necessarily short, and will not be of particular assistance in understanding one that is the subject of a proper archaeological analysis, the volumes do provide an extraordinary source of information that can be cross-referenced and comparisons made.

In a sense, Pevsner followed in the footsteps of a long line of other travellers interested in buildings to a greater or lesser extent, the first accessible one of which is John Leland, antiquary to Henry VIII at the time of the dissolution of the monasteries. His projected work on England and Wales was never finished, but his notes of his travels have been published and Leland's *Itinerary* should be a standard reference for any medieval building or site. Later works, which will usually only mention the more important buildings specifically but often do provide an interesting overview of the more important towns, include the late seventeenth-century *Journeys* of Celia Fiennes, Daniel Defoe's early eighteenth-century *Tour through the Whole Island of Great Britain*, Lord Torrington's late eighteenth-century *Torrington Diaries*, J. Britton's early nineteenth-century *Beauties of England and Wales*, and the slightly later *Topographical Dictionaries* of England and of Wales by Samuel Lewis.

Some counties are fortunate enough to still have an active *Victoria County History*. The VCH was set up in 1899 with the idea of producing a complete parish-by-parish historical encyclopaedia of the country to honour the ageing queen. It became organised on a county basis and has yet to fulfil its potential, even though over 200 volumes have now been published. Most counties produced the first or second introductory volumes early in the twentieth century but progress since has been erratic and the whole scheme has been rescued on more than one occasion by determined individuals. Where a VCH volume is available for the parish in which a building stands, it can be a source of specific information in its own right, and, perhaps even more usefully, another reference to many other sources.

All too few even luckier counties and more towns and cities have been looked at by the Royal Commissions on Historic Buildings. Their published gazetteer volumes provide a tremendous source of information about every substantially intact historic building before

119 Photographs tend to become more common, for the greater buildings at least, in the second half of the nineteenth century. This photograph of Lindisfarne Priory is probably from the 1870s, showing things had changed since the Bucks' engraving.

a certain date — originally 1714 for England. These are dealt with succinctly but in an archaeological manner, noting major changes and inserted openings, for example. As well as provided such specific information, they also provide a wealth of comparative material for buildings of similar types and periods. Latterly the Commissions began to publish more thematic studies, abandoning the gazetteers, which is rather a pity.

The VCH and other modern books on local history will usually make reference to any of the early antiquarian studies that may have been carried out in the county or town in which a particular building lies. These, like all books, vary in quality but can be extraordinarily useful. One of the earliest and most famous is John Stow's *Survey of London* first published in 1598. A particularly good and profusely illustrated later example is John Nicholl's *History of Leicestershire* of 1815.

One type of resource that spans the boundary between primary and secondary sources is the map. Some, like estate, enclosure and tithe maps, tend to be hand-drawn and thus could count as a primary source. Others, the printed maps, are really secondary sources. Both can be invaluable. Estate maps occasionally have the bonus of tiny watercolour paintings or sketches of some of the buildings in the vicinity. Detailed maps printed to accompany bills for canals or railways will often have useful information.

Britain is lucky to have excellent series of government-sponsored Ordnance Survey maps. The old 1in maps (now 1:50,000) are of little use in locating buildings, but all of the country was surveyed to a scale of 6in to the mile by the later nineteenth century and more details are shown. Apart from the astonishingly detailed 5ft to 1 mile survey of London finished in 1852, by far the best OS maps are the 1:500 scale ones produced in the later nineteenth century for most major towns, which show details as small as bay windows and lamp standards.

A special and crucial category of map is the tithe map, produced for most parishes in England and Wales in the 1830s and '40s as a result of the commutation of the traditional payments in kind or money (the tithes) for the upkeep of the church. The new legislation of 1836 resulted in an assessment, or apportionment, of the owners and occupiers of land to see how much everyone should pay. This was accompanied by a map showing all the fields and homesteads within the parish. Not only are these shown on the map, along with the main buildings, but each field or property is numbered and these numbers refer to the separate apportionment. This lists the owner, occupier, and type of field — arable, pastoral, garden, etc. — and its value. The detail on the maps differs from parish to parish. Most are reasonably well surveyed in terms of field boundaries, but the depiction of buildings differs greatly from map to map. In two similar Shropshire parishes, for example, the buildings on one were just sketched on dots or squares whilst on the other they were drawn with fine accuracy and the surveyors triangulation lines were still visible on the map.

Primary source material not only varies in usefulness but the ease of extracting the information varies too. Earlier material, written in Latin or older forms of handwriting in fading ink on vellum, can tax historians let alone archaeologists. Perseverance is the only answer if the information is thought to be crucial to understanding a particular phase of the building being studied. Fortunately, by no means all primary material is as difficult, and most documents from the early eighteenth century onwards should be easy to read, and most from the start of the twentieth century will have been typed.

The most common primary source for buildings are the documents relating to the sale and purchase of property. These all come under the generic name, deeds, but include a variety of different types of documents. Amongst these are leases and releases, bargain and sale deeds, rentals, and mortgages. Most will have the names and roles of all those concerned with the transaction, the property involved, any conditions on the lease or sale, and the money exchanging hands. Even more usefully, the deeds are often long-winded in repeating all the previous deeds relating to the property so that, with care, it is possible to just read a fairly late deed and get all the relevant information of previous ones from its preamble. Often the details of the buildings involved are sketchy or formulaic; typically terms such as 'capital messuage' occur again and again. Just occasionally there is a little more useful information, with entries such as 'all that newly erected dwellinghouse', or 'the site of the former priory of'.

If a building is or was part of a large estate, and that estate's records have survived, there will be a potentially huge amount of material, ranging from rental lists to building plans. Huge numbers of such estate records are fortunately now safe in county record offices and most have, or are being, catalogued.

Knowing the family who owned or lived in a particular building at a particular point in time helps in tracing them in the other standard primary sources such as the Census returns and the local Directories. Census returns became quite detailed in the mid-nineteenth century and give a good idea of the make up of individual households. Earlier and usually less useful standard sources for buildings include the Land Tax assessments and the late seventeenth-century Hearth Tax. For many towns and cities, rate books are also sometimes worthy of study.

Other personal documents that usually provide information on some buildings are to do with people's deaths. Wills are one obvious such source and sometimes provide details of other properties apart from the home of the deceased. Far more useful are the probate inventories that used to accompany most wills until the mid-eighteenth century. These were quite detailed inventories made of all the properties of the late departed; sometimes it is possible to trace the route of the assessors through a house as they listed each stick of furniture, brass lock and pictures, so building up a very useful idea of its layout and the functions of the rooms in the process. Sales inventories can sometimes be useful in the same way.

Another major type of documentary source are those specifically related to specific types of buildings. These include those related to churches, such as the archdeacon's 'visitations' which recorded the state of a church and any repairs needed to it; the 'terriers' listing the property of a parish church and its condition and the condition of the parsonage; the many and varied nonconformist records; licensed premises; almshouses; workhouses; industries; and schools.

Pictorial sources include many things, from old engravings to photographs, and finding them is more down to luck than with any other form of evidence. The more important the building the more likely it is to have been drawn, but if the building in question is close to such a building, it might just appear on the views as well. General town views are probably the most useful sorts but with engravings there must be a degree of caution. Plagiarism was rife in the eighteenth and nineteenth centuries; not only were written descriptions copied almost verbatim, but so were engravings.

Amongst the most famous series of views of historic buildings and towns were those produced in the first half of the eighteenth century by Nathanial and Samuel Buck. They were good — but not that good, and some of their perspectives were suspect and mistakes were made, but they were prolific and, for the time, reliable. Many prints purporting to date from the later part of the century were direct copies of the Bucks', often with the same minor mistakes as the originals and usually with more errors made in the copying. The date then becomes misleading, because whilst it may say 1790 on the engraving it is really a 1790 copy of a 1740 original. By and large it was only with the advent of practical photography in the 1840s and '50s that reliable visual evidence emerged.

Obviously the ideal visual source will be the complete plans and elevations of the building at the various stages of its development. For smaller and less important buildings these are very rare indeed until the later nineteenth century, unless the building happened to be part of a large estate or the drawings happened to survive as part of an architect's archive. There are not many such records of larger buildings either until the eighteenth century. There were a few exceptions such as the many plans drawn up by the surveyor John Thorpe in the early seventeenth century; it appears that he was only responsible for the design of a handful of these, the rest being surveys of other people's designs.

Proposal plans and elevations give an idea of how a building was designed to be and when, which can be compared to its present form. Equally, if the drawings are related to a major alteration or extension they will usually show the existing form of the building prior to the alterations. Obviously it is important to ensure that the proposals were actually carried out, and it was by no means uncommon for a client to reject several different schemes before finally agreeing to one — a situation most architects have to deal with today.

By the later nineteenth century many towns and cities had begun planning committees that controlled development within their districts, and as a result drawings of even fairly minor buildings or extensions had to be produced for their perusal. Some of these ink-wash drawings are works of art but their survival across the country is patchy, and many are still stored in council offices rather than in the public domain of a record office.

One final and little tapped source of information, suitable only when time is no object, is oral history: the recollections of people who knew the building in question. They may have lived, worked, or worshipped there and seen some of the more recent changes made to it. In many parts of the country there are active local history societies with an oral history section or archive, and these are always worth a try. They are particularly useful for information on industrial buildings, where many people would have worked over the years.

PART V: THE REPORT

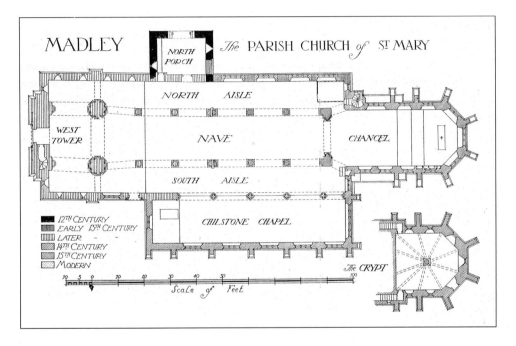

120   Illustrating the report with suitable extracts from the survey, photographs and some
interpretative drawings helps to explain the text. One of the most basic illustrations is the outline
phase plan — and the simple system developed by the Royal Commission on Historic
Monuments in the early 20th century is still as good as any. This is Madley church,
Herefordshire, surveyed in 1932

13   The written report

The written report is arguably the most important part of any archaeological exercise, yet one that seldom receives a great deal of attention. Even now there are still archaeological reports produced by professional consultants that are little more than a few sheets of badly typed A4 paper held together by a single staple. Some properly produced reports are often set out in a way that is difficult to use and riddled with jargon-ridden text that borders on the incomprehensible. Too many archaeologists of all persuasions seem to think that once they have recorded, phased and understood, their job is done; the report becomes a necessary evil at the end of the project and too little time and effort is expended on thinking about it.

A report is the point of contact between the archaeologist and the world; its primary purpose is to communicate, and if it does not do so then it is worse than useless. A badly written and badly produced report can devalue even the most accurate survey and incisive archaeological analysis. Once the interest of the reader has been lost, most of the report will just be skimmed and only the conclusions will ever be digested; the rest will lie unread in the archive. A well-written report will both inform and, hopefully, enthuse.

More importantly, the report summarises and explains the information gleaned from the survey and interpretation of the building. Always aiming to write a decent and publicly accessible report is one of the best ways of concentrating the mind. In it the evidence has to be clearly stated and the arguments logically presented, because if they are not the results will be questioned by others. This is especially so if an attempt has been made to bend the evidence to support a particular thesis, which is not as rare as it should be. If faults are found, the quality of the research will be questioned. For the amateur this may be a simple matter of pride, but for the professional it could be a matter of livelihood. In such a specialist field, reputation is everything, and anyone is only as good as their last job.

In most cases a report will have been commissioned when work is required to refurbish, restore, or alter a building. It will often put forward the evidence on which decisions made about such works will be made and should be a crucial part of the whole process. Therefore it needs to be understood by all those involved in the work, and this will include the client, the architect, the structural engineer, the quantity surveyor, the contractor and the planning authorities. A well-written report that can explain the building's history and archaeology to all these specialists should improve the chances of properly informed decision making.

Attempts have been made to regulate most aspects of the production and design of reports but fortunately so far all have more or less failed. Rigid conformity stifles individuality and as has been repeated elsewhere, buildings archaeology by its very nature loses a great deal when it is regimented. In the end, which type of reference system is used matters as little as the style of font or the justification of the text. But the individuality has to remain within a broad and very simple framework, and one that can be referred to easily. Any report, whether it is 2,000 words long or 50,000 words long, should be set out in the same way and be divided into the same three main sections — a beginning, a middle, and an end. This may seem obvious, but it is surprising how many reports fail to work to such a basic formula.

The beginning should outline the reason for the report. Where was the work done, why was the work done, what work was done, who requested it to be done, who paid for it, and who did it. The answers to these basic and fundamental questions should be outlined in the introduction, and this may also be the place to put on record any acknowledgements to those that have helped, such as the owners, an architect, or a particularly enthusiastic archivist. This part should also include a location map and an Ordnance Survey grid reference.

The main body of the report will be the description and analysis of the building in question. The way that this is organised is open to individual preferences but it should always be borne in mind that it is important to make the report readable. In some ways this is even more so when it comes to writing up building reports. Most other archaeological reports will be read more by other archaeologists than by the general public, simply because they are, usually, less easy to understand. This is because the often very subtle archaeological evidence within a trench is less tangible to most people than the evidence of a substantial three-dimensional structure. In addition, the written analysis of such evidence relies a great deal on the language of the Harris matrix and other necessary jargon, which is usually difficult to translate.

A lot of reports are produced in which all the illustrations (maps, photographs, reduced versions of the survey drawings, etc.) are in a group at the back, and sometimes the documentary history is introduced after the analysis. There are valid reasons for this. Being grouped together, an individual illustration is easier to find, and as, in good practice, the analysis should come before it could be unduly influenced by the documentary work, it seems logical to put it after the analysis in the report too. Unfortunately, such a layout leads to quite difficult reading. It seems better to put the history first, and to scatter the illustrations throughout the report so that they are close to the text that relates to them. It is always possible to append a complete set of the same drawings as an appendix anyway.

The style of writing is up to the writer but he or she has to accept that all the evidence needs to be put forward and properly explained, as must the thought-processes that led to the conclusions. This has to be done in a way that is relatively easy to understand. With a typical building it is usual to start with a simple outline description that will include its setting, basic dimensions, building materials, how many basic structural components it has, etc. If there are several components, each of these can then be described in more detail, usually taking each elevation in turn, followed by the roof, and then the interior floor by floor.

There have, and probably always will be, debates about architectural terminology. No doubt some colleagues would dispute some of those terms set out in the glossary of this book, and no glossary to date has escaped some criticism. Some of our terms have ancient origins, many were invented in the nineteenth century, and some have been 'rationalised'

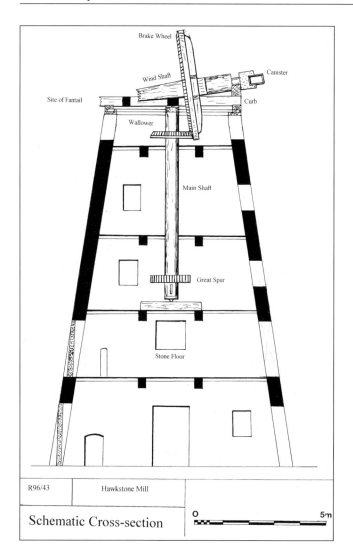

Brake Wheel

Wind Shaft

Canister

Site of Fantail

Curb

Wallower

Main Shaft

Great Spur

Stone Floor

R96/43   Hawkstone Mill

Schematic Cross-section

0   5m

121 Schematic diagrams based on the main survey drawing often help in a report, especially on a complicated structure that has many phases or has a specific function and workings, such as this late eighteenth-century oil seed mill in Shropshire

in the last few decades. To confuse matters, the meaning of some terms have changed. Reading an early architectural glossary, like that produced by Neve at the start of the eighteenth century, shows just how many have mutated over the past three centuries. As recently as the 1930s, for example, the Royal Commission described what are now referred to as crown posts as king posts, which now mean something completely different again.

There are many published books of current architectural terminology available and, by and large, providing the terms from one of these are used, they should be acceptable. Many technical terms are unavoidable, simply because they will be the right word for the right feature; for example, a bressumer is a perfectly acceptable architectural word and far more concise than 'the horizontal member projecting forward from the top of the framing of one floor level and forming the base of the next one above'. Nevertheless, great care must be taken not to be deliberately esoteric or to lapse into unnecessary jargon.

Once this evidence is down on paper, it can be followed by the objective analysis. This can be done component by component or as a general overview of the whole depending on the site and the style of the archaeologist. The arguments must make sense and be logical. Hunches and unsubstantiated ideas that may be relevant should only be used in the conclusions, and be referred to as such. Value judgements about the importance of the building should also be left until the end, or, if specifically requested, placed in a separate section, preferably as an appendix. Fundamentally, archaeology should not be judgemental about such matters.

At the end of the main text, the conclusions draw all the findings of the report together in a succinct summary. Depending on the length and layout of the report this can be just a single paragraph or several pages long. It could also include recommendations for further work, especially if it is felt that the main report has not been able to answer all the questions that it was intended to do.

Before and after the main sections of the report, the 'housekeeping' items should not be forgotten. At the very front of the report there should be a title sheet providing the name of the report, the date, the author(s), assistant(s) if any, and, if it is part of a series, the series number. There should be, after this, a contents page and, if appropriate, a list of figures and/or photographs. The pages should, of course, be numbered, as should the individual sections. At the end of the report there should be a full list of references, including all the works referred to in the text. On particularly large reports there may even be a need for an index, but this is rare.

Producing archaeological reports for clients and archives used to be rather expensive and tiresome but in the past fifteen years or so this has been completely revolutionised thanks to the astonishing development in computer technology. In the early 1980s personal computers were virtually unknown. Since then, they have not only become a standard household item, but also amazingly more powerful and much, much cheaper. Because of the ever-changing nature of the beast, the latest top of the range computer will be superseded within a few months and obsolete within a year. It will thus lose its value very quickly. All this is good news for those who do not need the latest machine to play the latest memory-sapping games or use highly complex drawing software. All most archaeologists will ever use a computer for is as a glorified typewriter.

The built-in obsolescence of computers means that there are huge stockpiles of new machines that have only just slipped off the cutting edge of technology, and these are available at quite ridiculously cheap prices. But even machines five years old or more will be perfectly capable of running very powerful word-processing packages. Guaranteed computers of this vintage, which would have cost well over £1000 when new will be widely available at a tenth of that price or less.

Word-processing software is also very cheap and older versions are often given away with computer magazines. Most packages are capable of working with the look of the text in any number of ways, and will have the facility for spell-checking, page numbering, headers and footers, justification, indentation, etc., all at the push of a few keys or a click on the mouse. Gone are the days of bottles of correction fluid and the waste bins full of screwed up paper!

The other vital piece of equipment is the printer. These have not come down in price as rapidly as the computer itself but are still now better than they were and reasonably

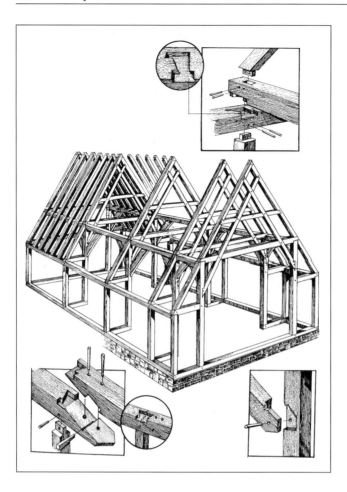

122   *Few individuals or archaeological units can rely on the skills of a suitably experienced artist to summarise the information gleaned in a project by the archaeologists so report drawings like this one are not surprisingly rare. This is a reconstruction by Brian Byron of the so-called 'Cathedral Barn' in Hereford, which began as an aisled high-status canonical house in the thirteenth century. Sketches of the structural details also help in the understanding of the building. (Archaeological Investigations Ltd., Hereford)*

priced. The cheapest printers used to be the dot-matrix type, whose output now looks decidedly amateurish. The colour ink-jet type of printers are now very cheap indeed and offer good quality for the price, but overall the laser printers are to be preferred for most high-volume output. Printers are judged by the resolution of their print, calculated in dpi (dots per inch); the lower priced lasers are usually 300dpi as opposed to the newer and more expensive ones of 600dpi and above. However, for written work the difference is not worth worrying about.

Reduced versions of the survey drawings, and selected photographs, can either be scanned onto the computer if a scanner is available, or if not they can be photocopied. Even photocopiers have come down to very affordable prices now, and all towns and most sizeable villages will have at least a shop offering photocopying facilities.

Most reports will be in A4 portrait (ie. upright) format and there will seldom be any logical reason to chose a different one. Some drawings, however, may not reduce down neatly to A4 size without losing some of their detail or a logical reduced scale. If necessary, these can be photocopied onto A3 sheets and simply folded into the main report.

A report needs a cover, even if it is only front and back covers of cardboard with the title on. The pages of a report need to be held together, of course, and this can be done in several ways. By far the simplest is to use staples, but it is worth spending a little more to get all but the shortest of reports properly spiral bound, either with plastic or metal bindings. Many professional print shops can carry out this work and it does not cost a fortune. Cost cannot, therefore, be a reason for not using a computer and a good laser printer in the production of reports.

Normally copies of reports should be sent to the clients, planning authorities, the local record office and the National Monuments Record. Local libraries are usually grateful to receive copies too, as are local archaeological societies and history groups. Obviously cost may be a factor and needs to be sorted out before reports are produced, and permission may be needed from whoever paid for the work in the first place.

Some more important building studies may warrant inclusion to a wider audience through the pages of a national of local archaeological journal. However, costs then become a more significant problem. Unless there are generous funds available, the writer will usually have to write the article in his or her own time. Just copying the report itself will not do; not only will the journal want a more readable text, the number of pages will usually be limited by its production costs.

Partly because of the cost of producing articles, and partly to help broadcast the ever increasing amount of archaeological work now being undertaken, there are several national and regional summary publications that will accept short notes on work done. These offer a good way of ensuring the fact that a particular building has been studied is known, and provide information on how to gain access to it.

Examples

Clun Castle

The degree of detail required in a building survey relies on two main factors that are not always interrelated — the amount of time available and the need of the individual project. Sometimes costs are not a problem. The archaeological recording of Clun Castle, Shropshire, commissioned by English Heritage soon after they took the monument into their care, is one such example. Two critical factors influenced the decisions about the recording strategy. One was the fact that the repairs needed to be comprehensive and would inevitably affect the historic fabric. The other was that in order for this to be achieved the whole monument, inside and out, needed to be scaffolded.

Originally it had been intended to use an existing photogrammetric outline survey as the basis for a more detailed survey of the areas to be consolidated and repaired. However, in practice, combining two different survey methods can have its problems and this was found to be the case when a few test areas were measured by hand and compared to the photogrammetric plots. As minor as these discrepancies may have been, they could and would have become cumulative during the recording programme.

It was decided that a complete new hand-taped stone-by-stone survey of the castle would be undertaken, using the scaffolding before the repair works started, and during it for a 'watching brief'. The survey took several weeks in bitterly cold weather, but all drawings were plotted on site before being redrawn in ink on permatrace back in the archaeological unit's offices in Hereford.

Whilst the drawings provided a detailed survey of the building in its pre-repair state, and formed the basis for overlaid 'post-repair' drawings, the irony of the situation was that only two major phases of masonry were found on the main building — the primary phase and some late nineteenth century repairs. However, the interpretation of the evidence, even without a parallel campaign of historical research, did allow the main 'keep' to be reassessed. From its appearance it looked like a typical Norman stone keep, even though its position on the side of the motte was a little odd. The archaeological survey — the first to have the benefit of actually getting inside small mural rooms high up in the building — identified fragments of cusped window tracery and quadripartite vaulting that were not Norman in character but had to be primary to the building. This, coupled with the surviving fragments of a large spiral stair and the other features related to the plan of the building, suggested that it was probably built around 1300 as a high-status lodging tower with separate lodgings on each of its main floors. The style was deliberately anachronistic, and the reasons for that

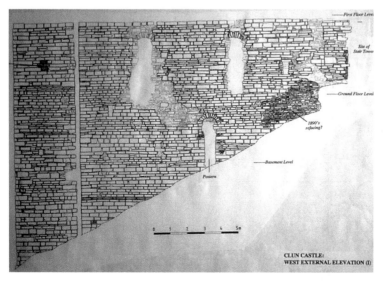

Part of the detailed stone-by-stone survey of Clun Castle, Shropshire, undertaken by the City of Hereford Archaeology Unit for English Hertitage

can only be assumed — but there are other examples of similar date in Shropshire. It may have been a less than subtle reminder to the only recently (and indeed, temporarily) subdued Welsh over the nearby border of the strength of the English at that time and a reminder of the earlier domination of the Norman barons.

A Shropshire Cottage

At the other end of the broad spectrum of archaeological recording is the rapid survey. This can vary enormously from site to site and building to building. One of the most useful examples is the 'assembly' or 'setting out' survey of timber-framed buildings as discussed above (pp.138-9).

This small west Shropshire cottage was surveyed in this manner. A fuller and more detailed levelled survey of the building would have been quite expensive and the historic carcass of the building was in any case largely hidden by later cladding. A full set of drawings of the building in this state would have showed little more than a good set of photographs.

The results of the 'setting out' survey, concentrating on the original frame design, could, in this case, quickly ascertain the original design of the building and the major changes made to it. By providing such a survey, coupled with photographs and a thorough interpretation, the client was able to provide sufficient information to the planning authority at a mere fraction of the cost of a much fuller levelled survey.

This late 17th-century Shropshire cottage had suffered major changes over the years. To properly understand the building, a fully detailed survey would have been inappropriate

Hardwick Hall, Derbyshire

Some surveys concentrate on certain aspects of a building or site. Hardwick Hall, 'more window than wall', is one of the great houses of England, built by the redoubtable Bess of Hardwick at the end of the sixteenth century and designed by Robert Smythson (see p.145). As with most buildings of this date and size there have been several campaigns of repairs over the centuries, the latest being by the National Trust.

The original stone was quarried in the park, but a large amount of the facing stone, and most of the window frames that give Hardwick its distinctive character, were replaced in repairs of the eighteenth and nineteenth century using a stone called Mansfield Red. Early in the twentieth century some repairs were carried out using the philosophy of the Society for the Protection of Ancient Buildings. This

A5(E)

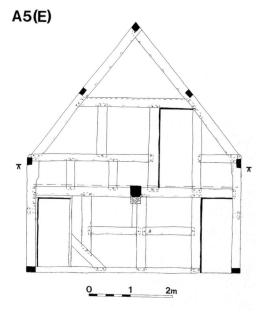

The outline 'assembly' survey was far cheaper and more informative

A detailed study of the masons' marks on Hardwick Hall, Derbyshire, carried out for the National Trust, has helped the identification of the surviving original work. Unusually, each stone had two marks on its face

involved 'honest' repairs, deliberately not designed to blend in and using materials such as clay tile and render. More radical refacing was carried out in the 1960s using more Hardwick stone, and the exterior was also sandblasted.

In the present ongoing work, the opportunity has been taken to study the fabric in more depth, mainly to allow a better understanding of the dates of the facing stones and, especially, to identify those that are original. The building has been recorded using photogrammetry, which has produced a detailed stone-by-stone elevation of each face. As the scaffolding for each phase of works is erected, an archaeologist has taken advantage of the access to amend the plots as necessary, and then to assess the various dates of the stones. Most of the phases have proven to be relatively straightforward to identify, though the differences between separate campaigns of the Mansfield Red are very subtle and the 'new' Hardwick stone has shown itself prone to weathering that makes some of the blocks appear as old as the originals.

Identifying original stone has been helped enormously by the fact that every one originally had mason's marks on the face rather than on the beds. What is even more unusual is that each stone originally had two separate marks. Curiously, mason's marks also appear on the finest of internal features, such as doorcases. Perhaps Bess was paranoid about not paying over the odds to her masons! The sandblasting of the 1960s has unfortunately destroyed some marks but a large percentage have survived. One of the two marks, a semicircle is the same for each stone, though not necessarily the same size. The other marks differ. In all, about 25 different designs of these marks have been identified so far; of these, three or four occur far more than the others and one occurs far more than any other. This has been nicknamed the hunting horn or hang-glider. It would appear that one mark is the banker mark from the quarry and the other that of the fixer mason.

The recording process has been straightforward, relying on the co-operation of the archaeological contractor and the architect. The architect has supplied copies of the rectified photography drawings. The archaeologist then checks and amends these on site, roughly colours in the various dates of each stone, and, using a simple numerical code to identify the individual marks, adds those numbers onto the drawing. These roughs are then sent back to the architect, whose staff translate the colours and numbers onto the digitised plot; the neat final drawings are then sent back to the archaeologist to be used in the interpretative report for each section under repair.

Usually each section of the building takes just a day of the archaeologist's time on site, and the office work is about two days in all. Yet for such a small outlay the Trust are building up a very detailed record of the exteriors of Hardwick and a detailed inventory that will eventually record every single mason's mark on the building.

Caradoc Court, Herefordshire

One of the sadder aspects of buildings archaeology concerns the recording of those buildings that are lost or badly damaged by neglect or, more dramatically, by fire. Often such survey work is necessarily swift, emergency recording prior to the total loss of the building. Other projects can be more leisurely, though each presents its own challenge. The only benefit of such losses is the amount of hitherto hidden information that comes to light. Caradoc Court, Herefordshire, is a

Understanding the inherent structural logic of a timber frame is a vital archaeological skill. This section of the survey of Caradoc Court was surveyed 'as is' (above), whilst a reconstruction based on the evidence of peg holes and mortises could be quickly generated (below). Using such evidence in standing frames, or in the debris, allowed a comprehensive rebuilding – on paper – of the building

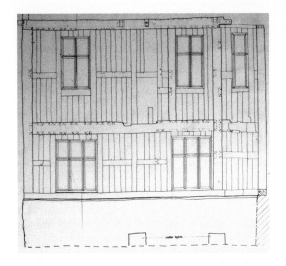

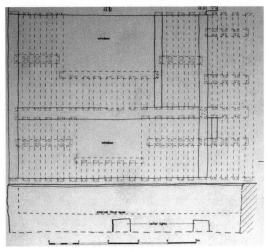

typical example and whilst the archaeological resources were not of the same level as those used at Windsor Castle or York Minster, pragmatic methods did help in a complete reassessment of the building.

The mansion, partly rebuilt in the 1860s, was mainly faced in stone, but there were some exposed sections of the original timber-framed building of about 1600. Gutted by fire before any analysis could take place, all of the debris from the interior had to be removed and the building made safe. Clearly this debris contained much of the archaeological evidence, and needed to be removed with care.

The ground plan of the house was recreated, in tape, on the Italian Garden. The rooms were then numbered in the house and in what became known as the 'timber field'. Each piece of significant material in the ruin was labelled with the room number, prefixed if possible by a letter signifying which floor the piece had originally been on, and a consecutive piece number. The number, a brief description, and, if relevant, a note of its relationship to other pieces, were then entered into the site notebook. The piece, whether it was a fragment of window mullion or a whole girding beam, was then manhandled out of the ruins by the contractors staff and placed, under archaeological supervision, in the 'timber-field' where it could be assessed in more detail and more safely.

Being able to move them around in the 'timber-field' it was possible to associate most of the scattered fragments with each other and recreate whole frames — on paper at least. This was helped by the uniqueness of hand-cut mortise and tenon joints, and of the burn patterns caused by the fire immediately before the frames collapsed. Once the interior had been cleared and made safe, there was a full survey and analysis of the standing walls. Reconstruction drawings could be produced combining surveys of standing and collapsed fabric, and particularly framing. The fire also exposed most of the important construction breaks and other architectural evidence within the shell of the building, from obvious vertical breaks in masonry to subtle stave grooves in charred rails.

Using all this available data allowed a much better understanding of the building's development, and led to one major surprise. It had been thought that the original building was L-shaped, and a stone wing had been added a generation later to create a half-H plan. Instead, it was originally built as a close-studded half-H-shaped mansion, a main hall block flanked by two parallel wings, with a grave design flaw. The tie-beams of the roof trusses, instead of resting on top of the wall-plates, were tenoned into their sides. All of the trusses in the stone wing were of identical form to those in the timber-framed section but had evidently been reused. The logical conclusion was that in this wing the design defect had proved fatal; movement in the wall-plates led to the collapse of the trusses soon after the house was finished, resulting in the need to rebuild the wing, reusing the principal floor beams and repaired trusses.

The archaeological study demonstrated two things. Firstly, despite the degree of damage to the house caused by the fire there was still enough surviving archaeological evidence to allow a reasonably comprehensive interpretation of the building. Secondly, in such cases, it is possible to use a simple tagging and salvage operation that, using contractors labour under careful archaeological supervision, need not be extraordinarily expensive. Obviously, there will be cases where a much more thorough salvage and sieving operation is needed, but such cases are fairly rare.

Select glossary

Terminology is never fixed, and is often the cause of much debate. The following terms should, therefore, be only taken as a working guide. It is also a short and basic glossary and many of the more specific and specialist words already dealt with in the text have been omitted.

Aisle: a space to one side of a larger space, such as a medieval open hall or the nave of a church, and usually separated from the larger space by a row of posts or columns.

Aisled Building: a building, such as an early medieval hall or a large threshing barn, with aisles along one or both sides.

Arcade: a row of posts or columns etc., either 'open' or 'blind'.

Arch: head of an opening, of many variants, most described according to the number of 'centres' used to create their profile: two-centred, three-centred, etc. Variants included 'stilted' and 'ogee'. In later building, 'flat' arches become popular. (see Figs. A1 etc)

Architrave: the lowest part of a classical entablature, but also used more commonly to refer to the moulded frame around a doorway or window.

Arris: the sharp edge of a brick or stone; the junction of two surfaces.

Ashlar: well-worked regular masonry with flat external face and straight joints.

Ashlar Piece, or Post: in a roof, a short vertical timber rising from the wall plate to the underside of a common rafter.

Attic: in vernacular use, a usable roof-space; in high status use, sometimes the lower, uppermost, floor of a house.

Bailey: an outer defended area of a castle, especially in motte-and-bailey castles.

Baluster: upright member in a balustrade, supporting the rail or coping; also part of a stair, supporting the handrail.

Balustrade: rail or coping supported by series of balusters, often used on the edges of garden terraces or at the tops of walls to hide roof structures.

Barbican: a strongly fortified outwork protecting the main entrance of a castle.

Bargeboard: fascia boards protecting the overhanging gable ends of pitched roofs, usually attached to the ends of the purlins; often wood and richly carved and cusped.

Bastion: tower or defended platform projecting from the main defended walls, usually of a castle and especially at corners.

Batter: outwards sloping base of a wall, particularly of castles; designed to improve stability and offer additional protection; hence 'battered'.

Battlement: a parapet, developed for fortifications, consisting of a series of alternating merlons and embrasures.

Bay: a structural unit in a framed building, delineated by the position of the main cross-frames and bay posts or stanchions. Also used architecturally to describe the number of windows in the width of an elevation.

Bay Window: window that projects from the main plane of a wall, either with canted or rounded sides. Can be one or more storeys high.

Beam: usually, a horizontal structural member.

Bed: the plane of the layers or 'bedding' in sedimentary rock, naturally horizontal. Also used for the mortar or cement onto which a stone is laid.

Blade(s): term used occasionally for the main members of a cruck frame.

Blocking Course: top course above a pediment or parapet, usually plain ashlar.

Bolection Moulding: moulding that projects from the feature that it decorates, such as a fireplace or panelling.

Bond: the manner in which bricks are laid.

Bond or Binding timbers: thin horizontal timbers placed in the coursing of brickwork.

Bonder: large stone bridging the rubble infill between the two outer leafs of masonry.

Bow Window: type of bay window with rounded sides.

Brace: curved or diagonal timber in vertical frames designed to stiffen them, usually tenoned at one end into a post and at the other into a plate or rail. Generally described in the manner in which they relate to the

BRICK BONDS

←Streche

←Header

←English

←Flemish

English ←Garden Wall

Flemish ←Garden Wall

main posts as 'up' or 'down' braces.

Bracket: small usually curved piece supporting a projecting rail such as a bresummer, or any such support in masonry or brick.

Bressumer: usually confined now to the bottom rail or plate of a jettied section of timber framing.

Brick bonds: the manner of laying bricks (see Fig.Betc..)

Brick Nogging: bricks used to infill the panels in a timber-frame.

Buttery: one of the two main service rooms of a medieval house, where 'wet' goods were stored.

Buttress: narrow masonry projection supporting a wall, especially in churches. A plain buttress has a simple sloping profile but most are stepped. A flying buttress is really a type of half arch, transmitting the loading down a solid pile of masonry. Corner buttresses are common on churchtowers and are of three main types: angle, in which paired buttresses meet at right-angles on the corner; set-back, in which the buttresses are at right-angles to each other but are set-back slightly from the corner; and diagonal, in which a single buttress projects at 45 degrees from the corner.

Camber: the slight upward bend of a relatively level member, especially a tie-beam or collar.

Capital: the top part of a column; in classical buildings the main key to the Order being used.

Carcass: the main structural skeleton of a framed building.

Carpenter's Marks: numerical assembly marks on timber structures.

Casement: simple opening window.

Cavetto: type of hollow moulding; opposite of ovolo.

Chamfer: cut away of a plain right-angled edge of wood or masonry, varying in

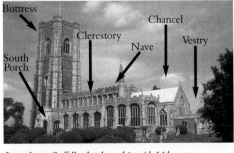

Lavenham, Suffolk, the chancel is mid-14th century Decorated and most of the rest was rebuilt in the Perpendicular style during the 15th

185

complexity from a plain surface to elaborate moulding. Ends usually marked by chamfer 'stops'.

Chancel: usually the east end of a parish church, where the altar is located.

Chimneypiece: proper term for the decorated surround to a fireplace.

Cladding: separately fixed surface covering to a wall, such as weatherboarding.

Clerestory: the top of the walls, usually of a church, with windows above the tops of the roofs of the adjacent aisles.

Close-studding: type of timber-framing using closely set verticals, either 'storey high' or with a mid-rail.

Cob: generic term for any solid walling of mud or clay.

Collar: a horizontal member between the principals but above the tie-beam of a roof truss.

Collar Purlin: in a crown-post roof, a longitudinal horizontal timber supporting the collars of the common trussed rafters.

Colonnade: a series of columns of, usually, an open-fronted building.

Colonette: a small column.

Composite: see **Orders**.

Console: type of bracket, especially in classical architecture.

Coping: the protective top of a wall, parapet or balustrade.

Corbel: small projection from a wall to support another feature, such as a wall-post or plate. A corbel table is a series of corbels, usually supporting a horizontal timber.

Cornice: in classical architecture, the top section of the entablature; in common use, the decoration at the head of a wall, especially inside where it is usually of wood or plaster.

Cross-Mullioned Window: window with mullion and transom, forming a cross shape; also used for windows of more than two lights.

Crown Post: the vertical post in a Crown Post Roof supporting the collar purlin.

Cruck(s): paired curved blade forming the main cross-frame in a cruck building, usually halved from the same tree bough.

Curtain Wall: external wall around a castle.

Cusp: small and usually decorated curve-sided projection in an arch or foil.

Dado: the lower part of internal wainscot or wall panelling, from the ground to the Dado (or Chair) rail.

Deal: generic term for the cheaper sorts of softwoods.

Decorated: architectural period, roughly

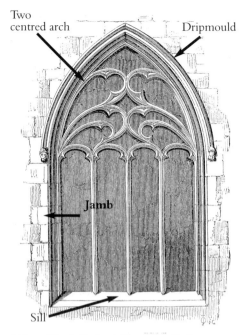

Melrose Abbey in Roxburghshire was rebuilt after an English raid in 1385. Unusually for Scotland it boasts mostly Decorated windows

from the late thirteenth to mid-fourteenth centuries.

Dormer: small window projecting from the angled slope of a roof to light attics.

Dragon Beam: angled beam at the junction of two jettied elevations, providing the inward support for the jetty joists of both.

Dripmould: protective moulding above a window or doorway. Also called a 'dripstone', a 'hoodmould', and, on flat-headed openings, a 'label'.

Early English: architectural period, mainly of the thirteenth century.

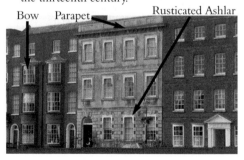

Houses in North Brink, Wisbech, Cambridgeshire. The central house is of three storeys and four bays faced in ashlar, rusticated on the ground floor

Eaves: the underside of the shallow projection of a roof.

Entablature: in classical terms, the horizontal members above and supported by a column, the main parts of which are the architrave, frieze and cornice; the top of an Order.

Facework: the visible surface of a masonry or brick wall, also called 'facing'.

Fanlight: window, usually fixed, within a doorway above a door.

Fenestration: the window pattern of a building.

Gable: the end of a roof, usually triangular, but shapes can vary. In a coped gable the roof is hidden by a low upstand of masonry.

A formal planned street in Dundee, built in the late 1820s for the city's middle class

Garderobe: latrine in medieval and post-medieval buildings, often projecting out from an external wall.

Girding Beam: in a framed building, a main intermediate horizontal beam, usually at the level(s) of the upper floor(s).

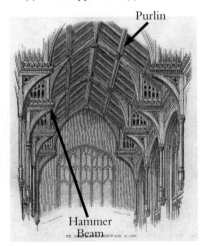

The hammer beam roof of St. Stephen's church, Norwich, a late medieval example

Gothic Revival: architectural style reviving medieval design, especially in the nineteenth century.

Gothick: a playful use of medieval themes, mainly for picturesque effect.

Greek Revival: architectural style influenced by the rediscovery of Greek antiquities in the late eighteenth century and particularly popular in the early nineteenth in England and Scotland.

Hammer Beam Roof: type of roof in which some truss members (struts and braces, for example) rise from short horizontal cantilevered timbers from the wall-tops.

Herringbone: Masonry or brickwork laid in diagonal courses of alternating direction.

Hipped Roof: roof in which the ends are sloped instead of gabled; the slopes are the 'hips'.

Hopper Head: top of a rainwater downpipe, often ornately cast lead on high quality buildings.

Impost: that part of a jamb or column from which an arch 'springs'.

Jamb: the sides of a window, doorway or other opening.

Jetty, Jettying: form of framing in which an upper storey frame is set further forward than the one below, its bressumer supported by projecting jetty joists.

Joist: horizontal 'common' timber supporting a floor or ceiling structure.

Jowl: the thickening of the head of a post in order to provide great support for junction of the horizontal members that it supports, such as a truss tie-beam and a wall-plate. Gently cuving jowls are usually described as 'flared'; stepped-profiled ones as 'gun-stock'.

Keep: the main fortified focal point of a traditional castle, often on top of the motte.

Keystone: the top stone or brick voussoir of an arch, often decorated and larger than the others.

King Post: type of truss based on a main vertical post between the tie-beam and the heads of the principal rafters.

Lancet: tall and narrow window with a two-centred head.

Lights: the spaces between the mullions of windows, hence a two light, or three light window, etc.

Lintel: the horizontal beam spanning the top of an opening.

Loggia: an open-fronted structure, often built alongside a house or wall and boasting a colonnade.

Long and Short Work: typical Saxon and early Norman quoins of alternating

Neo-classical streetscape in Bath, built in the 1790s by
Thomas Baldwin. The continuous loggias provided covered
walks along the whole street

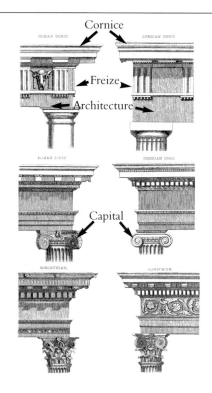

horizontal and vertical stones.

Loop: narrow window or ventilation opening.

Mansard: type of roof of two pitches, the
lower ones steeper than the upper.

Mezzanine: a floor level set between the
principal ones.

Mid-rail: in timber-framing, a rail between
floor levels in both square and close-
studded frames.

Motte: the defended mound of a motte and
bailey castle.

Mullion: the vertical intermediate uprights in
a window.

*Comparative Greek and Roman Orders, taken from a mid-
19th century architectural glossary*

*Typical Norman work in the west door of Tutbury church,
Staffordshire, of c. 1165*

*A fine oriel
window at
Montacute House,
Somerset, built in
the 1590s*

Nave: the main public part of a church, west
of the chancel.

Neo-classical: architectural style using
classical motifs fairly loosely in a
contemporary form, developed particularly
in the second half of the eighteenth century.

Newel: a main post in a stair, especially in a
spiral 'vice', and also the posts at the ends of

the balustrades at the landings of larger
stairs. In those cases they could be decorated
with finials on top of pendants below.

Norman: architectural period, also called
Romanesque, from the Conquest to the
early thirteenth century.

Order: in classical architecture an attempt to

The Palladian bridge in the grounds of Prior Park, Somerset, one of several early 18th-century copies of the design in Palladio's Four Books

define various types of styles, now usually divided in turn into Greek and Roman groups. Influential in the various classical revivals from the sixteenth century onwards.

Oriel: type of bay window, but on an upper floor and requiring some corbelled support below.

Ovolo: a convex moulding, as opposed to a cavetto; also used loosely for all rounded mouldings.

Palladian: term used for buildings influenced by the writings of Andrea Palladio, especially in the British Isles and North America.

Panels: the spaces between the timbers in a timber-framed buildings; also the spaces between the vertical and horizontal members of wainscot or doors.

Pantile: curve profiled type of ceramic roof

Inigo Jones's portico at the end of his St. Paul's church Covent Garden, of 1631, is one of the earliest in Britain

tile, usually a flattened S-shape in section.

Pantry: one of the main medieval service rooms, in which dry goods were stored.

Parapet: low wall, either solid, battlemented or balustraded, to hide a roof structure or protect a drop. Common on terraces, bridges, etc.

Pargetting: decorated external plasterwork, often in high relief.

Pediment: type of gable, especially in classical architecture, over a portico or opening; either triangular or segmental. There are several variants, included broken, scrolled and open.

Perpendicular: architectural period, from the mid-fourteenth to mid-sixteenth centuries.

Plank and Muntin: Type of internal partition, basically a frame of close-set studs (the muntins) with the thinner planks in between them. The sides of the muntins were usually moulded.

Pilaster: a shallow column projecting from a wall.

Pitch: the angle of a roof slope, for example.

Plasterwork: generic name for all internal plasterwork, decorative or plain.

Plate: general term for any main horizontal timber, such as a sole plate or wall plate.

Plinth: the projecting base of a masonry or brick wall, or of a column, and usually topped by a moulding.

Portico: the centrepiece of a classical or neo-classical building usually of columns supporting a pediment. The columns could be freestanding, or attached, or little more than pilasters according to the design. Usually built to one of the Orders.

Post: in timber-framing, the main vertical timbers, at the corners and the bay posts at the ends of the cross-frames.

Purlin: horizontal roof member, usually in pairs on each slope and in one or more tiers. They support the common rafters and are supported by the trusses.

Quarry: small piece of glass.

Queen Post Truss: type of truss in which there is a pair of posts rising from the tie-beam and directly supporting the side purlins.

Queen Strut Truss: type of truss in which there are two or more main vertical struts (as opposed to posts) rising from the tie-beam, usually to a collar.

Quoin: brick or stones at the corners of a building. The quality varies; in rubblestone the quoins may simply be larger, but usually quoins are well-wrought. Stone quoins are often used to decorate brick buildings, and brick quoins to decorate rubblestone ones.

Rafter: timber following the line of the slope of a roof; principal rafters belong to trusses, the rest being common rafters.

Relieving Arch: masonry or brick arch in a wall designed to spread and redirect the weight away from an opening below.

Render: externally applied plaster or stucco covering to a wall.

Reveal: the internal opening of a window or doorway, and especially the jambs.

Ridge: the top of a roof.

Rubble: type of masonry varying in quality from randon to well worked.

Rustication: deliberate decoration of stonework, and especially of ashlar. The two main types are surface dressing of the stones, or the dressing simply of their arrises.

Sash: type of sliding window, most commonly vertically 'balanced' sashes. A common name for horizontally sliding sashes is the 'Yorkshire sash'.

Scagliola: a material of cement, marble fragments and colouring smoothed and polished to resemble solid marble.

Scantling: the dimensions of a piece of timber.

Scarf Joint: joint to unite two pieces of timber end on.

Screens Passage: entrance at the end of a medieval hall, next to the services.

Sill: the bottom of a window opening.

Soffit: the underside of a timber, lintel, etc.

Solar: the traditional main upper chamber in a medieval building.

Spandrel: the roughly triangular area above the sides of an arch, and also between arches in a colonnade or arcade.

Splay: a larger version of a chamfer, for example in 'splayed reveals'.

Springing: the height from which an arch starts.

String course: horizontal projecting course on the outside of a building, also sometimes called a band course.

Strut: a vertical (or slightly angled) timber, usually in a truss.

Stucco: originally the term for all plaster work, but not mainly used for external rendering.

Stud: secondary vertical member in a timber frame, as opposed to a post.

Tie-beam: the horizontal beam at the base of a truss between the wall-plates.

Timber-framing: important and long-lasting form of construction, broadly divided into cruck-framing, square framing and close-

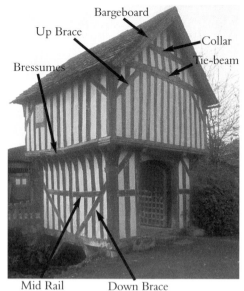

Late medieval timber-framing in the gatehouse to Lower Brockhampton, Herefordshire

studding.

Tracery: general term for the design of the ribs within windows, especially masonry ones.

Transept: the arms of larger churches running north and south of the crossing, and at right angles to the nave and chancel.

Transom: a horizontal member in a window.

Tread: the horizontal part of a step or stair.

Triforium: the usually arcaded part on the inward side of a nave wall above the top of the aisle arcade and below the clerestorey.

Trimmer: horizontal timber around an opening in a floor, such as a stair hole or hearth.

Truss: principal structural element in all but the simplest of roofs.

Tympanum: the area between the lintel of a door and the top of the arch above; in medieval work often richly decorated.

Voussoir: one of the stones or bricks making up the ring of an arch.

Wainscot: wooden internal wall panelling.

Wattle and Daub: standard panel infill in square-framed timber-framed buildings.

Weather Boarding: externally applied, and usually horizontal, boarding.

Weathering: sloping profiles of sills, steps to buttresses, etc. to aid water runoff.

Wind-brace: straight or curved support from truss to purlin in the roof.

Select bibliography

There are hundreds of books relating to buildings, their construction, design and use, though relatively few concerned with their interpretation. However without a basic understanding of its architectural and constructional context it is impossible to properly interpret any structure. The following is only a very short and fairly subjective selection of titles, confined to national rather than local studies. As a result, several fine regional and local books have been excluded, such as the series pioneered in England by Nikolaus Pevsner and later followed in Scotland and Wales. The various Royal Commissions on Historic Buildings in the individual countries produce works of the highest academic quality, and there are many important and useful articles published every year in both national and local journals. Perhaps the most useful of these is that of the Vernacular Architecture Group.

General

Alcock, N.W., Barley, M.W., Dixon, P.W., & Meeson, R.A., *Recording Timber-framed buildings: An Illustrated Glossary*

Buchanan, T., *Photographing Historic Buildings* (1983)

Cruickshank, D., & Burton, N., *Life in the Georgian City* (1990)

Elton, A., Harrison, B., & Wark, K., *Researching the Country House* (1992)

RCHM(E), *Recording Historic Buildings: a Descriptive Specification* (3rd ed. 1996)

Richardson, J., *The Local Historian's Encyclopedia* (2nd ed. 1986)

Wood, J., (ed), *Buildings Archaeology: Applications in Practise* (1994)

Architecture

Colvin, H., *A Biographical Dictionary of British Architects 1600-1840* (1995 ed.)

Craig, M., *The Architecture of Ireland* (1982)

Dixon, R., & Muthesius, S., *Victorian Architecture* (1978)

Dunbar, J.G., *The Architecture of Scotland* (2nd ed. 1978)

Fawcett, R., *Scottish Architecture: From the Accession of the Stewarts to the Reformation, 1371-1560* (1994)

Harvey, J., *English Medieval Architects* (2nd ed. 1984)

Hitchcock, H.R., *Architecture: Nineteenth and Twentieth Centuries* (4th ed. 1977)

Service, A., *Edwardian Architecture* (1977)

Summerson, J., *Architecture in Britain, 1530-1830* (9th ed. 1993)

Webb, J., *Architecture in Britain: The Middle Ages* (1956)

Construction

Airs, M., *The Tudor & Jacobean Country House: A Building History* (1995)

Alcock, N.W., *Cruck Construction: An Introduction and Catalogue* (1981)

Billett, M., *Thatch and Thatched Buildings* (1979)

Brunskill, R.W., *Illustrated Handbook of Vernacular Architecture* (3rd ed. 1987)

Brunskill, R.W., *Timber Building in Britain* (1985)

Brunskill, R.W., *Brick Building in Britain* (1994)

Charles, F.W.B., *Medieval Cruck-building and its Derivatives* (1967)

Clifton-Taylor, A., *The Pattern of English Building* (4th ed. 1987)

Clifton-Taylor, A., & Ireson, A.S., *English Stone Building* (2nd ed. 1994)

Davey, N., *Building Stones of England and Wales* (1976)

Fellows, R., *Edwardian Architecture: Style and Technology* (1995)

Gloag, J.E., & Bridgwater, D.L., *A History of Cast Iron in Architecture* (1948)

Harris, R., *Discovering Timber-framed Buildings* (1978)

Hewett, C.A., *English Historical Carpentry* (1980)

Hollister-Short, G.J., *Discovering Wrought Iron* (1970)

Innocent, C.F., *The Development of English Building Construction* (reprint 1975)

McCann, J., *Clay and Cob Buildings* (1983)

Mercer, E., *English Vernacular Houses* (1975)

Nash, J., *Thatchers and Thatching* (1991)

Salzman, L.F., *Building in England down to 1540* (1952)

Stratton, M., *The Terracotta Revival* (1991)

Wright, J.A., *Brick Building in England from the Middle Ages to 1550* (1972)

Yeomans, D., *Construction Since 1900: Materials* (1997)

Houses

Brown, R.J., *The English Country Cottage* (1979)

Fenton, A., & Walker, B., *The Rural Architecture of Scotland* (1981)

Girouard, M., *Life in the English Country House* (1978)

Muthesius, S., *The English Terraced House* (1982)

Reid, R., *The Shell Book of Cottages* (1986)

Smith, J.T., *Houses of the Welsh Countryside* (1975)

Tarn, J.N., *Working Class Housing in Nineteenth Century Britain* (1971)

Wood, M., *The English Medieval House* (1981)

Interior Decoration

Beard, G., *The English House Interior* (1990)

Clive Rouse, E., *Medieval Wall Paintings* (4th ed. 1991)

Hamilton, J., *An Introduction to Wallpaper* (1983)

Lewis, P., & Darley, G., *Dictionary of Ornament* (1986)

Osborne, J., *Stained Glass in England* (2nd ed. 1993)

Farms

Brunskill, R.W., *Traditional Farm Buildings of Britain* (3rd ed. 1999)

Harvey, N., *The Industrial Archaeology of Farming in England and Wales* (1980)

Morton, R.S., *Traditional Farm Architecture in Scotland* (1976)

Peters, J.E.C., *Discovering Traditional Farm Buildings* (1981)

Wiliam, E., *The Historical Farm Buildings of Wales* (1986)

Military Buildings

Bottomley, F., *The Castle Explorer's Guide* (1979)

Cruden, S., *The Scottish Castle* (3rd ed. 1986)

Evans, L., *The Castles of Wales* (1998)

Hughes, Q., *Military Architecture* (1991)

Thompson, M.W., *The Decline of the Castle* (1987)

Thompson, M.W., *The Rise of the Castle* (1991)

Kenyon, J.R., *Medieval Fortifications* (1990)

Platt, C., *The Castle in Medieval England and Wales* (1982)

Renn, D., *Norman Castles in Britain* (1973)

Religious Buildings

Addleshaw, G., & Etchells, F., *The Architectural Setting of Anglican Worship* (1948)

Betjeman, J., *Guide to English Parish Churches (rev. N. Kerr)* (1993)

Clifton-Taylor, A., *The Cathedrals of England* (1986 ed.)

Cruden, S., *Scottish Medieval Churches* (1986)

Curl, J.S., *English Heritage Book of Victorian Churches* (1995)

Fawcett, R., *Scottish Medieval Churches* (1985)

Friar, S., *A Companion to the English Parish Church* (1996)

Jones, A., *Welsh Chapels* (1984)

Knowles, D., & Hadcock, R.N., *Medieval Religious Houses: England and Wales* (1953)

Morris, R.K., *Churches in the Landscape* (1989)

Parsons, D., *Churches and Chapels: Investigating Places of Worship* (1989)

Pickford, C.J., *Bellframes: A Practical Guide to Inspection and Recording* (1993)

Platt, C., *The Parish Churches of Medieval England* (1981)

Platt, C., *The Abbeys and Priories of Medieval England* (1984)

Randall, G., *Church Furnishings and Decoration in England and Wales* (1980)

Robinson, J.M., *Treasures of the English Churches* (1995)

Rodwell, W., *Church Archaeology* (1989)

Southall, K.H., *Our Quaker Heritage: Early Meeting Houses*

Tatton-Brown, T., *Great Cathedrals of Britain* (1989)

Industrial Buildings

Binney, M., & Pearce, D. (eds.), *Railway Architecture* (1979)

Butt, J., *The Industrial Archaeology of Scotland* (1967)

Cossins, N., *The BP Book of Industrial Archaeology* (2nd ed. 1987)

Harris, R., *Canals and their Architecture* (2nd ed. 1981)

Hughes, S., Malaws, B., Parry, M., & Wakelin, P., *Collieries of Wales* (c.1996)

Morriss, R.K., *The Archaeology of Railways* (1999)

Pannell, J.P.M., *The Techniques of Industrial Archaeology* (2nd ed. 1973)

Rees, D.M., *The Industrial Archaeology of Wales* (1975)

Richards, J.M., *The Functional Tradition in Early Industrial Buildings* (1958)

Syson, L., *The Watermills of Britain* (1980)

Tann, J., *The Development of the Factory* (1970)

Trinder, B., *The Making of the Industrial Landscape* (1982)

Wailes, R., *The English Windmill* (1967)

Index

bold=illustration
S prefix=colour section no.
G = possibly used in Glossary
E=used in 'examples' appendix